**Psychological Theories
and Human Learning:
Kongor's Report**

Core Books in Psychology Series
Edward L. Walker, Editor

Psychological Theories and Human Learning: Kongor's Report

Guy R. Lefrancois

The University of Alberta

Brooks/Cole Publishing Company
Monterey, California

A Division of Wadsworth Publishing Company, Inc.
Belmont, California

This book was edited by Adrienne Harris and designed by Linda Marcetti. The cartoons were drawn by Tom Durfee, and technical art was drawn by John Foster. The book was typeset, printed, and bound by Kingsport Press, Kingsport, Tennessee.

L.C. Cat. Card No.: 76-164998
ISBN 0-8185-0014-X
Printed in the United States of America

3 4 5 6 7 8 9 10 — 76 75 74

This book is gratefully dedicated to my Blip, Can,
on Koros of the Androneas system,
and to
Marie, Laurier, and Claire

*(The good doctor probably deserves some recognition,
but his heart is so hard that the royalties, however
meager, will suffice.)*

Preface

Isaac Asimov made the interesting observation that those things which are understood need to be simpler than those which understand them. Attempting to understand the workings of the human mind puts man in the unenviable position of having to use his mind in order to understand its activities. Thus, since the mind is equal to itself, it may never be understood. This confounding of subject and object is the perennial dilemma of psychological investigation, and it is largely because of this dilemma that this report is so apt. The report was written by an extraterrestrial being. More precisely, its author was a Koron from the Androneas system by the name of Kongor M-III, 216,784,912, LVKX4. Only the footnotes, a short prologue, the epilogue, and this preface were written by me. The bulk of the book was written by Kongor.

The report is essentially a survey and interpretation of many of the theoretical positions that have evolved in the study of the psychology of learning in the past fifty years. It is not intended as a detailed encyclopedia of current "learning" research; it was written primarily for students of human learning, for teachers, counselors, social workers, industrial psychologists, nurses, social psychologists, doctors, lawyers, dentists, engineers, housewives, farmers, judges, fishermen, and all others—in that order. And, of course, it was also written for Korons.

Kongor has asked me to express his gratitude to Edward L. Walker of The University of Michigan for his many helpful suggestions and for his encouraging reaction to a manuscript produced by an extra-terrestrial being. He is also grateful to Walcott H. Beatty of San Francisco State College, Larry R. Goulet of the University of Illinois, and Robert D. Strom of Arizona State University for their reviews of the manuscript. Despite his customary immodesty, he readily acknowledges his indebtedness to Diane Gunderman and to Arlane Murphy for their part in typing the manuscript, to Adrienne Harris without whose copy-editing the manuscript might well have remained obscure even for Korons, and to Terry Hendrix for initiating and facilitating the project. Because of his lack of modesty, however, Kongor also wanted me to indicate that he is not responsible for any errors and misinterpretations that remain in the text. Allow me to clarify that point; any weaknesses of the book are, indeed, Kongor's (the royalties are mine, however).

GRL

Contents

Psychological Theories
and Human Learning:
Kongor's Report

1a

Lefrancois' Prologue

It rained during the early part of the evening—a gentle, refreshing, mistlike rain. Later the air was warm and quiet except for an occasional breeze that rippled the water's surface, scattering the reflected city lights in a million directions before passing on. The water then smoothed itself and gathered in the lights, rearranging them in their rightful patterns. I lay on the quiet banks of the river, watched the breezes play with the lights, and listened to them whispering in the shadows; a slow lethargy crept over me, and I closed my eyes.

In the space between waking and sleeping, the human mind is easily deceived; it responds to the unreal as though it were real; occasionally it assumes that reality is a dream. Thus, I was not particularly frightened when I felt a gentle tug at my foot and, looking down, saw an extremely strange little creature. I should say that I *fancied* that I saw it, since the thought that this creature was real did not immediately enter my mind. I remember quite clearly that I examined it very closely, marveling at the exquisite imaginativeness of my dream. Here was a fully colored dream object quite unlike anything that I had seen or

1

imagined in my waking hours. The creature's skin was an almost translucent sky blue. His appearance was somewhat humanoid, although his arms and legs were very short and his head rather large. His chest was covered by a thin matting of pink hair very similar to the tufts that perched above each of his ears. He stood at my feet, smiling and looking at me with huge, bulbous blue eyes—eyes that were easily the most striking part of his anatomy, for they moved constantly in coordination with a pair of extremely mobile ears. Then he spoke in a Koronian voice, saying softly, "My name is Kongor M-III 216,784,912,LVKX4."

It was with a great deal of difficulty that Kongor M-III LVKX4, as his friends call him, convinced me that he was real—but he was, and is, real. Kongor M-III LVKX4 is from a planet in the third solar system (Androneas). He is a behavioral scientist who was sent to explore Earth and to examine the behavior of the dominant life form thereon.

He was my guest for about one year. In the course of that time he prepared a number of reports, one of which attempted to summarize the present state of Earth knowledge about learning. His intention was clearly to employ this summary simply as a means of helping us to understand human learning as he himself understood it. Unfortunately, he was ordered to go to Mars prior to the completion of that report. He gave me this much of the manuscript, in the form *Kongor's Report*, with his complete and unrestricted permission to use the material as I saw fit. As is evident in Kongor's frequent use of illustrations taken from experiences I related to him or from his observations of our home life, we became very close friends in the course of the year that he spent here. Our friendship is also evident in the following introduction that he wrote specially for this text. I was extremely sorry to see Kongor leave, not only because he was a good friend, but also because his knowledge would be of tremendous value to us on Earth. He has promised to transmit the remainder of this text, however, and has left with me a sonarduct receiver for that purpose. Pending receipt and publication of that material, the reader is advised to study Kongor's present report very carefully.

Kongor's Prologue

My name is Kongor M-III 216,784,912,LVKX4. My friends call me Kongor M-III LVKX4 for short. You know what your name is. For short, I will call you Reader in the manner of your textbooks.

I am an inhabitant of a small, highly developed planet on the rim of the third solar system, Androneas. Our life form is high on the phylogenetic scale — our substance is almost pure intelligence. The physical attributes that we retain consist almost entirely of specialized sensors; for example, our vision and hearing are remarkably sensitive. On the other hand, we have lost much physical and manual dexterity. The appendages that we still possess are not often used since most of our locomotion is accomplished by means of the machines we have invented.

I left our planet, Koros, in the sixth Androneas time cube.* My

---

*More specifically, it was the thirty-first hexalog of the sixth Androneas time cube. Korons long ago abandoned a linear measurement of time. We have not moved simply to a three-dimensional concept — as would be implied by a human understanding of the physical attributes of a cube. Cubes have many more than three dimensions; unfortunately, however, the human mind seems unable to understand more than three (K).

destination—Earth; my mission—to study its inhabitants. I was the first Koron to discover your planet; I planted a flag at locus 4-21-3-Z and claimed it for our governing body. You might be interested in knowing that you now belong to us and that I was to be given a medal for my work here, which surprised me. Your inhabitants spend too much time trying to kill each other directly in wars or indirectly through planned ecological imbalance for your planet to be of value to us.

The order to abandon Earth arrived from Koros last hexalog. That same order stipulated that I should summarize my documents and sonarduct them to my home planet before proceeding to another inhabited planet in this same solar system, Mars. I desperately hope that Mars turns out to be more profitable than Earth.

My superiors have also asked me to leave copies of my records if I think they might benefit you. This textbook is one of a series of reports that I have chosen to leave with my friend Guy Lefrancois. This first report deals with psychological theories about human learning. The other reports will be released as the need for them becomes apparent.

When I arrived on your planet, I was struck first by the physical characteristics of the dominant life form—you are quite unlike anything that I have ever seen or read about. I was also amazed at the complexity of your existence. On our planet—since we are mostly *intelligence*—our behavior is largely rational. When it isn't, we naturally destroy the individual whose behavior is no longer predictable. It seemed to me, at least in the beginning, that very little of your behavior is rational—that is, very little of it can be predicted logically. It was with some considerable consternation and, indeed, frustration, that I tried in vain to apply our laws of learning to your behavior. If I did nothing else while on this planet, I did establish that our learning principles *are not universal.* It occurred to me much later that this discovery might be a good reason for my receiving a medal! In addition, I was later able to discover the variable that should be added to our Koron equations in order to make them valid. That variable has a variety of labels in your language, such as will, emotion, affect, and idiosyncrasy. It was after I determined that human emotion is neither constant nor measurable that the rulers on Koros ordered me to proceed to Mars.*

Before I present my report, I want to tell you about myself. Something seems to have happened to me on your planet. Sometimes I get vague stirrings of undefinable longings, which make me think that I

---

*Kongor was so struck by the contrast between us and Korons that he tended to exaggerate our emotionality and underestimate our rationality. This is obvious from the tenor of this report (GRL).

must be less rational and more emotional than I was when I arrived. I'm almost sure that I would not have wanted to include this autobiography a year ago. I wrote the following autobiography when I was in my last year of formal education (corresponding to the age level of your nursery schools).

The Life of Kongor M-III 216,784,912,LVKX4.

My name is Kongor M-III 216,784,912,LVKX4. My friends call me Kongor M-III LVKX4 for short. I live in residence with all other immature Korons, series LVKX4. An occasional LVKX5 or LVKX3 is allowed to spend some time in our residence.

I am learning about behavior. When I am mature, my duties will be to engineer behavior and to destroy those whose actions do not conform to the Laws. There is talk that some behavioral scientists will be sent as explorers to other planets. I may be one of these.

A behavioral scientist on Koros studies the Eleven Great Laws of behavior and their corollaries. His responsibility is to predict responses and to advise against situations that will lead to undesirable behavior. Behavioral science is a very undemanding field since electronic brains are assuming an ever-increasing degree of responsibility in areas that were once the sole province of the behavioral scientist.

Behavioral scientists, like all other Koron professionals, are selected by series numbers. That is why I will be a behavioral scientist.

My immediate origin is test tube LV2X, 316, 789, series LVKX4. Geneticists might find it of interest that my progenitors were Bleeba Y I, 216,741,376,XKV16 and Burbos A-VII,308,222,300,624,325MNKV7. I am a mutation, since obviously no LVKX4 series ordinarily result from XKV16's and MNKV7's. Nevertheless, I assure you that I am a very normal LVKX4.

All of us look alike on Koros; we all have very large ears and bulbous eyes. Our nostrils are flared and mobile. Among our useless appendages are vestigial arms and legs. Some of us have hair on our chests. Our skin is mostly blue. It matches our eyes and makes for a very aesthetic effect.

I have spent most of the first six time cubes of my life in the behavioral division of the electronic brain complex. I now know everything there is to know about the behavior of Korons. I await my orders.

My orders to visit Earth and to explore it and its inhabitants arrived soon after I wrote that short autobiography. Subsequently I boarded ship and made my way to your planet. There I met and was befriended by Lefrancois, with whom I am leaving this manuscript and a sonarduct receiver. I plan to transmit the Koron store of knowledge about behavior via sonarduct in the near future.

This manuscript is the text of a report that I have submitted to my

A Koron

superiors on Koros. It deals with the extent of the knowledge which your scientists possess about your own behavior. My superiors found it amusing that the state of behavior theory on Earth is remarkably similar to that of our ancestors, the Blips, several thousand years ago. It is for this reason that they requested me to summarize your theories. Had I substituted Burako for Skinner, Gleeba for Hull, Loreno for Hebb, and so on, the report would read like one of their ancient college text-books.

Since the report itself was written primarily for my superiors, all of whom have a vast amount of knowledge about psychology, it was unnecessary for me to spend much time in explaining the scope of learning theories, the major theoretical divisions, or the terms commonly employed to describe these divisions. Since, however, the Earth reader is less likely to have the same degree of sophistication in psychology, the following section is intended to clarify the scope and purposes of the report.

Learning

A variety of definitions have been offered for the term *learning*. The layman's notion is most often that learning is the *acquisition of information*. If I tell you that Koros is 48 billion years old, and you can then repeat that Koros is 48 billion years old, it could be inferred that learning has taken place. In this case the nature of the information that you have acquired is obvious. Consider, however, what would happen if police recruits were presented with a different image for each eye — one neutral and the other depicting some form of violence (Toch & Schulte, 1961). When this experiment was conducted, third-year trainees reported seeing significantly larger numbers of violent pictures than did novices. Had the trainees learned? What had they learned? What specific information had they acquired? Obviously the term *learning* is more complex than the initial definition would suggest. The police-recruit illustration involves a change in perception or behavior that may have resulted from the acquisition of new information, although the specific information acquired is not clear. Nor did the learning simply manifest itself in the regurgitation of information; instead, behavior changed. We need a second definition of learning — learning is a change in behavior or in perceptions. When I first visited the Lefrancois house, their dog reacted to me in a most peculiar and embarrassing fashion. As I moved around to the back of the house the dog followed, her nose to the ground, her tail wagging in excitement. Whenever I stopped she would raise her paw, stretch her nose to within an inch of my face, raise her tail high into the air, and remain rigid until I moved again. It was with some fear that I noticed saliva flowing copiously from her mouth as she stalked me to the door.

Eventually, the dog realized that I was not a new species of game bird and abandoned her attempts to "point" me. This change in behavior can be construed as an example of learning. Consider, on the other hand, the case of the student who after taking LSD believes that the streetlights have become serpents and who runs madly down the street shouting "Help!" Here is a rather striking change in behavior, but to say that this change is an example of learning is to stretch the inclusiveness of the term beyond reasonable limits.

A somewhat more precise, although not entirely satisfactory, definition is that *learning comprises all changes in behavior that are due to experience*. Such changes include not only the acquisition of new information but also those modifications in behavior whose causes are unknown. The definition excludes changes due to maturation (genetically determined changes) or artificial chemical changes such as those that can result from taking drugs.

Theory

Theory is a global term often employed to signify a particular way of looking at things, of explaining observations, or of solving problems. It is not uncommon to hear people saying, "I have a theory about that," when all they really mean is that they are willing to guess the explanation for some phenomenon. The student who says he has a theory about the way professors deliver lectures is simply saying that he knows why one or perhaps two lecturers behave in a certain manner. Despite the widespread use of the word *theory,* it assumes a fearsome and threatening stature when placed in a scientific or quasi-scientific context. Students have so often been exposed to complex jargon-laden attempts to "theorize" that the term *theory* has become almost synonymous with "incomprehensibility." Theories seem to occasion an avoidance reaction in students, whereas the terms *principles* and *laws* usually meet with less resistance.

The irony of this situation is that *theory* is intended to be a parsimonious simplification of observations—it is the observations that are complex, not the theory—at least theoretically. If the observations are simpler than the theory, then theory should be scrapped.

Korons do not deal in artificially complex theorizing.*

Theories can be defined as *systematic interpretations of an area of knowledge* (Hill, 1963). Obviously they will ultimately be based on the substantive knowledge or on the techniques for acquiring knowledge that are peculiar to a particular discipline. The sciences are collections of knowledge derived from experimentation or observations of natural phenomena, organized into principles and laws (statements of relationships among observations), and finally simplified in the form of theories. The theory itself may be a collection of several laws or principles (the terms are used synonymously in this report). Hence, theories are really nothing more than attempts to organize observations.

Hill (1963) discusses three criteria of a useful theory. First, a theory serves as a means of approaching an area of knowledge. That is, it draws attention to facts, laws, or principles that the theorist considers important and provides a language to describe these aspects of knowledge. It is clear that different theories, since they deal with different information, may lead to different approaches to the same subject matter. For example, a theory of human behavior that describes the emotional aspects of man not only reveals the theorist's position but also leads the students of that theory in the same direction.

Second, theories should be parsimonious summaries of knowledge. Obviously there is little merit in a theoretical position that generates a body of abstractions more complex and numerous than the observations that first gave rise to the theory. A parsimonious statement is the simplest and shortest statement that adequately covers the facts. Accordingly, a parsimonious theory is the simplest and shortest set of summarizing concepts available.

Third, a theory should *explain* observations as well as summarize them. The best test of the worth of a psychological theory is the extent to which it explains and predicts the phenomena it deals with. This predictive aspect of theories can be viewed as their fourth function.

Allport (1955), in his discussion of criteria that can be used in assessing psychological theories, lists factors to be considered in addition to the four mentioned above. He includes such considerations as whether there are testable hypotheses in the theory and whether the

---

*Although I sometimes find his smugness to be somewhat irritating, I realize that Kongor isn't really trying to be superior—he simply thinks he is being honest (GRL).

theory is logically consistent. Obviously a theory that contradicts itself should enjoy a short life in terms of psychological popularity. It is not so obvious that a theory that does not give rise to testable hypotheses is also of limited value. A hypothesis is essentially a prediction about the outcome of situations, and it is (hopefully) derived logically from theory. When the hypothesis is supported, it lends credence to theory; when it is not supported, the result may be to invalidate it.

The Psychology of Learning

Since learning is defined as changes in behavior that result from experience, the psychology of learning is concerned with observations of behavior and behavior change. Interestingly, the terms *learning theory* and *behavior theory* are essentially synonymous in psychological literature. Learning theories (or behavior theories) are attempts to systematize and organize what is known about learning. Typically, these theories are statements about the conditions under which learning will take place — they are essentially predictions that are testable in most cases.

Learning theories have become increasingly complex as psychologists have come to recognize that earlier positions were not inclusive enough to account for all the facts. It is important to note, however, that rarely were the early theories discarded completely. Surprisingly often, they were not even altered significantly but were instead simply incorporated into larger theoretical frameworks. But that story comes later.

The earliest learning theories that retain more than historical interest were the stimulus-response (S-R) theories. They were the attempts of the pioneers of twentieth-century psychology to objectify the study of man. Stimuli (conditions that lead to behavior) and responses (actual behavior) are the *observable* aspects of behavior; hence they are the objective variables that can be employed in developing a science of behavior. This early preoccupation with the *observables* of behavior gave rise to the *behavioristic* movement. *Behaviorism* is simply used to denote concern with stimuli and responses and with discovering the relationships between them. Behavioristic theories include those of Watson, Guthrie, and Thorndike (Chapter 4), and Skinner (Chapter 5). More recent concern with what occurs between the presentation of a stimulus and the occurrence of a response has led to the use of a second label, *neobehaviorism*. Neobehaviorists include Spence and Hull (Chapter 6), Hebb (Chapter 7), and Osgood (Chapter 8). The last division in learning theory included in this report is labeled *cognitivism*. Cognitive psychologists are typically interested in perception, decision making, information processing, and understanding. They include the Gestalts (Chapter 9), Bruner and Ausubel (Chapter 10), and Piaget (Chapter 11).

Psychological Theories and Science

It is commonly accepted that science is both a collection of information and a way of dealing with it and/or obtaining it. It is also popularly believed that a discipline is more or less scientific according to the validity of the information it claims as its own and the rigor with which it obtains that information. Lefrancois relates an anecdote to his eager students on the first day of classes — an anecdote that is hilarious despite the fact that most of the students don't laugh.* The story is intended to illustrate the precision and rigor with which psychologists approach their subject. He tells of a brilliant young investigator who conditioned a flea to respond to the command "Jump" and then experimented with variations of the procedure. Specifically, he wanted to discover what the relationship is between the removal of a flea's legs and its response to the command "Jump." At every step of the experiment he made careful and detailed notes in his lab book:

Time.   1:30.7

Procedure.   The two hind legs of the flea were grasped securely between thumb and forefinger of the right hand. The flea was held gently in the left hand with the thumb of that hand underneath the abdomen. Both legs were removed simultaneously by means of a sharp pull. The flea was placed on the conditioning table at 1:32.8 in position 3-Y, facing north. The experimenter then said "Jump" in a normal tone.

Observation.   The flea jumped.

The experimenter "delegged" the flea in three stages (Earth fleas have six legs). After the first two pairs of legs were removed it still jumped vigorously. After the last two legs had been pulled off, however, the flea remained quivering on the table even when the command was repeated. The last recorded observation was this:

Observation.   When a flea has six legs removed, it becomes deaf.

*Kongor is exaggerating. Many do indeed laugh (GRL).

This illustration suggests that the validity of conclusions does not always follow from careful experimental procedures, although it is certainly true that such procedures increase the likelihood that inferences will be accurate.

The scientific method in psychology is similar to that employed in the natural sciences. The investigator first formulates a problem, often in the form of a hypothesis (prediction), and proceeds to gather data (observations) that will serve to substantiate or refute the prediction. Typically, the data deal with two kinds of variables: dependent and independent. Independent variables include those conditions that are directly under the control of the experimenter; dependent variables are thought to be affected by the independent variables. For example, if a psychologist wishes to investigate the effect of sex (as a category, not an activity) on the learning of language skills, he can manipulate the sex of the groups used in his study (on Koros this might not sound quite so confusing). In other words, he can decide that one of his groups will consist of males and another of females. The sex of these groups is an *independent* variable. The hypothesis predicts that achievement in the learning of language skills is *dependent* upon sex. A test of the hypothesis can be obtained by comparing the achievement of the two groups.

This *design*, in which two groups that differ on one relevant independent variable are compared on a dependent variable, is one of the simplest and most common designs used in psychological experimentation. Many other experimental designs are also possible. One possibility is to compare one group to itself in a before-and-after type of design. For example, a group of fat women can be given shock treatments in order to reduce their weights and their *avoirdupois* compared before and after treatment. Another design is the comparison of a *control* group with an *experimental* group. The experimental group is subjected to some form of treatment, whereas the control group is comparable to the experimental group in every way except that it is not subjected to any treatment. Final differences between the groups may be assumed to be due to the treatment. Numerous other more complex designs may also be devised. (See Campbell & Stanley, 1963.)

One of the principal limiting features of experimentation in psychology is that many of the observations dealt with in the discipline do not constitute incontestable facts. It is a fact that apples fall down when they become detached from a tree, and it follows that if a lazy Newton is sleeping below that tree directly under the apple, it *will* hit him on the head. Is it also a fact that 6-year-old North American children have a vocabulary of 3,000 words? Is it a fact that 3-year-old boys love their mothers whereas 4-year-olds love their fathers? Is it a fact that women are more verbose than men? On Koros, yes; on Earth, maybe, sometimes, perhaps, usually, frequently, and occasionally. In other words, the subject matter of psychology often represents no more than the most logical affirmations that can be made on the basis of the data available. Sometimes the affirmations are less than logical.*

A second limitation that makes psychological investigations less than completely scientific is the fact that the subject matter is confounded by the subject. The investigator has some difficulty disentangling himself from the subject he proposes to study. Pre-twentieth-century psychologists—like James (1890) and Titchener (1898)—who were less concerned with the division between object and subject, were able to employ the relatively unscientific, but intuitively satisfying, tool of introspection. The technique involves subjectively analyzing one's own thought processes, feelings, and sensations and extrapolating from them to the behavior of others. Contemporary psychologists usually actively avoid this practice and are consequently forced to employ stratagems that are sometimes relatively inappropriate and wasteful, although highly objective. Consider, for example, the Turkey-Whiff test described by Lefrancois (1972).

> Konorski (1968) has argued that the data of subjective experience should be as valid in the scientific investigation of human behavior as the more objective data which commonly forms the basis of that science. His contention is that in order to discover something as obvious as, for example, the fact that a connection is formed between the smell of turkey and the image of that noble bird, it is not necessary to assemble a group of hungry subjects. It is true, however, that the volume of printed *research* is probably often a function of the use of objective rather than subjective data. Imagine the amount of prose which can result from a detailed analysis of the salivation of twenty hungry subjects who are allowed to catch a whiff of turkey from the laboratory kitchen. To this can be added a detailed examination of changes in pupil size of these subjects, and a correlation of these changes with movements of the eyeballs. The conclusion—20 pages, $4000, and 5 months later—might well be: "There is evidence to suggest that in some cases, perhaps, some degree of measurable change in pupil size results from turkey-whiffing. These changes are not correlated with either salivation or eye movements. There is also some tentative evidence that salivation increases

---

*It should not be inferred from this statement that physical facts are more "factual" than psychological facts. Indeed, in this relativistic and inexact world, "fact"—be it physical or psychological—is a statistical concept of varying probability. Perhaps Kongor's point is that while it is simple to observe an apple falling, it is less easy to ascertain the vocabulary of a child or to measure his attachment to his mama (GRL).

as subjects undergo the turkey-whiffing test." The original question, interestingly, had to do with whether or not a whiff of turkey would evoke an image of turkey. Subjective experience says clearly that if a person has been exposed to turkey sufficiently often, its odor "reminds" him of it.

Psychological investigations are also limited by the amount of control that can be exercised over relevant variables. Two rats who are reared in identical cages and subject to the same daily routines from the time of birth may reasonably be assumed to have had highly comparable experiences. The same assumption cannot be made as confidently about two children who are raised in middle-class homes. Their parents, friends, siblings, and peers are all different. Thus, the concept of *control* in psychological experimentation should take into account relevant differences among subjects.

Consider the following illustration:

Problem. To determine the effect of age on problem-solving behavior.

Subjects. Two groups selected from a private school are chosen for the study. One group comprises older subjects; the other group is made up of younger children.

Hypothesis. Older subjects will perform significantly better on a test of problem-solving behavior.

Method. Subjects are administered the test, and the two groups are compared.

Results. The older group does significantly better.

Is the conclusion that age is related to problem-solving ability warranted? The answer is "yes," *providing that a number of other relevant variables have also been controlled.* If, for example, the older group is generally more intelligent, or is all male, or has had previous training in problem solving, these variables could also account for the differences in test performance. It would then not be logical to conclude that age is the significant factor. One way to control for relevant variables is to match the groups on them. If all subjects are similarly intelligent, balanced by sex, and without any previous training, then the conclusion is more justifiable. However, since it is usually impossible to account for all relevant variables in psychological experimentation, the possibility that results may be confounded by uncontrolled factors remains a limiting feature.

Thus, while psychology attempts to be scientific, it is limited in that attempt by the nature of the subject with which it deals. Nevertheless, psychologists continue to make interesting and useful observations and are increasingly successful in organizing these observations into systematic interpretations of human behavior.

Animals as Subjects

For ethical and practical reasons, it is often necessary to make use of animals in the psychological laboratory as a means of approaching the study of human behavior. The degree to which conclusions derived from animal studies can validly be generalized to man cannot be easily determined, for human behavior is ordinarily infinitely more complex than the behavior of lower animal forms. In addition, despite the fact that the term is largely avoided in contemporary psychology, man is assumed to possess a degree of *awareness* not possessed by a rat, for example. However, it can reasonably be argued that there is little evidence to suggest that many conclusions based on studies of animal behavior should *not* be generalized to man, although the converse is not true. (See Bandura, 1967.) Despite the disadvantages of using animals, it is often necessary. Small children cannot be reared in cages with carefully controlled environments; rats can. Humans do not produce eight generations in several years; rats do. Severe electric shocks should not be administered to students if they fail to learn; they can be administered to dogs and monkeys with more impunity. Adult humans should not have their brains removed and frozen for a count of neurons, particularly when they are still alive; rats don't seem to mind.*

Overview of the Report

This report is a summary of psychological theory on Earth, particularly in North America; it is *not* a summary of learning theory on Koros. Our Eleven Great Laws would be quite incomprehensible to you on Earth without a careful study of this report first. The text deals, in order, with stimulus-response theories, cognitive explanations, and

---

*It should be mentioned that Kongor had some difficulty understanding this distinction since Korons apparently do not hesitate to employ other Korons in scientific investigations (GRL).

computer models, and finally, it attempts to integrate these theories. Lefrancois could not be dissuaded from adding his minor contribution at the end.

Preview of the Text

Following an idea taken from Lefrancois (1972), this section presents short previews of each of the following thirteen chapters. The previews are in the form of brief descriptions of behavioral phenomena or of experiments related to the chapter in question.

Chapter 2. Man: A History and Description

In a carefully guarded psychological laboratory of a large American university, a small, bespectacled, heavily bearded, shabbily dressed undergraduate student sits on a straight-backed kitchen chair. In front of him there is a dish filled with curled, greyish pieces of food. The student doesn't know what the food is, but when well salted and peppered it is quite palatable. He has not been fed for 24 hours and is now busily eating.

Prior to being given this meal, the student was presented with a simple problem in advanced calculus. Much to his embarrassment, he failed miserably. Now, after eating four dishes of the unnamed food, he is expected to be able to solve the problem. Why?

Chapter 3. Human Motivation

Three radical student leaders are cleverly coerced into volunteering for a psychological investigation. They later discover that they will be required to write an essay strongly advocating a pro-Establishment, nonradical point of view. None of them dares refuse for fear of incurring the wrath of his psychology instructor. One student is paid fifty dollars for his essay, the second is paid ten dollars, and the third is presented with a crumpled one-dollar bill. Each student is told that his essay is quite good and that the authorities would like to see it published. The money is ostensibly payment for this right of publication. Each student agrees to allow his work to be published. A day later a skilled interviewer casually uncovers how each of the subjects really feels about the Establishment. A human grandmother (grandmothers appear to be the largest source of real psychological knowledge on Earth)* would almost certainly predict that the student who was paid fifty dollars would be most likely to feel better about the Establishment—but grandmother is wrong. Why? She isn't stupid.

Chapter 4. Early Behaviorism: Watson, Guthrie, and Thorndike

Thorndike once had the human urge to impress his friends with the intelligence of his dog. To this end he knelt with the dog at suppertime one evening, and he proceeded to fill the air with the kind of barking sounds that might be expected of a particularly intelligent dog. The dog listened politely and then ate ferociously. The following evening Thorndike repeated the procedure. He knelt and bayed, barked, howled, whined, and yipped with wild abandon. Again the dog listened attentively and then effectively demolished his supper. Thorndike was obviously trying to teach the dog to bark—not just in an ordinary way but in an *intelligent* manner—for his supper. This procedure is referred to as conditioning. It half worked. At the end of 2 weeks the dog still would not bark, but it absolutely refused to eat until Thorndike had knelt and vocalized in canine fashion. Why?

Chapter 5. Skinner and Operant Conditioning

A bright psychologist once decided that he would show a rat how to eat. "Pshaw," his well-behaved grandmother croaked, "rats already know how to eat." She was obviously not *au courant* (whatever that means). Her grandson explained to her that he intended to teach this rat how to eat properly, how to use a knife and fork, how to tuck in a napkin, how to sit at a table, and how to chew with his mouth closed. He also expected that the rat would eventually learn how to wipe his chops delicately with the napkin after a particularly mouth-watering chew.

The psychologist tried and almost succeeded. Unfortunately, both the rat and the grandmother died of old age before the learning program was completed.

How was the rat trained?

---

*Among Kongor's hang-ups was his constant need to belittle the efforts of honest psychologists by comparing their work to the wisdom of human grandmothers. This should not be taken too seriously (GRL).

Chapter 6.   Neobehaviorism: Hull and Spence

Lefrancois' classes often go to sleep when he presents a magnificent lecture on Hull and Spence. They think that they are bored. He thinks that most of them are simply suffering from symbol shock.

What does this mean: $_sE_R = {_sH_R} \times D \times V \times K$?

Chapter 7.   Neobehaviorism: Hebb

A poverty-stricken graduate student in psychology was compelled by his increasing hunger to seek employment one summer. It was with some excitement that he accepted a position with the forestry division. His duties were simply to man a fire-lookout tower for 2 months. He was flown to the tower by helicopter and left alone in the peaceful grandeur of a world unblemished by men. From his vantage point atop the tower, he looked out over unbroken forest as far as the eye could see.

> There he was—alone,
> It was quiet and peaceful,
> Tranquil even.

A man, the forest, and his soul.
A soul can't talk—nor can a forest
And the radio died the second morning.

There he was, alone.
It *was* quiet.

Four days later the helicopter flew in with a radio repairman—but the student was gone. Three hundred miles of impenetrable forest and muskeg. He was never seen again.

Why? Not why was he never seen again, but why did he leave? He was not stupid.

Chapter 8.   Neobehaviorism: Osgood

The first twenty-two steps in a stairway are each 7 inches high. The twenty-third step is only 4 inches high. An experimental subject is asked to climb the stairs. He trips on the twenty-third step and kills himself (on the second).

Why?

Chapter 9.   Gestalt and Cognitive-Field Psychology

Humans had their first world *war* beginning in the year 1914. A war is a method of destroying people—a highly irrational method since it is quite nonselective.

At the time that this war broke out, a young German found himself marooned on an island off the coast of West Africa, unable to return to his home because of the war. His name was Wolfgang Kohler; he was a psychologist. The name of the island was Tenerife; it was inhabited by numerous apes. During the 4 years that Kohler spent on Tenerife he studied apes, and the apes studied him. Kohler reported his studies in a book entitled *The Mentality of the Apes*. It is uncertain what the apes did with their observations.

What did Kohler discover?

Chapter 10.   Cognitivism: Bruner and Ausubel

If a man sees a head with long blond hair and an attractive face smiling at him over a sea of foam in a pink bathtub, does he simply see a head with long blond hair and a smiling face over a sea of foam in a pink bathtub? (The question is surely of more than passing academic interest.)*

---

*A good example of Kongor's strange sense of humor (GRL).

Chapter 11. Cognitivism: Piaget

An interesting game is often played by psychologists with their wise and ancient grandmothers. The grandmother is asked whether a child will solve the following problem correctly: Two equal balls of plasticene are shown to a 5-year-old; one of them is flattened; the child is then asked whether the balls still contain the same amount of plasticene. Much to the psychologist's delight, a grandmother will often make the wrong prediction, since most 5-year-old children will answer incorrectly. As a sort of *coup de grace*, the grandmother is then challenged to teach the child to answer correctly. She will probably not succeed.

Why?

Chapter 12. Feedback, Machines, and Men

Can machines think?

Chapter 14. Human Socialization

Chapter 15.   An Integration and Evaluation

The integration and evaluation should be the reader's own.

Summary of Chapter 1

This chapter has presented a prologue, a part of which was written by Lefrancois, as well as definitions of learning, theory, and learning theory. In addition, the role of science in developing theories of learning and the use of animals in the psychological laboratory were discussed. A preview of the remaining thirteen chapters of the text was also given.

1. I, Kongor M-III 216,784,912,LVKX4, wrote this report. Guy Lefrancois was of some assistance to me—not much, but some.
2. Learning can be defined as changes in behavior that are due to experience.
3. Theories are systematic interpretations of phenomena intended to be a description of an approach to subject matter, a summary of knowledge about a subject, and an explanation of observations related to the subject.
4. Learning theories are attempts to systematize and organize what is known about human learning.
5. The traditional divisions in theories of learning are based on the primary concerns of different theorists. *Behaviorism* describes an approach that deals primarily with the observable aspects of human functioning; *neobehaviorism* also deals with observables, but, in addition, is concerned with processes that occur in the "black box" (the mind); *cognitivism* refers to a preoccupation with such topics as perception, information processing, concept formation, awareness, and understanding.
6. Psychologists attempt to employ scientific methods for gathering, interpreting, and reporting data. The scientific character of psychology is limited, however, by the nature of the subject matter. Observations do not always constitute incontrovertible fact, nor can the investigator always isolate himself from his subject.
7. The report consists of thirteen more chapters but has no Chapter 13.

Psychological Theories and Human Learning: Kongor's Report

Presented to the

**Koron Space Exploration Department
Division of Behavioral Sciences**

Prepared by Kongor M-III 216,784,912, LVKX4

*(Transmitted by Sonarduct in the
Sixth Androneas Time Cube)*

1

Introduction: Memory, Attention, and Motivation

2

Man: A History and Description

The Landing

I approached the planet Earth at the thirtieth hexalog but did not land until I'd moved into the thirty-first hexalog of the time cube. In the meantime, I drifted slowly over the continents, accelerating as I crossed the oceans, searching for the most pleasing place to set down. As you know, I have always been greatly influenced by aesthetic considerations. Eventually I floated over the North American continent, a most remarkable and striking landmass. A great spine of rugged mountains stretches across its length, rising from warm waters in the south and burying itself in the harsh forbidding cold of the arctic wastes. The majesty and grandeur of these mountains increase as one moves north. Everywhere they look upon vast farm-dotted prairies, rugged hills, or impenetrable forests. Their beauty and the beauty of the surrounding countryside is difficult to imagine for anyone who has known only the bleak desolation of the Koron landscape.

The area I selected as a landing site was a considerable distance from the frozen arctic. I was afraid to brave that fierce cold. It was a fortunate choice, for not only is it one of the most beautiful areas on this planet, but it was there that I met the human who has been most helpful to me during this past year. His name is Guy Lefrancois—a strange name, particularly inasmuch as it has no numbers following it. Occasionally several letters are placed at the end in order to increase its stature.

Humans

Appearance. The dominant life form on Earth is self-named *Homo sapiens.* The phrase derives from an archaic Earth language and is very obviously a misnomer—it means *wise man.* Man, as he is popularly called, is an ugly, foul-smelling creature that walks upright on two long legs. It is never blue unless very cold or dying but does come in a variety of colors. It stands, when mature, as high as three or more Korons and has very long *functional* arms and legs. The ends of the arms terminate in separate mobile rods called *fingers.* These are assumed to have been instrumental in determining the position of humans on Earth's phylogenetic scale.

One of the peculiarities of this animal is that it spends a great deal of time grunting, bellowing, and making other strange noises through a large orifice in the front of its head. It communicates remarkably well by means of different combinations of these noises, but it is incapable of intertelepathic communication. Lefrancois and I had no trouble whatsoever in communicating by ordinary Earth means, however. This ability to communicate is partly why I suspect that man is a phylogenetic precursor of Korons.

It is somewhat ironic that this species has survived and become the dominant life form on this planet *because of its superior intellectual capability* since it is so limited in that area. Its physical prowess relative to subdominant life forms is also quite unremarkable. Nevertheless, it has survived well, although there is considerable evidence that it will eventually destroy itself by fouling its environment or by means of some other irrational act. The most striking difference between man and us is that he is not completely rational. *In fact, our Eleven Great Laws are not entirely applicable on Earth!* It appears that another variable, referred to here as *emotion,* needs to be incorporated into the laws. I have not yet worked it out but propose to do so after I leave and to sonarduct the revised laws back to Earth later.

Development of a Human. Human babies are produced in a strange manner, which I cannot describe in detail here since knowledge of it has been difficult to obtain. Suffice it to say that the entire process is quite unlike that employed by Korons and is much less reliable. Nor is the progeny predictable. Indeed, the entire affair reminds me somewhat of the amusing behavior of our pets, the Blips.

When a human child first appears he is almost completely helpless. He must be fed, clothed, and sheltered for a long period of time — sometimes as long as 20 years. During that time he learns a great deal of what he must know to adapt to his world. Interestingly, the human child has only recently become an important subject in psychological research. Previously a small rodent, *rattus norvegicus,* was the most frequently used subject.

Contemporary theories which attempt to explain human development often assume that it involves a series of stages through which all children progress (see Chapter 11). The forces that account for development are considered to include maturation (genetic endowment) and experience (environmental factors). The relative contribution of each has not yet been discovered. (See, for example, Anastasi, 1958, and Jensen, 1968.)

Theories of development form an important part of the body of psychological knowledge on Earth. Such theories are often not clearly distinguishable from *learning* theories, however, except that they are more concerned with describing learning at different ages rather than learning in general. Discussions of developmental theories are provided by Baldwin (1967), Maier (1965), and Hurlock (1964).

Senses. It is interesting that the senses through which man gets most of his information about the world are the two that are most important for Korons — vision and hearing. Man, however, has not evolved the visual and auditory sensitivity we possess. Man's contacts with the world are limited to his apprehension of its physical properties through one or more of the senses. One of the central problems of learning theory is to explain how raw data from the senses is transformed into meaning. Given that psychology is an emerging science, any answers given here are either incomplete or speculative or both. These answers inevitably implicate the nervous system.

It appears that the human nervous system consists of billions of nerve cells arranged in interconnected pathways and systems in the spinal cord, throughout the body, and in the brain. Major nerve trunks (arrangements of neurons or nerve cells) connect the sense organs directly to different parts of the brain. For example, the optic nerve links the eyes to the visual area of the cortex whereas auditory nerves link the ears to the auditory parts of the brain. That the brain is directly involved in vision and hearing as well as in numerous other functions can readily be demonstrated by means of several techniques. *Ablation* refers to the surgical technique of removing parts of the brain in order to observe the effect on behavior or memory. A second technique involves the *electrical or chemical stimulation* of the brain in order to bring about behavioral change. A third approach is to *record activity of the brain* that occurs in response to external stimulation. Most of what man knows about his brain derives from the application of one of these techniques or from the physical examination of actual brains in people or animals.

The Human Brain

Unlike the Koron brain which is a beautiful blue, the human brain is gray and white. The term *gray matter* is employed to refer to the cortex (or outer covering of the brain), which is composed of millions of cell bodies that are gray in appearance. The general appearance of the human brain relative to the Koron brain is shown in Figure 1. It is readily apparent that the human brain is simpler, smaller, less convoluted (wrinkled), and less attractive than the Koron brain. At birth, the human brain weighs approximately 12 ounces. At maturity it weighs an average of $3\frac{1}{4}$ pounds in the male of the species. Interestingly, the female brain weighs only 90% as much as the male brain. Humans are quick to point out that the gross body weight of the female is only 90% that of the male and that therefore the ratio of brain-to-body weight is the same. It is sometimes argued that this ratio is the best indicator of intelligence, since a number of animals have larger brains than man but appear to be less intelligent—for example, the elephant and the whale, whose brains can weigh as much as 13 and 19 pounds respectively. The ratio of brain-to-body weight in man is close to 1 to 50, whereas it approaches 1 to 10,000 in whales and elephants. However, the argument that this ratio is closely linked to intelligence is somewhat misleading if based solely on this evidence. For example, some small monkeys have much more favorable brain-body ratios than man—as low as 1 to 18. Despite this fact, these monkeys do not appear to be particularly intelligent—maybe due to the fact that the absolute size of their brains is actually extremely small. It appears, then, that on Earth those nonhuman creatures with large brains also have extra-

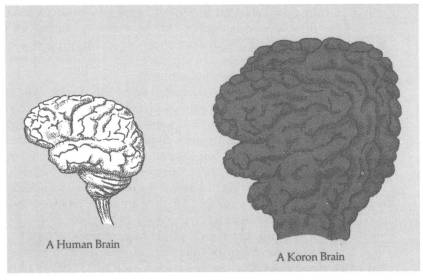

A Human Brain

A Koron Brain

Figure 1

ordinarily large bodies that must be supported by these brains. In addition, where the brain-body ratio is optimal, the absolute size of the brain is too small. There is one exception. The dolphin weighs almost as much as an average human adult; his brain is somewhat heavier ($3\frac{3}{4}$ pounds), and it is more convoluted. Is it more intelligent? As incredible as it seems, no human has yet spoken with a dolphin to find out!

The Koron brain weighs 15 pounds at maturity. An adult Koron weighs 30 pounds; hence 15 pounds of brain for 15 pounds of body.*

Split-Brain Experiments

One of the striking features about human beings is that they appear to consist of two complementary halves, with all parts duplicated in both halves. If a man were separated down the middle, front to back, each half would have one arm, one leg, one eye, one nostril, one ear, one lung, and so on. It is true, however, that the heart and a few other organs would not divide equally (as is the case in Korons).

---

*Kongor constantly reminded us of this fact when he first arrived (GRL).

It is interesting to note that almost all terrestrial animals are characterized by this same dual symmetry. In addition, almost all manufactured items on Earth, however complex, also comprise two complementary halves (for example, automobiles, airplanes, pens, many trees and houses, and most simple tools).

The human brain is also characterized by this duality. The cerebral hemispheres, which are the two complementary halves of the cortex, are not only similar physically, but appear to have duplicate functions as well. Damage to one hemisphere does not necessarily produce lasting behavioral impairment, but instead often leads to a transference of function to the other hemisphere. A number of recent studies have investigated the nature of this transfer and the conditions under which it will occur. The classical studies in this area are reported by Sperry (1964). These studies essentially involved cutting the *corpus callosum*, which serves as a link between the two hemispheres.

Ordinarily, these hemispheres act in coordination as *one* brain, but when the corpus callosum is severed, each half receives input from the side of the body to which it is directly linked. It is generally true that in man the left hemisphere controls the right half of the body, whereas the right hemisphere controls the left half. Interestingly, the retina of each eye is linked to both halves of the brain, with the right half of the retina feeding into the left hemisphere, while the left half is linked to the right hemisphere. When an animal's brain has been "split," however, and the optic nerve is also physically separated, each eye is functionally linked only to the cerebral hemisphere on that side. In this way, the right hemisphere receives input only from the right eye, whereas the left hemisphere is linked to the left eye. No problem arises if both eyes are operative. When one eye is covered, however, and the brain is "split," it is possible to "teach" one hemisphere while the other remains ignorant. Sperry (1964) has successfully taught monkeys to avoid a square and choose a circle with the left eye. The same animal can then be taught to avoid a circle and choose a square with the right eye. As Hebb (1966) points out, it is theoretically possible to produce a completely schizophrenic (split-minded) monkey by providing him with different experiences for each eye from the time of birth.

Functions of the Brain

It is widely accepted that the human brain is not only responsible for sensation (vision, hearing, tasting, feeling, and smelling), for learning in its many forms, and for reasoning and related thought processes, but that it is ultimately responsible for maintaining life in an organism. How it accomplishes this is not always clear. Since this report deals with human learning and since memory, attention, and motivation are closely related to learning, these functions are considered in some detail. The "learning" function of the brain is covered implicitly in most of the report. Memory and attention will be discussed in the remaining sections of this chapter; motivation is the subject of the next chapter.

Human Memory

It is sometimes said that there are two kinds of memory—good and bad—and that most ordinary people possess the latter. When referring to "good" memory, people often mention professional entertainers who can perform the feat of faultlessly recalling the names of dozens of objects listed by an audience. On occasion reference is also made to the so-called *idiot savant*, the mentally defective human who possesses remarkable but highly specific talent. For example, such a person could watch a freight train pass by and memorize all of the serial numbers on the boxcars.

Another example of extraordinary memory is the well-documented case described in *The Mind of a Mnemonist* by A. R. Luria (1968). Luria describes in clinical detail the phenomenal memory of an otherwise ordinary man who had not been very successful as a musician or as a journalist, but who did become an accomplished mnemonist (a professional memorizer). The man could, within 35 to 40 seconds, memorize a table of twenty numbers. Given more time he could easily remember fifty numbers. The absolutely remarkable thing about his memory was not so much that he could memorize these tables so quickly but that he could remember them *without error* at any time in the future.

What would be accepted as commonplace on Koros is an exception on Earth.

Man's memory is a relatively unremarkable thing in absolute terms, although relative to other Earth animals he fares quite well. Consequently, I cannot understand why he chooses to compare a member of his species favored with a good memory to an animal— as in "He has an elephant's memory."

The rather unphenomenal nature of human memory is well illustrated by "memory curves," which have been plotted in connection with experiments on retention since the pioneering work of Ebbinghaus (1885). A hypothetical summary of these curves is presented in Figure 2. The most striking item of information to be derived from it is that humans tend to forget most of what they learn almost immediately after learning it. It must be pointed out, however, that some information is retained over rather long periods of time. This has led to the establishment of two general areas of investigation in this field—*short-term memory* and *long-term memory*. Before summarizing some of the research in these two areas, a number of expressions must be clarified:

Memory.   The term *memory* ordinarily refers to the availability of information. Memory presupposes learning and retrieval in that material obviously cannot be remembered unless it has been learned. (This statement is somewhat tautological since it is difficult to ascertain that learning has occurred without implicating memory.) Equally obvious is the fact that remembering implies being able to retrieve information from storage. Considerable confusion arises when memory researchers attempt to determine whether failure to remember results from not learning, from having originally learned but then losing whatever "trace" learning leaves, or from simply being unable to retrieve information from storage. This last alternative is supported by the observation that subjects under hypnosis can often recall events so remote that they would probably not be remembered outside of a hypnotic state.

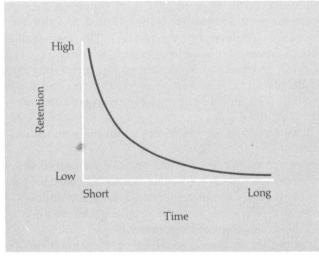

Figure 2

Retention.   The term *retention* is often considered to be synonymous with *memory* and is used in that manner in this text. However, some confusion does result when the term *forgetting* is defined in terms of learning and retention. Deese and Hulse (1967), for example, present the following equation (p. 371):

Amount forgotten = amount learned − amount retained.

It is evident that what a subject ostensibly retains is not necessarily equal to what he has in memory. If, in fact, failure to remember is at least in part a result of failure to retrieve, the amount learned and maintained in memory may be considerably greater than the amount recalled.

Forgetting.   Whereas memory involves retention, *forgetting* is defined as a loss of information after it has been learned. Skinner, for example, defines forgetting as the elimination of some behavior as a result of a slow decaying process due to the passage of time. He does not specify exactly what the nature of the decay is. Nor can he, or anyone else, clearly demonstrate that forgetting does take place. Since subjects can sometimes be made to recall items they would otherwise be assumed to have forgotten through questioning, or hypnosis, or both, it is not unreasonable to argue that nothing is ever forgotten (as did Guthrie, 1935), but that it simply is not recalled.

How much simpler it would be if humans, like Korons, remembered and recalled everything.

Memory as a Behavioral Phenomenon

It can be said that a person remembers if his behavior or responses reflect previous learning. For the sake of simplicity, however, most studies on memory deal only with the subject's ability or inability to reproduce items of information that are presented to him. One of the possible contaminating factors in these studies is the amount of previous *related* learning that a subject has. Thus, an attempt is usually made to present subjects with material that is entirely new to them. This material typically takes the form of *nonsense syllables*, which are novel arrangements of letters. The originator of this approach was Ebbinghaus (1885), who devised over 600 of these syllables (for example, *lar, gur, kiv*). For a number of years, he sat faithfully at his desk at periodic intervals, memorizing lists of nonsense syllables and testing his retention of these. The plotted results of these experiments, with Ebbinghaus as the sole subject, provided the first memory curve (see Figure 2) — the striking feature of this curve being that it indicates that the bulk of what is forgotten is lost very rapidly. At the same time, however, what is retained for a longer period of time (say 10 days) is less likely to be forgotten even after a much longer passage of time (for example, 40 days). It appears that humans possess short-term and long-term memories whereas we have only long-term memories. People often place telephone numbers in short-term storage — sometimes so short that the number is forgotten before the last digit has been dialed. On the other hand, particularly striking or important information may be placed in long-term storage. Hence, the *type* of material that is to be learned often determines whether it is retained for a longer or shorter period of time. In general, organized, related material is more easily remembered than unrelated material. Thus, nonsense syllables are largely unsuitable for studies of long-term memory.

Short-Term Memory. The most frequently employed technique for studying short-term memory was developed by Peterson and Peterson (1959). The experimenter presents the subject with a single nonsense syllable (sometimes by spelling it for him) and later asks him to recall the syllable. Immediate recall comes close to, but seldom reaches, 100%. Errors are usually due to misperception of the original syllable. (As I have pointed out, a human's ears are not nearly so well developed as the ears of a Koron.) Greater delay between the presentation of the word and its recall usually results in considerably lower levels of retention, *depending on the subject's activities in the meantime.* If he is not asked to do anything and *knows* that the experimenter will ask for recall, the subject will probably *rehearse* the syllable, thereby ensuring that it will be retained in memory. If, on the other hand, the subject is asked to engage in some unrelated activity, such as counting backwards in time to a metronome, *immediately* after the syllable has been presented, retention will be less. In this case the amount retained will be a function of time lapse. After sufficient time has passed, very few subjects recall the nonsense letters accurately. For example, in the Peterson and Peterson (1959) study, after 18 seconds subjects recalled less than 10% of the material correctly.

Numerous variations of short-term memory studies have been performed. While there is some disagreement on whether short-term memory really differs from long-term memory (see Melton, 1963), a number of findings that are presumably of more relevance for short-term than for long-term memory can be gleaned from the research. (1) As has already been mentioned, time lapse reduces retention very considerably. By definition, this is not the case for long-term memory. (2) Repetition of the stimulus (the nonsense syllable) increases retention over time (Hellyer, 1962). (3) Forcing subjects to recall slowly (speak slowly) interferes with retention (Conrad & Hille, 1958). (4) Retention is frequently poorer as a function of the number of items that intervene between the presentation of a word and its recall (Norman, 1969). (5) If a series of words is presented, the first word in the list is often most easily recalled (Loess, 1964). (6) The complexity of the stimulus is directly related to the correctness with which it is recalled (Murdock, 1961).

We have seen that short-term memory is of tremendous importance for humans. Not only is it often sufficient that a stimulus be kept in mind for only a few seconds (as is the case for a typist who needs to remember a letter or word for only as long as it takes to type it), but it also appears impossible for many humans to keep anything in mind for longer than that.

Long-Term Memory. Human psychologists have recently been greatly concerned with precision, rigor, and the "scientificness" of their discipline. Consequently, less work is currently being done on long-term than on short-term memory, for it is virtually impossible to control the experiences that occur between the presentation of a stimulus and its recall, unless the time lapse is relatively short. But, by definition, long-term memory involves long time lapses.

That long-term memory exists is obvious. Humans retain numerous items of information almost indefinitely. Some items of information are rehearsed frequently (a person's name, his age, and so on), while others are rehearsed less often (a striking experience like a car accident, for example). Interestingly, even those items of information that are rehearsed frequently are often forgotten very rapidly when they cease to be rehearsed. When I asked Lefrancois to list all of the telephone numbers he had had in the past 10 years, he could only list those that he had currently (he may be a poor sample, heh! heh!).*

Although it is generally accepted that material that is organized and meaningful (that is, related to other material) is remembered for longer periods of time (see Ausubel, 1968; and Ausubel & Robinson, 1969), it is nevertheless true that relatively meaningless material can also be remembered over several years. Lefrancois, who often does

---

*Heh, heh! (GRL)

absurd things out of the mistaken notion that the absurd is comic, always begins an undergraduate course by firing a miniature cannon. He offers no explanation to the students for this behavior. Despite the fact that during the ensuing course he delivers a series of stimulating and highly meaningful lectures, years later many students recall only that he was the professor who fired the cannon; few remember the content of his course.*

One of the characteristics of long-term memory is that what is recalled is often not simply what was seen or heard but a *modification* of the initial learning. Changes in memory were extensively investigated by Bartlett (1932) and more recently by Piaget (1968) and Neisser (1967). It seems that remembering involves not only recall but also an attempt to restructure what was originally learned (see Chapter 10 for a Gestalt discussion of this restructuring). It is probably inevitable that the restructuring will be influenced by learning that has taken place in the intervening period. Piaget and Inhelder (1956) demonstrated, for example, that very young children who are asked to draw lines representing the level of water in tilted jars (see Figure 3) are typically unable to remember what the appearance of the water is, despite the fact that they have just been shown the tilted jar with water in it. Only after the child has learned that water remains horizontal does he *re-member* correctly. Memory can therefore be assumed to interact with other learning.

Memory as a Physiological Phenomenon

It can be accepted as self-evident that learning results in some sort of change in the brain, for otherwise it would logically be necessary that the brain *not be* involved in learning. Since learning and memory are two ways of looking at this phenomenon of acquiring information, it can also be accepted as axiomatic that *memory* involves some change in the brain. Unfortunately, the exact nature of that change is not known with any certainty. However, there is some fascinating and potentially useful evidence that sheds some light on the question.

First, it is likely that short-term memory does not involve the same mechanisms as long-term memory. The most widely accepted theory that presents different explanations for the two aspects of memory is

---

*Kongor is exaggerating again (GRL).

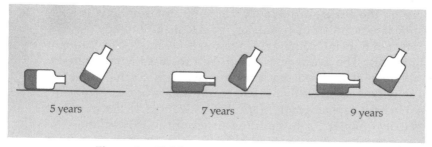

Figure 3. *Children's Drawings of Water Lines*

advanced by Hebb (1949, 1966). His contention is that short-term memory involves nothing more than sustained electrochemical activity in a series of cortical neurons which reactivate one another in a loop (see Figure 4). When activity in the loop ceases, the item of information is lost. Long-term memory, on the other hand, involves more permanent changes of *facilitation of conduction among neurons* (see Chapter 7).

This dual theory represents the two alternative explanations that have received the greatest amount of attention. The first alternative is that learning involves some continuing electrochemical activity; the other is that structural changes in neural cells account for retention. What happens to the human brain as a person learns? Two related answers are given here: the first involves rats, and the second planaria. No directly comparable experiments have been undertaken with humans.

Rats. The first studies, performed by Krech and his associates (1960, 1962, 1966), were designed primarily to investigate the effects

Figure 4. *A Reverberatory Loop: Short-Term Memory*

of learning on the brain of the lowly white rat. Interestingly, the rat brain is sufficiently similar to the human brain to make its study reasonable. In rats and humans neural transmission is accomplished through similar processes. The exact nature of these processes is not entirely known, although it is a fact that cortical activity is accompanied by electrical activity that can easily be detected by means of an instrument called the electroencephalograph (EEG). (The EEG will be discussed in more detail in Chapter 3.) In addition to electrical activity, there is evidence of chemical changes in the brain as a function of neural transmission. The prevailing theory is that transmission from one nerve cell to another is made possible by a chemical change at the juncture (synapse) of these cells. (See Chapter 7 for a more detailed account of neural conduction.) Among the chemicals involved is an acid with the forbidding label *acetylcholine* and its enzyme with the even more awesome name of *acetylcholinesterase*. Prior to transmission, there is a rapid buildup of acetylcholine. When it reaches a sufficient level, transmission occurs. The function of the acetylcholinesterase is to break down the cholinesterase in order to prevent repeated firing.

In the first of a series of replicated experiments, Krech took pairs of 25-day-old rats and assigned one randomly to what was termed the Environmental Complexity and Training Group (ECT) and the other to the Isolated Control Group (IC). The first group (ECT) consisted of rats who were housed in large, airy, well-lit cages that were equipped with the latest in rat furnishing: poles to gnaw on, toys to play with, ladders to climb, and tunnel mazes to explore. The rats could observe from their cages all of the activity in the lab. In addition, they were taken out of the cage for 30 minutes each day and allowed to explore a variety of mazes. Not only were the barriers in the mazes moved frequently but the furnishings of the cage were also changed daily. Rats in the IC group, on the other hand, were placed in isolation in small cages, and the cages were lined so that the occupants could not see other rats or witness any activity around them. Nor were they ever allowed to leave their cages.

At the age of 105 days, all rats, ECT and IC, were humanely executed and delivered to a laboratory for dissection and analysis. Three of the findings of the study are particularly striking and significant.

1. The ECT rats showed a 2% increase in acetylcholinesterase when compared with the IC rats. This finding has been replicated many times, suggesting that learning does result in changes in brain chemistry. It cannot be inferred from the evidence how this chemical affects memory, but it would appear reasonable to assume that it *is* in some way involved.

2. The actual weight of the cortex of an average ECT rat was 4% greater than that of an IC rat. This increase in weight could not be accounted for simply in terms of the increase in acetylcholinesterase. (Interestingly, these effects were most pronounced in the visual areas of the cortex.)

3. There was an increase in the size of the ECT cortex that could be accounted for by an increase in the number of *glial* cells. *Glial* cells serve as a blood-brain barrier. It is suspected that they may also be involved in learning.

The most obvious conclusion to be derived from the Krech studies is that learning *does* change the brain; the nature of these changes may serve as a clue to the physiology of memory. A second inference, which is of considerable significance for human learning, is that if an enriched environment can produce measurable changes in the brain of a rat in 80 days, there is no reason to believe that humans cannot similarly be affected. Hunt (1961), among others, has stressed the importance of varied and rich sensory environments for young children—a point of view supported by the experiences of *rattus norvegicus*.

Cannibals. It is written in human history that the North American Indians and the African tribesmen of another generation always ate the hearts of the animals they killed in order to take full advantage of the spirits of strength that dwell in all hearts and leave soon after death. The liver, the eyes, and the brains were also occasionally eaten in order to benefit from other spirits.

It is also written in human history that men have frequently eaten other men, not only when they were desperately hungry but often as a matter of course. There are reports that even today in the jungles of Africa and South America there remain tribes that prefer a well-prepared human to any other meat. Even the North American Indian is believed to have indulged in the heart of the bravest of the missionaries whom he is alleged to have killed.

Until recently such practices would have been looked upon as barbaric, cruel, tasteless, and repulsive at best. As the only Koron to religiously eat planaria (flatworms) every morning, I can safely predict that man may become a surreptitious cannibal within the next decade.* In order to understand this prediction it is necessary to know of the "cannibal" experiments that have been conducted with planaria and, more recently, with rats. In order to understand these experiments, it is

---

*This statement is not really true; Kongor never did eat planaria. It simply serves to further illustrate his rather bizarre sense of humor (GRL).

necessary to understand something about ribonucleic acid (RNA). In order to understand RNA, it is probably necessary to be a Koron.

The notion that memory may involve chemical changes in a neuron has led to the hypothesis that RNA may well be the agent of memory. RNA is present in neurons in sufficiently large quantity, and it is constructed in such a way that it can assume any one of billions of combinations. It is conceivable that any given combination could represent one unit in memory. This possibility is further corroborated by the fact that the concentration of RNA increases as humans age but decreases in old age, in the same manner as learning ability increases and decreases. Additional support for the hypothesis derives from the controversial planaria (flatworm) studies. McConnell (1962) and his associates began these experiments by training planaria to turn or curl up in response to a light. Trained planaria were then minced and fed to other planaria. "Untrained" planaria were prepared in the same fashion and served to a second group of eaters. Amazingly, the planaria who were fed the "trained" food outperformed those who had eaten only untrained planaria. Later refinements (Zelman et al., 1963) have ostensibly demonstrated that simply extracting RNA from trained planaria and injecting it into naive subjects has the same effect.

However, not all researchers have been able to duplicate these

results (Bennett & Calvin, 1964). It appears that, like an inoculation, a meal of planaria—however well trained they might be—does not always "take."

More recently, RNA memory-transfer experiments have been successfully performed with rats (Babich et al., 1965; Jacobson et al., 1965). The next step is obviously to revert to the practice of some African and South American Bushmen. An injection of RNA from a human genius is probably no more unappealing than is the heart of an antelope.

Planaria don't taste much worse than any other human food if they are well salted.and peppered. I still do not curl up when I see a light, however.*

Attention

A great deal of contemporary learning-related research is concerned with the phenomenon of attention. Indeed, as is made clear toward the end of this report, today's "cognitive" psychologists appear to be more concerned with the investigation of such topics as attention and memory and with the formulation of theories applicable specifically to these phenomena than with the elaboration of the more inclusive theories that have traditionally characterized learning psychology. While this focus may be partly due to the fact that it is considerably easier to deal with smaller aspects of human functioning than with the whole of human behavior, it is also in part a reflection of the relative significance of the topics. The processes involved in memory, learning, attention, and motivation are so closely related as to be logically necessary to one another. Even as learning cannot be said to have taken place unless it can be shown that there is something in memory, so there will be nothing in memory unless the individual has attended.

Interestingly, the psychological investigation of attention dates back to the work of William James (1890), a contemporary of Ebbinghaus, who pioneered studies of human memory. James' definition of attention as the holding in mind of one among a number of competing objects or "trains of thought" (p. 403) is still valid. Quite simply, an organism is attending to an event when he is aware of it. Equally interesting is the historical fact that the systematic investigation of attention was not undertaken until the fifth decade of the twentieth century. Among the first of a large number of related experiments were those conducted by Cherry (1953, 1954) in an attempt to answer two ques-

*Heh, heh! (GRL)

tions: how do humans select what they will attend to, and how much of what is not attended to will be retained in memory? The questions make the assumption that selective attention is, in fact, an ever-present reality.

Cherry (1953) makes frequent reference to what is called the "cocktail-party problem" (Broadbent, 1952). This problem refers to the characteristic ability of a human at a cocktail party* to attend to the speech of only one of the many people who are speaking. Ostensibly he understands no other conversations, although they are clearly audible, but he is nevertheless able to respond to certain auditory signals that are not part of the conversation to which he is then attending. For example, if his name is called, he may respond immediately; if someone else's name is called, he may give no indication whatsoever of having heard.

Cherry's investigations introduced the use of headphones where different sounds could be fed to each of the subject's ears simultaneously. Under these conditions humans seem to be able to listen to either ear simply by *intending* to do so. A second type of experiment, also designed by Cherry, attempts to duplicate some of the features of a cocktail party by taping two messages on the same sound track and playing the tape from one speaker. If the same person records both messages—which serves to remove such additional cues as intonation, accent, facial characteristics, direction of speaker, or lip movements—the subject has a great deal of difficulty in sorting out the messages. There is some evidence from studies employing this technique that the processes of attention are affected by syntactical structure and the related expectations of the listener.

A number of interesting findings have emerged from the first type of study (in which the subject has different messages fed to each ear). In order to discover the effect, if any, of the material that is not attended to, subjects are instructed to repeat everything that they hear on one side as quickly as they can. The exercise is referred to as "shadowing." Surprisingly, it is an extremely simple task—even for humans. Employing this approach, Broadbent (1952) discovered that subjects do not remember what transpires in their other ear. Indeed, when the language was changed from English to German, the subject was quite unaware of it. Moray (1959) found that even if the same word were repeated as many as 35 times, the subject was not able to remember

---

*The *cocktail party* is a social institution where humans stand in noisy rooms holding glasses of intoxicating beverages from which they drink continually, regardless of thirst (K).

having heard it. If the subject's *name* were used, however, usually one presentation sufficed to alter attention.

The results of this last study indicate that there is probably some short-term retention of sensory events, even when they are not being attended to. Neisser (1967) labels this kind of retention *echoic memory*. That it exists has been demonstrated in a number of studies (for example, Pollack, 1959; Eriksen & Johnson, 1964). Eriksen and Johnson attempted to measure the length of time that unattended signals are retained by sounding a signal tone when subjects were reading and then asking the subjects whether they had just heard something. The length of time between the stimulus and the question was varied. Results showed that with longer time lapses the likelihood of recalling the signal lessened.

Among the first theoretical explanations for attention and consequent retention was the "filter" model advanced by Broadbent (1958). This theory maintains essentially that some mechanism serves to *filter* out irrelevant stimuli entirely. It assumes that humans select an input on the basis of its *physical* characteristics. The "filter" model has been shown to be wrong (see Deutsch & Deutsch, 1963; Treisman, 1964). Treisman proposed an alternative model that suggested that attention is not effected simply on the basis of physical attributes but involves the ongoing analysis of stimulus input from all sources and the rejection of that which is irrelevant. Neisser (1967) refers to this proposal as the *filter-amplitude* theory, and a variation of this theory has been advanced by Deutsch and Deutsch (1963). A theory of attention has also been advanced by Zeaman and House (1963) specifically as an explanation of some of the learning problems of mental retardates. More detailed reviews of these theories are provided by Norman (1969) and Neisser (1967).

It is evident from the current literature that the processes involved in human attention are not yet completely understood, although great advances are currently being made. It may well be that when man understands these processes he will at the same time have discovered what memory and learning really involve — and psychology will then be much closer to attaining the goals it has set for itself.

Summary of Chapter 2

This chapter has presented a brief discussion of the physical and physiological characteristics of man and of how he interacts with the world. His brain and its functions were described with special reference to memory. A brief discussion of human attention was also given.

1. Man is an unattractive creature that has survived and become the dominant life form on his planet largely because of lack of *intelligent* competition. He has misnamed himself *Homo sapiens*.
2. Humans are formed in a strange and bizarre manner (much like Blips). Their development after birth is a long process that is assumed to involve a series of stages. Various theories have been advanced as descriptions and/or explanations of these stages.
3. Man derives most of his information about the world from two senses, *vision* and *hearing*. These are referred to as *distance receptors*.
4. The human nervous system consists of millions of nerve cells (neurons) arranged in systems and pathways throughout the body. Concentrations of neurons are found in the spinal chord, the brain stem, and the brain.
5. The adult male human brain weighs $3\frac{1}{4}$ pounds. Female brains weigh approximately 10% less. Man has the most favorable brain-to-body weight ratio of all Earth animals — except for some small monkeys, whose brains are too minute for them to be very "intelligent," and dolphins and porpoises *who may be extremely intelligent*.
6. The brain of a mature Koron weighs as much as the remainder of his body — around 15 pounds. It is a lovely robin-egg blue.
7. The human cortex is characterized by a duality of structure and function. The complementary halves are labeled *cerebral hemispheres*. Split-brain experiments are employed to investigate the relationships between the halves.
8. Memory is ordinarily defined as the availability of information (recall or retrievability). There is some evidence that it may be either short-term or long-term. The physiological processes involved in each are assumed to be different.
9. Ebbinghaus pioneered the early *scientific* investigation of memory. Contemporary psychologists have inherited from him nonsense syllables (which are meaningless) and memory curves (which are unimpressive).
10. Long-term memory is assumed to involve some permanent structural changes in the units of memory. Short-term recall, on the other hand, may involve no more than temporary electrical activity. This is essentially Hebb's theory.
11. Memory involves more than simple recall of information that was learned earlier *as perceived at that time*. It can easily be shown that remembered material undergoes changes over time as evidenced in later reproductions of it.
12. Studies involving rats have demonstrated that learning causes some measurable physiological changes in the cortex. Among these are an increase in the concentration of acetylcholinesterase, an increase in glial cells, and an increase in brain weight.
13. There is some interesting (and contested) evidence that the agent of memory is ribonucleic acid (RNA) and that memory can be transferred by transferring RNA from one organism to another. One way to effect this transfer is to have one individual eat another. The human expression for this is "dog eat dog."
14. Planaria taste much like any other human food if they are sufficiently salted and peppered.

15. Man attends selectively to stimulus input. Ordinarily he responds to only one "message."
16. There is considerable evidence that input that is not attended to is not filtered out completely but instead remains in short-term storage.
17. Several models have been advanced to explain selective attending. Among these are the theories of Broadbent, Treisman, Deutsch and Deutsch, and Zeaman and House.

3

Human Motivation

I have now been with the Lefrancois family for almost 6 months. They are very good to me, although I sometimes find their behavior extremely difficult to understand. They are not much more rational than other humans I have observed. While I understand reasonable behavior very well, emotional reactions are beyond my comprehension at the present time. Judging from Earth literature on the subject, emotions are also beyond the comprehension of most humans. Nevertheless, it is necessary to know something about emotion if one is to achieve any understanding of people.

The term *motivation* is derived from the same archaic language from which man chose his generic title *Homo sapiens*. It relates to the verb *motere*, which means to *move*. Accordingly, it is concerned with the question "what moves man?" Why does he behave the way he does? This question is related to learning theory because explaining how man learns necessitates answering the question of *why* he learns. This section of the report discusses the various answers that have been proposed for the question of human motivation, with special emphasis on the physiology and functioning of the brain as it relates to the regulation of behavior.

Emotion

Emotion is unknown on Koros; behavior there is reasonable and therefore predictable. Reason is unknown on Earth; behavior here is emotional and unpredictable—at least to some extent.* One of the self-imposed goals of psychology is to increase the accuracy of predictions about behavior through the acquisition of more information. Unfortunately for the behavioral scientist (but perhaps fortunately for man), his progress toward this goal is impeded by the interaction of emotion and reason in behavior. Therefore, it is necessary for him to attempt to understand emotion.

While emotion and reason are often contrasted, they are not necessarily incompatible. Indeed, it is often abundantly *reasonable* to react on the basis of emotions and quite unreasonable not to do so.** To run, fight, or pray when afraid is to respond to *fear;* in many cases, ignoring that fear would be irrational.

Emotion is commonly defined as a subjective reaction to external stimuli—a reaction that can take the form of common *feelings* like fear, rage, love, anger, disgust, and so on. A second way of defining emotion is to relate it to physiological changes that occur in response to emotion-producing situations. These changes can involve heart and respiration rates, blood pressure, glandular secretions, and changes in cortical activity. (They are discussed more fully in the section on *arousal* later in this chapter.)

The earliest psychological theory of emotions is the James-Lange theory, labeled for its two independent proponents, William James and Carl Lange. The theory holds that conscious emotional reaction follows after overt bodily reactions. For example, a human who is confronted by an angry cow moose does not feel fear and then run but rather runs in response to such physiological changes as accelerated heart rate and the rapid secretion of adrenalin *and then* feels *fear.* The reaction occurs as a result of the bodily changes rather than vice versa.

From the outset (around 1884) the James-Lange theory was subjected to severe criticism. Walter Cannon (1929, 1939), the main critic, demonstrated, for example, that severing the appropriate neural links between an animal's body and his brain to prevent the animal from being aware of changes in his body does not prevent emotional re-

---

*It is ironic that a mind as clever and coldly rational as Kongor's would make so obvious an error as is implied by this statement. It is clear that reason is not unknown on Earth; it is simply a little rare (GRL).

**Kongor himself too frequently forgets this point. Throughout this text he tends to compare emotion unfavorably with reason (GRL).

actions. In addition, it is possible to produce the changes that ordinarily accompany emotions by injecting the subjects with certain drugs (usually adrenalin or forms thereof). This procedure does not necessarily result in an emotional reaction.

Schachter and Singer (1962) carried on a study designed to investigate the role of cognitive (intellectual) factors in the production of emotional states. Their study was based on the assumption that while physiological changes are responsible for the fact that humans feel emotion, *cognition* (awareness of the meaning of the situation) determines what the emotion will be.

The experimental procedure attempted to produce identical physiological states in a number of subjects while simultaneously providing them with different explanations for these physiological changes. The investigators predicted that the emotion reported by the subjects would be related to the explanation they had for it. The physiological changes were induced through the injection of adrenalin in the bloodstream. Adrenalin is a *sympathomimetic* drug, meaning that the drug acts on the sympathetic nervous system, which is responsible for such functions as respiration, heartbeat, and maintenance of blood pressure. A subject injected with adrenalin reacts *physiologically* as he would when confronted with an emotion-related situation—that is, he experiences an increase in blood pressure, heart rate, and respiration rate.

In the Schachter and Singer experiment some subjects received adrenalin injections, while others were given a placebo.* Some of the experimental and placebo groups were then subjected to experiences designed to provide them with a number of different explanations for the bodily changes they experienced, while others were simply used as control groups. Attempts were made to provide cognitions related to two emotions: euphoria and anger. For the first emotion, subjects were placed individually in a room with a stooge (an experimenter's helper who is ostensibly another subject) who followed a prescribed pattern of behavior. He doodled and played "basketball" with crumpled pieces of paper and asked the subject to join him if he didn't do so of his own accord. In addition, the stooge made spitballs, flew paper airplanes, played with a hula hoop, and generally gave the impression that life is a great deal of fun. In other words, his actions suggested euphoria.

In the *anger* situation, the stooge and subject were asked to answer a long, complicated, extremely personal, and somewhat insulting questionnaire. The last question, for example, was:

> With how many men (other than your father) has your mother had extramarital relationships?
>
> 4 and under _____; 5–9 _____; 10 and over _____.

The stooge was instructed to make comments indicative of increasing anger as he worked through the questionnaire, pacing himself so that he was always working on the same question as the subject. By the time he finished the questionnaire he was in a complete rage.

The results of the study strongly suggest that the explanation one has for a physiological change determines the nature of the emotion that is felt. The euphoria group and anger group differed significantly on reported emotions, with the euphoria group reporting more joy and less anger than the anger group. Subjects who had been injected with the placebo reported significantly less emotion. Presumably the physiological state of a person is related to the degree of emotion he feels, despite the fact that the cognitive label for the change determines

---

Placebo is the term employed to describe an experimental condition in which the subject is made to believe that he is being treated in the same manner as everyone else. But in reality he receives some *neutral* treatment. When testing the effects of a new pill, for example, it is not uncommon to employ a "sugar" pill as a placebo in order to control for "psychological" effects (K).

the nature of the emotion. This last point is illustrated more clearly by one additional observation made by the experimenters. At the beginning of the experimental session some of the subjects were told precisely what physiological changes they would undergo as a result of the injections; others were left in ignorance or were misinformed. Not surprisingly, there was a tendency for those who knew what to expect to report a lower degree of emotional reaction. Evidently, subjects who had no adequate explanation for physiological changes were more likely to account for them in terms of anger or euphoria.

The role of emotions in behavior can be summarized in Piaget's (1967) terms. He sees emotion or affect as the force that energizes behavior whereas reason or more intellectual factors determine the course of the behavior.* It appears axiomatic that learning will not occur unless there is *interest* — and interest is an emotion. But emotion is not the only force that energizes behavior — given the highly imprecise nature of man's knowledge about his emotions, it is probably profitable to look at motivation in other ways as well.

Instincts, Imprinting, and Reflexes

Instincts. When the Lefrancois' English setter followed me around their backyard trying desperately to get me to stop so that she could "point" me as a decent bird dog should (and probably hoping that her master would hurry with the gun), she was demonstrating a primitive, unlearned form of behavior referred to as instinct. Perhaps it is not true that humans behave only because they have learned to act in certain ways or because of emotions that lead them to act or not to act — it may be that they, like animals, act out of instinct. Indeed, among the earliest explanations of human behavior were the instinct theories of McDougall (1908) and Bernard (1924). Employing rather loose definitions of instinct, they attempted to explain all human behavior as resulting from unlearned tendencies to react in given ways. Lists of human instincts typically include such qualities as gregariousness, pugnacity, flight, self-assertion, self-abasement, and hunger. Their explanatory and predictive value is severely limited by the fact that typical definitions are circular. For example, the instinct for survival is manifested in the fact that humans avoid dangerous situations. How is it known that there is an instinct for survival? Because people avoid

---

*Kongor had a great deal of difficulty believing this fact when he first arrived. He seemed to understand it more clearly (and perhaps more subjectively) later (GRL).

dangerous situations. Why do they avoid dangerous situations? Because they have an instinct for survival. Ad infinitum.

How much simpler it would be if humans, like Korons, clearly had no instincts.

More recently, the concept of instincts has been limited to a discussion of complex, species specific, unlearned, and relatively unmodifiable behavior patterns that are particularly evident in lower animal forms (Thorpe, 1963) — such behaviors as nest building, migration, hibernation, and mating rituals. When defined in this manner, it is not at all clear that humans possess instincts. It may be that they do but that the instincts have become so confounded by culture that they are no longer distinguishable from learned behavior.

Imprinting. Imprinting is a term related to *instinct* that has recently been coined by ethologists (people who are concerned primarily with investigating the behavior of lower animal forms). Tinbergen (1951) and Lorenz (1952) describe imprinting as unlearned behavior that is specific to a species and does not appear until an animal has been exposed to the appropriate stimulus (called a releaser), providing that exposure occurs at the right period in the animal's life (the critical period). The classic example of imprinting is that of the "following" behavior of ducks, chickens, or geese (Hess, 1958). It appears that the young of these birds typically follow the first moving object they see. Fortunately, that object is usually their mother—but it need not be. Lorenz (1952) reports the case of a greyleg gosling that imprinted on him and followed him around much as dogs follow humans or Blips follow Korons. As the time for mating approached, much to Lorenz's embarrassment, this goose insisted on foisting its affections upon him.

While imprinting behavior is of relevance for animals, it is not clearly evident in the behavior of humans. Although attempts have been made to extrapolate to man conclusions derived from studies of critical periods in imprinting, no such periods have unequivocally been identified. There is some evidence, however, that there may be times during which some types of learning are accomplished more easily than at others. The work of Spitz and Wolf (1946) and of Bowlby (1951) with children in orphanages has been interpreted to indicate that the first 6 months of a child's life are crucial for the formation of maternal attachment. That this observation, if valid, is analogous to that of critical periods in animal imprinting is not at all certain.

Reflexes. Some human behavior is explainable in terms of reflexes. A reflex is a simple unlearned act that occurs in response to a specific stimulus. It is not as complex as instincts or imprinted behavior, nor does it need to be established through the presentation of a releaser during a critical period. Human children are born with a limited number of reflexes which, with some exceptions, are usually retained into maturity. These include blinking in response to air blown on the eye, the knee-jerk reflex, withdrawal from pain, and startle reactions. In addition, at least three human reflexes are present at birth but disappear shortly thereafter—the Babinsky reflex (curling of the toes when the sole is tickled), the grasping reflex, and the sucking reflex. If an object is placed in the hand of a newborn child, he will automatically grasp it; if the same object is placed in his mouth, or if his lips are otherwise stimulated, he will suck it. All three of these reflexes are usually absent in mature adults.

Another type of reflexive behavior, the orienting reflex (OR), has been identified by some Russian psychologists, beginning with Pavlov. More recently, Razran (1961) has reviewed the history and properties of this reaction. In general an orienting reaction is the first response made by an organism to any stimulus to which it reacts. It appears to take the form of increased sensitivity and awareness and may be reflected in such physiological changes as increased pupil size, alterations in heart and respiration rate, and changes in cortical activity. In animals like dogs, orienting reflexes have observable components. When a dog is presented with a novel stimulus, he is likely to move his ears as well as to assume an "attentive" posture. Because of these aspects of the orienting reflex it is often referred to as the "what-is-it?" reaction.

It is interesting to note that the overt OR of a dog is very similar to that of a Koron, particularly the positioning of the ears. The mobility of human ears is rather unimpressive.

To say that some human behaviors are reflexive in nature is to explain only those specific behaviors that are, in fact, reflexive. As an explanatory concept, however, the notion of reflexes is obviously of limited generality. Attempts to explain more complex human behavior usually take some other form—for example, psychological hedonism, which is borrowed from philosophy and remains less psychological than philosophical.

Psychological Hedonism

If humans were like Korons and always selected the most reasonable alternative, their computers (although these are rather primitive) could quite simply and accurately predict behavior. There is considerable evidence, however, that human behavior often tends toward that which is pleasant and seeks to avoid that which is unpleasant. This notion is referred to as psychological hedonism. It was borrowed from the work of Jeremy Bentham in an effort to arrive at some *general* explanation for most human behavior. Unfortunately, despite the fact that the idea is intuitively appealing — particularly since humans do seem to try to avoid pain and to obtain pleasure — it remains relatively valueless when taken in isolation. The central problem with the notion is that it cannot be employed to predict or even to explain behavior unless pain and pleasure can clearly be defined *a priori* (from that same archaic language, meaning beforehand). Such definition is not usually easy. While it might appear wise to say that a man braves the arctic cold in an uninsulated cabin because he derives pleasure from it, it is quite another matter to predict beforehand that it will be this specific man who will retire to that cabin. The difficulty is that pain and pleasure are subjective emotional reactions. While it might be true that humans are hedonistic, motivational theory can profit from this bit of knowledge only if pain and pleasure can be described more objectively.

How much simpler it would be if humans, like Korons, were rational rather than hedonistic.*

Need-Drive Theories

Numerous theories have been advanced that attempt to account for behavior in terms of needs and drives. These theories can be related directly to the hedonistic position in that they are attempts to specify what the nature of pain and pleasure is.

A *need* is usually defined in terms of a deficit or lack which gives rise to a desire for satisfaction. Need can be viewed as a state of the organism that bears the seeds of its own destruction. For example, a hungry person is in a state of need; this need leads him to eat; the need then disappears. A *drive* is the tendency toward activity that is aroused by a need. Need for food gives rise to a hunger drive, need for love gives rise to the sex drive, and need for water gives rise to thirst.

The relationship of need-drive theories to hedonism is implicit in the assumption that to be in a state of need is unpleasant, whereas to satisfy a need is pleasant. Hence, listing needs is one way of defining the nature of pain and pleasure.

It is commonly accepted that man has a number of *physical needs*, most of which are necessary for survival. Mouly (1968) lists the follow-

*Simpler, but how very unexciting (GRL).

ing: food, water, sleep and rest, activity, and sex. These are referred to as physiological or organic needs. The assumption is that they are *basic needs*, which are manifested in the form of actual tissue changes. Lefrancois has been heard to say that it is his nonexpert opinion that the last need may be at least partly psychological.

Although there is relatively little disagreement about what the physiological needs of humans are, there is considerably less agreement about *psychological* needs. The essential difference between physical and psychological needs is that the physical need — and its satisfaction — result in tissue changes. Psychological needs, on the other hand, are not necessarily manifested in bodily changes, but pertain more to cognitive or intellectual aspects of human functioning. In addition, physiological needs can be completely satisfied whereas psychological needs are relatively insatiable. A person can eat until he is not at all hungry, but he seldom receives affection until he desires absolutely no more.

Mouly (1968) lists six psychological needs also — the need for affection, belonging, achievement, independence, social recognition, and self-esteem. Numerous other lists of needs have also been presented (for example, Raths & Burrell, 1963; Murray, 1938; Maslow, 1954). Maslow's list contains five need systems as follows: physiological needs, safety needs, love and belongingness needs, self-esteem needs, and need for self-actualization. These are arranged in hierarchical order from what are presumed to be the lowest-level needs (physiological needs like hunger, thirst, and so on) to the highest-level system (need for self-actualization — that is, the need to fulfill or actualize inherent potential). The central assumption in this arrangement is that higher-level needs will not be attended to until lower-level needs have been relatively well satisfied. This assumption may have implications for explaining differences between cultures where hunger is a daily fact of life and those typical of the contemporary affluent North American society. It is obvious that the former will be more concerned with survival in a physical sense; perhaps the affluent cultures are, or should be, more concerned with high-level needs.

Despite the fact that need theory appears to have some relevance for explaining human behavior, there are a number of objections to it. The theory holds that behavior results from a need or deficiency in the organism, and it follows that the satisfaction of needs should lead to rest. However, this restfulness does not always follow satisfaction. Even rats which presumably are not in a state of need if they have just been fed, given drink, and loved, often do not simply curl up and go to sleep when in this state. Instead, they may even show increases in activity. A second objection is that there are numerous instances of behaviors that human beings engage in (and lower animals as well) with no possibility of immediate or delayed satisfaction of a need — as when a rat learns to run a maze in the absence of any reward (Tolman, 1951) or when a person seeks sensory stimulation (Hebb, 1966). Of course, Korons never need (heh, heh!).*

Although need theory is often criticized severely (for example, Hunt, 1961) and has certain shortcomings, it is probably descriptive of a great deal of human behavior. Nevertheless, it is not the only current theory of motivation — nor is it the most popular.

Cognitive Dissonance

A position that is less an alternative to need theory than an extension of it has been advanced by Leon Festinger (1957, 1962) and elaborated by Brehm and Cohen (1962). The theory of *cognitive dissonance* is an attempt to explain at least some human behavior on the basis of the motivating effect of dissonance between cognitions. In simpler English, when a person possesses two contradictory items of information (dissonant cognitions) simultaneously, he will be motivated to act. The theory goes one step further and specifies that the behavior engaged in will be designed to reduce the degree of contradiction between the items of information. In addition, it contends that the behavior will be related directly to the magnitude of the discrepancy that exists between the cognitions.

Several studies involving human subjects have been carried out in order to investigate dissonance theory. One such study (Festinger, 1962) was concerned with subjects whose behavior was at variance with their private opinions. A number of college students who volunteered for an experiment that ostensibly dealt with "motor performance" were subjected to an exhausting and boring hour session. Actually this session was designed to provide all subjects with an identical experience about which they would have a very unfavorable opinion. After the session, subjects were told that the experiment was over, but they were then individually asked to help the experimenter with the next subject. They were led to believe that it was important for the research that the incoming person think that the experiment was interesting and pleasant. The relationship between college instructors

---

*Heh, heh, indeed. That pun, of course, is Kongor's. It is not only weak but also inaccurate, since he was not as rational and needless as he thought (GRL).

and their students is such that none of the subjects could easily refuse. As a result, all of them, when they lied to their fellow classmates, created conflict between their behavior and their beliefs — one of the most common sources of dissonance in humans. The obvious prediction that can be made on the basis of theory is that subjects would try to reduce the dissonance by retracting the lie or by changing their private opinions. Since circumstances prevented an effective retraction, it would be highly likely that a change in belief would occur. That this change did indeed occur was determined by having another person interview the subject *after he had told his lie* in order to uncover his real feelings about the experiment.

Two variations were used in the experiment. All subjects were paid for their participation in the second part of the study (telling the lie), but some were given more money than others. In fact, members of one group were given twenty dollars for their help; the others received only one dollar. The effect of this differential treatment is remarkable. The obvious prediction (and the one which is almost invariably advanced by those unfamiliar with the theory) is that those who are paid twenty dollars would change their beliefs much more than those who are paid only one dollar. But the opposite is consistently true! Those who receive small sums often become quite convinced that the hour session was really enjoyable; those who are paid the larger sum remain truer to their original beliefs.

This finding has been corroborated in a number of replications and variations of this study. One such variation reported by Brehm and Cohen involved having college students write essays advocating points of view that were at variance with what they truly believed. Subjects were paid either ten dollars, five dollars, one dollar, or fifty cents for their efforts and were then asked to complete an anonymous questionnaire designed to reveal their true beliefs. As in the Festinger study, those subjects paid the smallest sum changed their opinions the most, whereas those paid twenty dollars did not change appreciably. Both of these studies lead to the interesting observation that if criminals (thieves, for example) initially know that their behavior is immoral, and if they are highly successful at their chosen vocation, they will be "better" people than if they are unsuccessful. In other words, if they make a lot of money by stealing, they are more likely to continue to believe that stealing is an immoral act.

The explanation for the rather unexpected results is simply that the magnitude of dissonance that is occasioned by a behavior counter to belief will be directly proportional to the justification that exists for the act. The student who is paid twenty dollars to lie has a very good reason for doing so and will therefore feel less dissonance (guilt) than if he had been paid only one dollar. He will therefore be less motivated to alter his belief.

A second series of investigations related to dissonance theory have studied the effects of resisting temptation. It follows from the theory that whenever temptation is withstood, there must arise some degree of conflict between desire and behavior. It also follows from theory that this conflict will give rise to behavior designed to reduce it and that the behavior will reflect the magnitude of the conflict. As in the previous studies, it can also be expected that dissonance will be greatest where there is the least amount of justification for resisting temptation. One study performed by Aronson and Carlsmith at Stanford (cited in Festinger, 1962) involved young children in a play situation. The children, who were about 4 years old, were brought into a room individually and allowed to play with any of five toys present in the room. Each child was asked to rank the toys in order of attractiveness and was then forbidden to play with the toy that he had designated the second most attractive. Three conditions were employed to "prohibit" the subject from playing with the toy. In the first situation, the toy was taken out of the room by the experimenter. In the other two, the toy was left on a table in the room, but the child was threatened with punishment if he played with it. In one case he was threatened with only mild punishment, while in the second he faced the possibility of severe punishment. In all cases the experimenter left the room and observed the subject through a one-way mirror for 10 minutes. At the end of that time he returned to the room, allowed the child to play with the toy for a few minutes, and then obtained a second ranking.

The first situation (where the experimenter removed the toy) would produce no dissonance since temptation would not be present. Thus, the prediction was that the child would not alter his ranking. In the "severe-threat" situation, dissonance would arise since the toy was left in the room and since none of the subjects succumbed to the temptation. In this case, however, the justification for resisting is very high; therefore, dissonance would be low, and the degree of change in the ranking should be slight. On the other hand, it is likely that in the "mild-threat" situation a great deal of dissonance would arise, and accordingly the attractiveness of the toy could be expected to become less. All three of these predictions were borne out. The "severe-threat" and "no-temptation" groups still found the forbidden toy highly attractive; the "mild-threat" group found it quite unattractive.

Humans tell an interesting story about a man who was tempted by a woman—to eat an apple, that is. I wonder what the consequences would have been had he resisted temptation?

There are numerous examples of dissonance in everyday life. Below are a couple that I have observed in the course of my stay on Earth.

1. Lefrancois once spent a considerable amount of time trying to decide what kind of car he should buy. Having eventually decided that in accordance with his position he should purchase a very old Volkswagen, he did so. Up to the moment of purchase, any number of other cars seemed almost equally attractive to him. However, after he had acquired this "pauper's Cadillac," he almost immediately *knew* that it was the best of all possible buys. The violence of his rejection of other alternatives *a posteriori* (from that old dead language, meaning "after the fact") serves as an indication that there really was considerable dissonance between his behavior and his desires.

2. An amusing situation developed last winter where a young human was offered the choice of two ladies as marriage partners.* Actually he was not exactly offered these two ladies, but rather he behaved in such a way as to ensure that he would have the choice of two. He wavered for some time but finally decided upon one of them. Almost immediately, she became more attractive in his estimation, whereas the other must have become much less desirable since he avoided her quite actively.

Reducing Dissonance

The illustrations and experiments discussed above offer some indication of how dissonance may be reduced. Festinger (1958), Brehm and Cohen (1962), and Berlyne (1960) suggest a number of additional means for lowering dissonance. Some of these are listed and described below:

Attitude Change. One illustration of this method is provided by the study in which students who had been compelled to lie subsequently changed their opinions. Another example is provided by Tom Blow, who dislikes school teachers quite intensely but who likes Mary

---

Marriage is the term employed to refer to the strange human practice of relatively permanent cohabitation. It is said to legalize certain practices that were not explained to me at all well and that I do not understand, although they may be similar to the behavior of Blips (K).

Jones. When he discovers that Mary is a teacher, he is confronted with a great deal of dissonance, which will disappear when he decides that he really doesn't like Miss Jones or that teachers really aren't that bad.

Compartmentalization. The example of Tom Blow can also illustrate compartmentalization. If Tom decides that Miss Jones is really not like other teachers, that she is a different type of person despite the fact that she teaches, in effect, he places her in a different "compartment." Compartmentalization is evidently a fairly common dissonance reducer employed by religious people who are also scientists and who are compelled, by virtue of the nature of the two areas, to apply different sets of criteria to each. The "compartments" here would involve symbolic truth versus literal truth or "scientific" versus "faith" beliefs.

Exposure to or Recall of Information. On occasion, where there is a conflict between two items of information, gaining more information may reduce that dissonance. If a rumor is circulated that wheat flour turns the human liver white, it will likely create some conflict in those who have been in the habit of eating food made with wheat flour. If a person were exposed to the information that white livers are really quite functional and also somewhat more attractive than the usual dull, dark red human liver, the dissonance might disappear. Koron livers are blue.

Behavioral Change. Situations characterized by dissonance often lead to changes in behavior. The smoker whose behavior is at odds with the information that he has about the effects of smoking may cease to smoke, thereby eliminating all dissonance. Quite frequently, however, humans find it simpler to use other techniques for coping with this problem. For example, it is not uncommon to hear smokers assure their listeners that they have read that there is yet no conclusive proof that smoking is harmful (selective exposure to information, or perceptual distortion). Others insist that all that has been clearly demonstrated by numerous smoking-related studies is that *rattus norvegicus* would do well to stay away from the weed.

In summary, cognitive dissonance is the *motivating* state that occurs when an individual is in conflict. Ordinary sources of dissonance are incompatibility between beliefs, between behavior and private opinion, or between two items of information. Dissonance theory holds that such a state leads to behavior intended to reduce the conflict and reflective of the amount of conflict that exists.

A more global approach to motivational theory that is somewhat imprecise but highly promising has recently been proposed by numerous psychologists. This approach is referred to as arousal theory. A brief introduction to arousal theory is presented in the following section.

Arousal Theory

Arousal theory is sometimes referred to as a single-drive theory in order to relate it to need theory and to make it more easily understandable. It will be recalled that needs are states of deprivation or lack that lead to activity designed to remedy that lack. Implicit in this need-drive theory is the notion that the body tends to maintain some sort of equilibrium or balance in terms of needs and their satisfaction. This tendency has been labeled *homeostasis,* meaning "equilibrium." With some modification, the concept can be applied to arousal.

Definition

The term *arousal* has both psychological and physiological meaning. As a psychological concept, it refers to the degree of alertness, wakefulness, or attentiveness of a person or animal. It varies in degree from sleep at the lowest level to panic or frenzy at the highest. As a physiological concept, it refers to the degree of activation of the organism. This activation is reflected primarily in electrical activity of the brain but also in such other physiological functions as heart rate, respiration rate, blood pressure, and electrical conductivity of the skin. With increasing arousal, there is a change in the pattern of electrical activity of the cortex as measured by an electroencephalograph (EEG). This change takes the form of increasingly rapid and shallow waves (called beta waves); at the lower levels of arousal (such as sleep), the waves are slow and deep (called alpha waves). Also, with increasing arousal there is an increase in the electrical conductivity of the skin, which is probably due to increased perspiration, as well as increases in heart and respiration rate and in blood pressure. Obviously these changes are highly similar to those which ordinarily accompany the intensification of emotions. Indeed, the relationship between emotions and arousal is so close that the terms are frequently used synonymously.

The following passages from Lefrancois (1972) are presented as behavioral illustrations of two extremes of arousal:

1. In the spring of 1969, the author and a friend came down an eighty
    mile stretch of river in a fifteen foot fiberglass canoe. This river, for
    most of its length, runs a leisurely course, displaying from its banks
    a vast panorama of peaceful, farm-dotted prairie. But, on occasion
    it plunges in wild abandon over boulder-strewn rapids and around
    corners where, in the boiling maelstrom, no man, and no beast, can
    easily survive.

    In the spring, the eighty-mile stretch of swollen river that
    courses from the foothills of the Mountains to the prairies is almost
    entirely covered with white-water which lashes in furious frenzy
    at floating beaver-cut logs as they tear among the precariously
    anchored rocks in its bed.

    This was the stretch that the author travelled that spring. It
    was here that, in the blinding rain of a freezing May morning, the
    canoe and its two toiling occupants plunged through the hellish,
    roaring, watery chaos which is known on detailed maps as the Blue
    Rapids. And, at the height of that insane dash through the tur-
    bulent waters, the author pierced the air with an animal scream
    of pure exhilaration.

2. In the spring of 1961 the author sat in the back row of an intro-
    ductory educational psychology course. The instructor, a nondescript,
    middle aged man who had almost mastered the art of the monotone,
    was reading from page 87 in a psychology text (the author has for-
    gotten its title). The instructor had begun, thirty-four minutes
    earlier, in the middle of the second paragraph on page 81 where he
    had been interrupted by the buzzer during the previous lecture. He
    would continue without pause until the next buzzer.

    Between the thirty-fourth and the thirty-eighth minute, 42
    of the 56 students in that class yawned. Four of the others were
    visibly sleeping. The remaining ten could not be seen by the author—
    he was one of those who yawned.

Arousal and Homeostasis

The relationship of the concept of homeostasis, or balance, to
arousal is implicit in the two assumptions that are ordinarily made
about levels of arousal. Since these two assumptions are central to all
theoretical positions that stem from arousal concepts, let us examine
each in turn.

1. There is an optimal level of arousal that differs for different tasks.

This conclusion seems to be obvious. Intense, concentrated types
of activity, like studying or competing on a television quiz program,
evidently demand higher levels of alertness (arousal) than more habit-

ual behaviors like driving a car. It is generally accepted that for most daily activities, moderate levels of arousal are probably optimum.

2. The organism behaves in such a way as to maintain the level of arousal that is most appropriate for the behavior in which it is then engaged.

The value of arousal as a motivational concept is based largely on the validity of this second assumption. If people do behave in order to maintain an optimal level of arousal (that is, if they seek homeostasis), then it is possible to predict, although somewhat imprecisely, what the behavior of individuals will be in some situations. Given that a moderate level of arousal is optimal, a class of students who are at too low an arousal level would be expected to engage in activities designed to increase their arousal. Such activities do, in fact, take place. They often take the form of such noble pursuits as daydreaming, throwing spitballs, or conversing with other bored students.

The assumed relationship between behavior and arousal can be expressed in terms of a law of behavior—a law that states that the effectiveness of behavior increases as arousal increases, until the optimal level is reached (Figure 1). Upon reaching this level, increas-

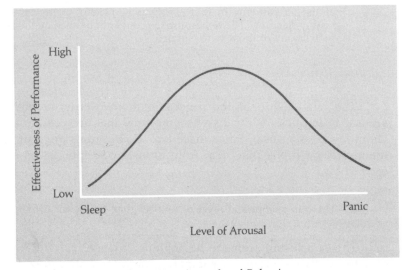

Figure 1. *Arousal and Behavior*

ing arousal merely serves to lower the effectiveness of behavior. There is almost limitless anecdotal evidence that extremely high levels of arousal are associated with sometimes extremely inappropriate behavior. There are instances of students in tense doctoral oral examinations being unable to remember anything and even sometimes being unable to speak. There is the example of the human who became so aroused when she first saw me that she turned and ran screaming into a lake. There are the cases of soldiers at war who are unable to fire their rifles and of hunters who, when confronted with their quarry, are unable to hold them. Too-low arousal levels are also related to inappropriate behavior, although sometimes of a different nature. Anyone who has observed humans sleeping and who has witnessed their amazing inability to answer even the simplest of questions when in that state, realizes how ineffective behavior can be when arousal is too low. Even after waking, there is often some considerable time lapse before humans are properly aroused.

Causes of Arousal

One of the central questions for motivational theory is what causes arousal. There are two ways of approaching this question: the first is to describe the situations that lead to higher or lower excitation; the second is to discuss the physiological mechanisms that are involved in arousal. Both are discussed below.

The RAS. The reticular activating system (RAS—also called the nonspecific projection system, NSPS) is a formation of the brain located in the brain stem (see Figure 2). There is considerable evidence that one of its functions is to regulate an organism's level of arousal (French, 1957; Berlyne, 1960; Hebron, 1966). It appears that stimuli received by the human brain are not simply transmitted directly to the cortex via specific neural pathways but are also diverted into the brain stem (more specifically, into the RAS). Hebb (1966) refers to two properties of stimuli. The *cue* function is the property that indicates to the organism what the nature of the stimulus is—that is, the "cue" is the message function of a stimulus. It is transmitted to the cortex via relatively direct neural pathways. The second function, *arousal*, is effected through the RAS. From each of the major nerve trunks there are branches that terminate in the RAS. When the RAS is stimulated, it in turn bombards the cortex in a *random, diffuse* manner. The effect of this bombardment is to increase arousal. It is widely accepted that

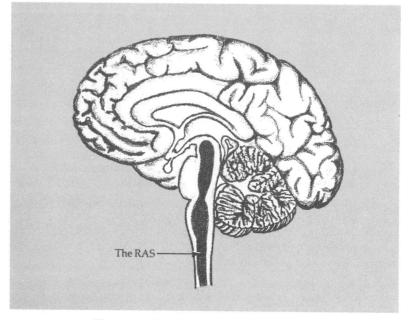

Figure 2. *The Reticular Activating System*

without this activation, the cortex would be unable to respond to the cue function of stimuli (see Hebb, 1958, and Berlyne, 1960). In other words, arousal is necessary for interaction with the environment.

Another function of the RAS is to control sleep and waking. Since sleep is simply a very low level of arousal (the lowest level short of death or of comatose states), it follows that during sleep the RAS is less active. In effect, it appears that the RAS is not at all dormant during sleep but simply serves to gate out stimuli. That it can respond and awaken its sleeping owner is made clear by the fact that a crying human baby can quite easily awaken its mother. Interestingly, the father usually cannot be awakened in the same fashion. French has reported that a sleeping cat can be awakened very gently by stimulating its RAS with very low voltage. Delgado (1969) reports the same phenomenon with humans.

The RAS, as has been pointed out, responds to incoming stimulation by bombarding the cortex and thereby arousing it. It follows from this observation that the amount and intensity of external stimulation should be directly related to the degree of arousal. Schultz (1965) has demonstrated this fact in his study of sensory deprivation. Sensory-deprivation studies typically isolate humans and subject them to prolonged periods of minimal and monotonous sensory stimulation. The effects on arousal are consistently marked, as is evident through EEG ratings and behavioral changes (see Chapter 7 for a more detailed discussion of one of these experiments).

Conflict and Arousal

In an attempt to relate arousal theory more directly to human behavior, Berlyne (1960, 1965) has advanced a theory based on the arousing properties of conflict. His contention is that a great deal of the curiosity and knowledge-oriented* behavior of humans is explainable on this basis. One of his major contributions is his description of the properties of stimuli that lead to arousal. It appears that it is not so much the amount or intensity of stimulation that activates the RAS as it is the *novelty, meaningfulness, surprisingness, ambiguity,* or *complexity* of stimuli. These properties are referred to as *collative* variables. Berlyne (1966) suggests that arousal is induced by stimuli that possess these characteristics because they create conceptual conflict. The individual then engages in behavior designed to reduce the conflict. Put quite simply, the collative properties of stimuli increase arousal, which in turn motivates the individual to behave. Since the behavior is designed to reduce conflict, it will usually take the form of activity that removes the *surprisingness, ambiguity, novelty,* or *uncertainty* of the stimulus. The most logical way of attenuating these collative variables is by acquiring information, for a stimulus is no longer surprising or complex once it is familiar. Hence this type of conflict leads to epistemic behavior (or learning) and can be used to explain such things as curiosity or exploratory behavior.

Summary of Arousal Theory

Arousal theory attempts to account for behavior in terms of the apparent need of humans to maintain optimal levels of arousal. Since arousal level is very much a function of stimulation, the theory is sometimes referred to as a stimulation theory of motivation (Mouly, 1968). Also, since the need for stimulation (or arousal) seems to explain such behaviors as are evident in exploration and problem solving, arousal concepts have been incorporated in most current cognitive theories of learning in an attempt to explain curiosity, problem solving, manipulation, or simply activity (Butler & Harlow, 1957; Bruner, 1957; Fowler,

*"Knowledge-oriented" behavior is called *epistemic* behavior by Berlyne (K).

1965; Hebron, 1966). As is made clearer in the following chapters, the concept of arousal shows exceptional promise in providing explanations for human behavior.

Motivation: An Integration

I must confess that as I wrote this chapter, I could not help wishing that human behavior might be as simple and straightforward as Koron behavior. It is obvious, from reviewing the literature and examining some of the many theories that have been advanced to account for human behavior, that its sheer unpredictability makes the task extremely difficult. Nevertheless, it is possible to summarize and integrate some of what is known about human motivation. The integration here takes the form of three propositions:

1. Emotion can usefully be interpreted in terms of arousal. Since behavior does not take place in the absence of either emotion or arousal and since both are accompanied by (or defined in terms of) the same physiological changes, it is theoretically economical and accurate to treat the concepts as equivalent.
2. Instinctive behavior (if it exists) and reflexive activity comprise very small portions of the total repertoire of human behavior. Hence, they assume a relatively insignificant role in explaining behavior, although they do explain a limited number of specific responses.
3. Cognitive dissonance can be related directly to arousal theory by making the assumption, as does Berlyne, that dissonance increases arousal. It is then possible to explain attempts to reduce dissonance in terms of the organism's need to remain at a relatively moderate level of arousal.

Applications of Motivation Theory

Knowledge about why people behave the way they do can greatly facilitate the psychologist's task of learning how to predict what a person will do in a given situation and to control his behavior when it is not unethical to do so. Consider, for example, the chaotic and confusing situation that would obtain if the ordinary activities of a person were not at least partly predictable. One human meeting another and saying "hello" expects that either the same greeting will be returned, some other greeting will be returned, or, at worst, he will be ignored. He would be greatly surprised if, instead of responding as expected, the person chose to kick him in the shins, run away, faint, or curse in some foreign language. Indeed, the ordinary business of day-to-day living requires that many of the implicit predictions that are made about the behavior of people be correct.

The second application involves the control of behavior, a subject which has led to considerable debate among Earth psychologists. Should behavior be controlled? How should it be controlled? Who should control it? To what end? And so on. Essentially the question is not whether behavior can be controlled but what the ethics of behavior control are (see Rogers & Skinner, 1956).

Despite the somewhat appealing humanistic arguments against behavior control, it is clear that not only is deliberate behavior control a reality but that it is also in many cases highly desirable. Few humans would deny that a child who is toilet trained is somewhat more desirable than one who isn't — toilet training frequently involves systematic and deliberate attempts to modify behavior. The role played by motivation theory in these attempts is related to the realization that a child can be toilet trained more easily when he comes to view cleanliness as a desirable condition (as a goal). In addition, rewards and punishments, which also relate to motivation (and to learning, as is made clear in the next section of this report), can be employed. Furthermore, cognitive dissonance may well be implicated in toilet training, since a child who realizes that being dirty is highly desirable will feel considerable dissonance occasioned by the contradiction between his behavior and his ideals when he does have what is euphemistically referred to as "an accident."

A second illustration related to behavior control is of considerable relevance for teachers, particularly since the function of the teacher is largely one of modifying the behavior of students (the astute reader will recall that this is precisely the definition given earlier for *learning*). His task can be facilitated considerably by a knowledge of the individual needs and goals of students, by a knowledge of the effects of cognitive dissonance, and by a knowledge of the role of arousal in learning and behavior. Cognitive dissonance, for example, often obtains when the student is aware of a discrepancy between his behavior and that which is described (perhaps by the teacher) as being ideal. Such dissonance may well lead to attempts to become more like the teacher's description of the ideal.

The role of arousal in behavior can be even more crucial for teaching. It will be recalled that among the important sources of arousal are the distance receptors of vision and hearing and that it is the combined novelty, intensity, and meaningfulness of stimuli that most affect level of arousal. A teacher in a classroom may be considered to be the most important single source of arousal-inducing stimulation for his students. The impact of what he says and does and how he says and does it is instrumental in determining whether his students are bored or sleeping (low arousal) or whether they are attentive (higher arousal). This consideration, of course, leads directly to a very strong and important argument for variety, meaningfulness, novelty, and intensity of classroom presentations.

Motivational theory can easily be applied to a variety of occupations. Indeed, wherever a profession demands interaction with humans, both predicting behavior and sometimes controlling it are probably of considerable importance.

Summary of Chapter 3

This chapter has presented a discussion of some of the various explanations that have been advanced for human behavior. Emotion, its nature, and its causes were discussed, as were instincts, reflexes, and imprinting. In addition, an introduction to need-drive theories, in the traditional sense, and to a single-drive arousal position was included. The theory of cognitive dissonance was presented as an explanation for some interesting, although not easily explainable, human behaviors.

1. Emotion is a subjective reaction in terms of *feeling* (affect). It is accompanied by physiological changes in most of the major systems of the body (brain, heart, lungs, and stomach).
2. Recent evidence suggests that although the fact that humans feel emotion may be at least partly a function of the physiological changes they undergo, the *nature* of the emotion is probably determined by the cognitive labels available as explanations for the changes. Hence, learning is involved in emotions.
3. Instincts are complex, unlearned patterns of behavior that appear to have more relevance for animal than for human behavior. Reflexes are simple stimulus-specific responses that explain some elementary human behavior.
4. Orienting reflex (OR) is the name given to the general *reflexive* response an organism makes to novel stimuli; it involves some physiological changes that are related to arousal.
5. Psychological hedonism is the motivational position which holds that the pain-pleasure principle is the moving force in human lives. The position is of limited value unless the nature of pain and pleasure can be determined more precisely.
6. Needs are states of deficiency or lack. They give rise to *drives,* which in turn impel the organism toward activities that will reduce the needs.
7. Numerous lists of physiological and psychological needs have been advanced by psychologists. These lists can be interpreted as one way of specifying the nature of pain and pleasure if it is true that unsatisfied needs are unpleasant and that their satisfaction is pleasant.

8. The theory of cognitive dissonance was advanced by Leon Festinger to account for the motivating effect of possessing simultaneously incompatible items of information. It is assumed that dissonance leads to behavior designed to reduce the conflict.

9. Arousal refers to the degree of alertness of an organism. It is a function of stimulation mediated by the reticular activating system (RAS). Its relation to motivation is implicit in the assumption that too-low or too-high arousal is related to less optimal behavior than a more moderate level of activation. Humans behave in such a way as to maintain arousal at the optimal level.

10. According to Berlyne, the novelty, meaningfulness, complexity, and surprisingness of stimuli lead to increases in arousal because they engender conceptual conflict. Such conflict may lead to knowledge-acquiring (epistemic) behavior.

11. The behavior of Korons is simple and logical—Korons are not *simple*, however.

2

Learning:
Stimulus-Response
Explanations

4

Early Behaviorism: Watson, Guthrie, and Thorndike

I have a Blip. His name is Can. He is a full-blooded XT, series M327. Like all other M327's, his genetic pool is such that it makes him a remarkably good watch-Blip. The XT designation indicates his coloration—mauve skin with green splotches. As he ages, the green becomes lighter. Unlike Earth dogs, our Blips are not covered with hair. Indeed, they are not covered with anything but skin.

Our Blips can speak. They are not born knowing how to speak, but must learn to do so. In this respect, they are much like humans and somewhat different from Korons. In fact, they are so much like humans that the elementary psychology texts written by earlier Blips are remarkably like those found in the behavioral-science division of the best Earth libraries. The history of Blip psychological thought is parallel to human history. A brief account of early human psychology as it relates to learning is given in this section of the report.

I do miss the companionship of my Blip.*

*Despite this kind of statement, Kongor would never admit that Korons might also be somewhat emotional (GRL).

Theories of Learning

Chapter 1 pointed out the distinctions among behaviorism, neo-behaviorism, and cognitivism. The real significance of the distinction is probably that it permits a simple classification of explanations of human learning and thereby makes easier the process of attempting to understand, remember, and apply learning theories. I pointed out earlier that learning theory has progressed from simple, rather mechanistic approaches toward more complex orientations. However, the sequence is not perfectly chronological, for the more recent positions are often as neobehavioristic as cognitive. In addition, cognitive positions have not clearly demonstrated that they improve upon the explanation, prediction, and control of human behavior. In line with the relative complexity and inclusiveness of the various approaches, studies of learning theory almost always begin with behaviorism and culminate in cognitivism.

Behaviorism focuses on the objective and observable components of human behavior—that is, the stimulus and response events that concerned Watson, Guthrie, Thorndike, and Skinner. *Neobehaviorism* deals with stimuli and responses as well but extends its sphere of interest to events that occur between stimuli and responses. In some

Table 1. *Divisions in Learning Theory*

	Symbolic Representation	*Variables of Concern*	*Representative Theorists*
Behaviorism	S-R	Stimuli Responses Reinforcement	Watson Thorndike Guthrie Skinner
Neobehaviorism	S O R	Stimuli Responses Reinforcement Mediation	Hull Spence Osgood Hebb
Cognitivism	O	Perception Organizing Information processing Decision making Problem solving Attention Memory	Gestaltists Ausubel Bruner Piaget

cases, discussion of the actual neurological units and their role in behavior forms an integral part of the neobehavioral system (Hebb, for example). In other cases, the theorists are content to assume that there must be some neurological mechanisms that correspond to the organizing and information-processing events assumed to occur in the human organism (for example, Osgood).

The essential difference between the cognitive approach and the neobehavioristic approach is that the cognitivist is not concerned with stimulus and response events so much as with organizing, information processing, and decision making. This distinction is illustrated in Table 1. The Reader should be warned, however, that behaviorism, neobehaviorism, and cognitivism exist only as convenient labels for extremely complex theories. No one theory can be said to be a clear example of any one theoretical division, for each position has characteristics corresponding to other positions with ostensibly different orientations.

Recent Origins of Learning Theory

Learning theory deals primarily with behavior change and attempts to explain changes in behavior as well as to predict them. Ultimately, the goal may well be one of control as well (for example, see Skinner, 1948).

When the observations, hypotheses, hunches, laws, principles, and guesses that have been made about man's behavior are organized, they comprise theories of behavior (and when they are not organized, they sometimes appear to be no more than old wives' tales at one extreme or common sense at the other). Among the origins of contemporary psychological theory are early attempts by psychologists to explain behavior on the basis of instincts and emotion. The rather loose (by contemporary scientific definition) approach of introspection was employed to investigate psychological phenomena. Early psychologists (for example, James, Titchener) relied heavily on introspection (examining one's own feelings and motives and generalizing from these) as a means of formulating their positions. Ironically, probably the most profound and long-lasting effect of this early work is the reaction to it at the turn of this century, particularly in the United States.

The establishment of a psychological laboratory in Leipzig, Germany, by Wilhelm Wundt in 1879 has been taken to mark the beginning of psychology as a science. Wundt and his followers—both in Europe and in America — continued to deal with mentalistic concepts: consciousness, sensation, feeling, imagining, and perceiving. By the early 1900s an orientation toward behavior rather than thought had begun to appear in the United States. This movement, which later became known as *behaviorism*, had as its primary leader John B. Watson (1878–1958). The influence of behaviorism on contemporary psychological thought throughout the world has been remarkable.

John B. Watson (1878–1958)

The term *behaviorism*, coined by Watson (1913), has come to mean concern with the observable aspects of behavior. More precisely, behaviorism assumes that behavior comprises responses that can be observed and related to other observable events, such as conditions that precede and follow behavior. The ultimate goal of a behavioristic position is to derive laws to explain the relationships existing among antecedent conditions (stimuli), behavior (responses), and consequent conditions (reward, punishment, or neutral effects). Accordingly, the validity of these positions can be judged by the extent to which they delineate these relationships.

Concerns of Behaviorism

Watson's (1930) explanation for learning was concerned with the antecedent conditions of behavior rather than its consequences. Much of his theorizing was based on the earlier work of the Russian physiologist Pavlov. In the course of his work with animals, Pavlov had observed that some of the dogs in his laboratory began to salivate before meat powder was placed in their mouths. This behavior occurred only in dogs who had been in the laboratory for some time. In attempting to arrive at some scientific explanation for this phenomenon, Pavlov developed the model of *classical conditioning*—a model that was the basis for a large number of early theoretical formulations and continues to form an accepted part of contemporary psychological knowledge.

In his experiments, Pavlov demonstrated that not only could the sight of food eventually bring about salivation in his dogs but almost any other distinctive stimulus could have the same effect, if paired with the presentation of food often enough. The food is referred to as the unconditioned stimulus (UCS); the initial salivation to the food is the unconditioned response (UCR). The UCS and UCR form an unlearned (reflexive) stimulus-response unit. If a buzzer is sounded every time food is presented to the dog, eventually the buzzer (now a conditioned stimulus, CS) will elicit the response of salivation (now a conditioned response, CR). An illustration of this procedure is given in Figure 1.

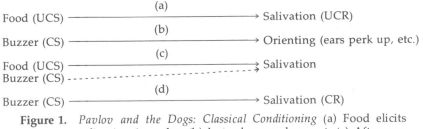

Figure 1. *Pavlov and the Dogs: Classical Conditioning* (a) Food elicits salivation in a dog (b) but a buzzer does not. (c) After successive pairings of food (UCS) and buzzer (CS), (d) the buzzer begins to elicit salivation.

This kind of learning is also referred to as learning through stimulus substitution, since the conditioned stimulus, after being paired with the unconditioned stimulus frequently enough, can then be substituted for it. It will evoke a similar, but weaker, response.

Lefrancois claims that it occurred to him some years ago that if Pavlov could teach a dog to salivate in response to the sound of a buzzer or a bell, then another stimulus that was slightly more sophisticated, but perhaps not so highly distinctive, might have the same effect. The stimulus he selected was the word "salivate." He took an attractive piece of moose meat (no artificial meat powder for his dog) and elicited a copious flow of saliva from a German short-haired pointer, all the while saying, clearly, distinctly, and authoritatively, "Salivate!" The training sessions took place in the seclusion of the garage. (Great steps in Earth science are often taken in secluded garages.) Some days later, after repeated pairings of moose meat and the command "Salivate," he brought the dog into the house. There, in front of his wife, the first (and last) person ever to witness this event, the dog drooled and slobbered profusely on a new carpet as her ecstatic master shouted repeatedly "Salivate, salivate, yahoo! Salivate, yippee!!"

The appreciation of scientific demonstrations is not universal.

Little Albert

Watson's emphasis on behaviorism, coupled with his reaction against mentalistic concepts, led him to abandon all nonobjective approaches to the explanation of human and animal behavior. For example, he considered emotional behavior to be simply another instance of classical conditioning. He assumed that individual differences are virtually nonexistent, and that all people are born with a limited number of reflexes. Among these reflexes are such unlearned behaviors as the knee-jerk reflex as well as the emotional reactions of fear, love, and rage. These reflexive behaviors occur in response to certain specific stimuli, such as loud noises and sudden loss of support, which he believed led to fear reactions; stroking and fondling, which elicit love; and confinement in tight clothing, which was thought to evoke rage. According to Watson's theory all later emotional reactions would be the result of classical conditioning involving these reflexive emotional responses.

In connection with his views on emotional development, Watson performed one of his most famous, if somewhat cruel, experiments. The subject of his experiment was Little Albert, an 11-month-old boy who had become friendly with a white rat, as some boys will. Watson proceeded to condition fear of the rat in Little Albert by repeatedly making a loud noise whenever the rat was presented to the boy. Eventually the mere sight of the white rat was sufficient to make Little Albert cower and attempt to crawl away, whimpering. To Watson's credit, it must be pointed out that he later successfully demonstrated that fear could be unlearned, and he used Little Albert in that demonstration.

Classical Conditioning and People

Watson's early theorizing about emotional development has not stood the test of objective inquiry, for, despite his attempts to deal only with objective variables, the fact remains that fear, rage, and love are emotional reactions that are difficult to identify in young children. A number of controlled studies have shown, for example, that babies left completely unclothed in temperature-regulated environments show as much rage as do babies wrapped in cumbersome clothing (Irwin & Weiss, 1934; Taylor, 1934).

It remains true, however, that many of man's behaviors are the result of classical conditioning. He reacts with fear to the sound of a dentist's drill, although the *sound* of the drill has never really hurt him; he presses on his car accelerator when the light becomes green; he salivates when he sees food (usually with more restraint than the German short-haired pointer); and he makes countless other responses automatically — probably because of previous stimulus pairings.

Below are descriptions of two experimental procedures that can be used to demonstrate classical conditioning.

Illustration I. Keller (1969) describes a procedure in which a subject is asked to dip his right hand in a pitcher of ice water. This immersion causes an immediate drop in the temperature of that hand and, interestingly, also causes a more easily measured drop in the temperature of the left hand. If the hand is dipped in the ice water at regular intervals (3 or 4 minutes) and each dip is preceded by a buzzer, after twenty or so pairings the buzzer alone will cause a measurable drop in hand temperature.

Illustration II. Pavlov's work on conditioning has influenced many Soviet psychologists, who have conducted experiments involving the conditioning of responses not ordinarily under control of the organism. For example, blood-vessel constriction or dilation, which is brought about by the external application of cold or hot packs, can be conditioned to a bell or a buzzer. Urination can also be classically conditioned. If air is introduced into a person's bladder in order to increase the pressure inside the bladder, urination occurs. If the introduction of air is paired with a bell or buzzer, after a relatively small number of pairings the bell alone will elicit urination. This procedure appears to have important implications for toilet training young humans.

Watson's contribution to the understanding of man is difficult to assess, largely because the behavioristic approach for which he was a strong spokesman continues to exert a profound influence on the direction of contemporary psychological thinking. Within the rather narrow perspective of psychological issues as they relate to learning theories, his contribution can be seen as an attempt to make the science more rigorous and more objective, the popularization of the notion that environmental experiences are potent forces in the shaping of people's behavior patterns, and the elaboration of a learning model (classical conditioning) that is adequate to explain at least some simple animal and human behaviors.

Watson and Environmentalism

A recurrent theme in psychological literature is the controversy over the nature-nurture question: is the human adult largely a product of his genetic makeup (nature) or is he molded and shaped mainly by his environment (nurture)? The chief spokesman for the nature position at the turn of this century was Francis Galton (1870), a cousin of Charles Darwin; the chief spokesman for the nurture camp was Watson (1930). Watson went so far as to say that given a dozen healthy infants of any background and given complete freedom to bring them up in any environment that he chose, he would make of them anything that he wished. In other words, he assumed that all human differences result from learning.

The controversy surrounding this question has received recent impetus in the writings of Arthur Jensen (1968) whose work implies that there is a strong genetic factor involved in intellectual makeup. While there remains considerable controversy, most psychologists readily admit that both heredity and environment are involved in the determination of many facets of human behavior and personality.

Edwin Guthrie (1886–1959)

Edwin Guthrie's approach to explaining human behavior is very similar to Watson's, for both theorists were highly preoccupied with being objective, and both dealt with observable aspects of behavior. Their explanations for learning were also identical in many ways.

Probably the most important theoretical distinction between the two behaviorists is Guthrie's denial of Watson's notion that practice strengthens learning. Guthrie's denial was actually less a contradiction of Watson's position than an expression of a different way of inter-preting learning.

Guthrie's (1952) explanation for learning is summarized in his one major law, which states simply that the stimulus or the combination of stimuli that have led to a response will tend to lead to that response again if repeated. He goes one step further to say that the full strength of the "bond" between a stimulus and a response is attained on the occasion of the first pairing and it will be neither weakened nor strengthened by practice. In other words, when an organism does something on one occasion, it will tend to do exactly the same thing if the occasion repeats itself. In behavioristic terms, if a stimulus leads to a specific response now, it will lead to the same response in the future. The interpretation of this law together with its subsidiary is summarized in the declaration that Guthrie's theory is that of "one-shot learning"—a description often applied to it in all seriousness. In other words, complete learning occurs in one trial.

For Guthrie, learning was a process of acquiring S-R bonds (he referred to these as habits) through pairing behavior with stimuli. His position does not provide a clear answer for the question of why specific behaviors occur to begin with. The charge is made that his law of learning is obviously incorrect since we often behave differently in the same situation. His answer appears to be both simple and plausible: if the responses to two stimuli are different, it is because the stimuli are not exactly identical—or it may be that through one of a number of procedures, an old habit has been replaced by a new one. The old one is not forgotten—it is merely replaced.

Breaking Habits

From a pedagogical point of view, Guthrie's suggestions about how one habit can be replaced with another are particularly relevant. He lists three techniques that can be effective in bringing about desirable responses in the place of undesirable ones. However, in order to be consistent with his theory, he maintains that in no case is the old response ever forgotten. It is merely replaced by a newer, more desirable response that is *incompatible* with the old one. Hence, only the newer response will take place in the future. The three techniques, described below, are the fatigue method, the threshold method, and the method of incompatible stimuli (Hill, 1963).

The Fatigue Method. This technique involves presenting the stimulus repeatedly in order to elicit continued repetition of the undesired response. Eventually the organism will become so fatigued that it can no longer perform the response; at that point a different response will be emitted, or the organism will do nothing. Doing nothing can also be interpreted as a kind of response — one which is probably incompatible with the undesirable response. It follows from Guthrie's theory of one-shot learning that as soon as the organism has emitted a response, that response, together with the stimulus or stimulus complex that elicited it, will have been learned. This response, since it is the most *recent* reaction to that stimulus, will be repeated if the stimulus is presented again. In this way the original undesirable habit has been broken.

The Threshold Method. The threshold technique involves presenting the stimulus that forms part of the undesirable S-R unit (habit) but presenting it so faintly that it does not elicit the undesirable response. If it doesn't elicit the undesirable behavior, then it probably elicits another response; again it may simply be the response of not reacting in an undesirable fashion. The stimulus is then presented repeatedly over a succession of trials, but its intensity is increased each time. The degree of increase, however, is carefully kept sufficiently small that the undesirable response will never be elicited. By the time an intensity is reached that would initially have stimulated the undesirable behavior a different habit has been formed.

The Method of Incompatible Stimuli. This technique involves presenting the stimulus when the response cannot occur. If the undesirable reaction cannot occur, then, again, a different response takes its place and eventually replaces the old habit entirely.

All three of these techniques can be illustrated in the training of horses. Hill (1963) describes one procedure for training horses (the fatigue method). There are two other methods. A bucking horse, most people will readily admit, has a bad habit. Rigid behaviorists will go so far as to say that a bucking horse has an S-R unit that should probably be modified. The stimulus part of this unit is represented by the various objects that are put onto a horse's back, leading him to react in an asocial, and sometimes antisocial, manner. The response part of the S-R unit is represented by the asocial activity — the bucking response. Within the context of Guthrie's theory, any attempt to modify a horse's behavior will take the form of one or more of the three techniques he describes.

The common "rodeo" technique of breaking a horse is simply to throw a saddle on his back and to ride the living _____ out of him.

The Fatigue Technique

When he gets sufficiently tired he will stop responding in an unde-sirable way, and if the rider is still on his back, the horse may eventually begin to respond by standing, walking, or running. This change in response is obviously an illustration of the application of Guthrie's fatigue technique.

The threshold method is also commonly used for breaking horses. It breaks as many horses as the rodeo technique but many fewer riders. This method involves "gentling" the horse—beginning by placing a light blanket on his back and increasing the weight (increasing the intensity of the stimulus) over successive trials. Given sufficient time and patience, a horse may be broken in this fashion.

The third technique of incompatible stimuli is probably used much less frequently with horses but can also be effective. It involves presenting the stimulus (saddle and rider on the horse's back) when the response cannot occur. The incompatible stimulus usually involves tying the horse to a post ("snubbing short") so that he cannot buck.

Breaking Habits and Humans

The above title does not refer to the breaking of habits *and* to the breaking of humans but to the breaking of human habits. (Heh, heh!)* Each of Guthrie's three techniques can be applied to people. Of course, it is quite unacceptable to break a child in the same manner that a horse would be broken. But even with due consideration for the *humanity* of the child, it is possible to remove certain bad habits that he may acquire, even in the very best of homes. Consider, for example, a small boy who habitually responds to the sight of his grandfather with very intense fear, which he acquired because the old grandfather was the first individual to punish him with a short whip. (Of course, this illustration is fictitious.) In the manner of Watson and Little Albert, one could remove the boy's fear by having him eat something pleasant while grandfather stands quietly in the distance. Over succeeding trials, grandpa can be invited to move a little closer each time but never close enough to bring about the old fear reaction (threshold method). Eventually the fear response would be replaced by a more desirable behavior.

Both the fatigue method and the method of incompatible stimuli can be employed in a similar manner. Each may be applied to discipline problems in the school or at home. The human Reader is invited to attempt to arrive at illustrations of each.

Evaluation of Guthrie and Watson

While Watson's and Guthrie's positions fall far short of their goal of explaining human learning, they both provide some valuable insight into human and animal functioning. They should probably not be dismissed on the basis of their failure to explain symbolic functioning or so-called "higher" mental processes — as could easily be done — but should, instead, be looked at in the light of their contribution to the development of a science that has never been adequate to explain all, or even most, human behavior, but which explains more behavior, more clearly, with each succeeding theoretical contribution. And the apparently minor contributions of men such as Watson and Guthrie are much more significant when viewed as the beginning of the development of this science.**

*Heh, heh! (GRL)
**See, for example, the elaboration of Guthrie's system in a series of articles by V. W. Voeks (1948, 1950, 1954) (K).

Contiguity and Reinforcement

In learning theories that are based on conditioning, one of two different explanations for learning have typically been advanced, or, more recently, a combination of the two is utilized. When Lefrancois' dog learned to salivate in response to the command "Salivate," why did the learning occur? The two alternative answers are contiguity or reinforcement. The first explanation maintains simply that an association was formed between the stimuli (the UCS, food, and the CS, "Salivate") because they were presented in contiguity (together, simultaneously, overlapping in time, or at least in close temporal proximity). This explanation is probably the most reasonable for this particular learning. The second alternative, reinforcement, is not a good explanation for the behavior of the pointer, however. This explanation maintains that learning occurs because of the consequences of the behavior — or, more specifically, because the behavior leads to pleasant consequences or to the elimination of something unpleasant or both. The presentation of a pleasant stimulus or the removal of a noxious (unpleasant) one is a clear and accurate definition of what is meant by reinforcement.

Both Watson and Guthrie used contiguity to explain learning. Watson maintained that the simultaneous presentation of two stimuli would lead to the development of some sort of equivalence between them. For example, the bell becomes at least partly equivalent to food when it elicits a response similar to that elicited by the food. Guthrie maintained that a link is formed between a stimulus and a response because they are simultaneous (in contiguity). In order to maintain this position in view of the apparent time lag between the presentation of most stimuli and responses, he posited the existence of minute responses that occur between an overt stimulus and a response. Thus, stimuli give rise to a series of responses in sequence, which in turn are somewhat similar to stimuli. For this reason the responses are called *movement-produced stimuli* (MPS). Each response in the chain overlaps with the next (temporally); therefore, through the mediation of these MPS, stimuli and responses are in contiguity.

Probably the major shortcoming of both these theoretical positions is that neither theorist paid much attention to the possible effects of the consequences of behavior on learning. Both were contiguity theorists — neither was a reinforcement theorist. It remained for Edward L. Thorndike to introduce the notion of reinforcement in psychological theory.

Edward L. Thorndike (1874–1949)

Thorndike's work is often given short coverage in psychology textbooks because aspects of his theorizing seem to have found a more popular spokesman in B. F. Skinner.

While Thorndike did not deny the relevance of much of the work of Watson and Guthrie, his final system relies heavily on the principle of reinforcement, which was essentially ignored by them. The effects of recency, frequency and contiguity were summarized by him in the form of his *Law of Exercise* (Thorndike, 1913), which stated that bonds between stimuli and responses would be strengthened through being exercised frequently, recently, and "vigorously." This law plays a relatively minor role in his final system, however.

Basic Notion of Learning

For Thorndike, learning consists of the formation of bonds between stimuli and responses—bonds that take the form of neural connections. Consequently, the term *connectionism* has been applied to the theory. Learning involves the "stamping in" of S-R connections; forgetting involves "stamping out" connections. Both processes—stamping in and stamping out—are subject to a number of laws that explain learning and forgetting, the most important of which is the *Law of Effect* (Thorndike, 1913). Simply stated, the Law of Effect maintains that *responses just prior to a satisfying state of affairs are more likely to be repeated.* The converse also applies, although it is of considerably less importance in explaining learning: *responses just prior to an annoying state of affairs are more likely not to be repeated.* In other words, whether or not a response will be stamped in or stamped out is largely a function of the consequences of that response.

In order to objectify the interpretation of the Law of Effect, Thorndike found it necessary to define what *satisfiers* and *annoyers* are. A satisfying state of affairs is one which the animal (or person) either does nothing to avoid or which he attempts to maintain. An annoying state of affairs, on the other hand, is one which the animal (person) does nothing to preserve or which he attempts to end.

The significance of the Law of Effect in the development of learning theory can hardly be overestimated. Bitterman (1969) describes it as one of Thorndike's two great contributions to psychology. The other is his notion of intelligence in man and animal—a notion that was essentially a denial of the belief that man is simply another animal that can reason. Instead, he maintained that intelligence can be defined solely in terms of greater or lesser ability to form connections. According to Bitterman (1960), this view has been widely and uncritically accepted until recently.

The Law of Effect is essentially one model of *instrumental learning*. An organism performs a response and establishes some connection between it and the stimulus preceding it if it is followed by satisfaction. The important aspect of this model from a theoretical point of view is that the connection is assumed to be formed between the stimulus and the response rather than between the reward and the response. As is made clear in succeeding chapters of this report, Hull accepted Thorndike's view and made it one of the central features of his system. Skinner, on the other hand, adopted the current notion that the reward and the response become associated. Numerous animal studies have been performed in attempts to substantiate one or the other point of view (see, for example, Crespi, 1942; Bitterman, 1967; Hulse, 1958; Postman, 1962). Some of these are reviewed by Bitterman (1969), who, interestingly, concludes with the speculation that perhaps the Law of Effect is a "perfectly general law of learning" and that human psychology may well be at the beginning rather than at the end of the Thorndikean era.

Subsidiary Laws

Five additional laws also form part of Thorndike's explanation for learning:

1. *Multiple Response.* This law states that in any given situation the organism will respond in a variety of ways if his first response does not lead immediately to a more satisfying state of affairs. In other words, it is through *trial and error* that an individual will attempt to solve problems.

Thorndike's most famous experiments are those which have been cited as an illustration of this principle. They typically involve a hungry cat in a cage that has been placed a short distance from a fragrant piece of fish. The cat can open the door leading out of the cage, and thereby acquire the fish, only if he pulls a looped string that hangs in his cage. The typical feline response to this situation is to pace up and down the cage, meowling and scratching at the walls. Eventually, the cat will accidentally pull the string and escape. Over succeeding trials, the amount of time required for the cat to escape becomes progressively shorter until he can finally open the door immediately upon being placed in the cage. Thorndike interprets this behavior as evidence that learning results from the slow process of stamping in a correct response, which was originally acquired through trial and error.

2. *Set or Attitude.* The second law makes the observation that learning is partly a function of attitude or set, set being defined as a predisposition to react in a given way. This law applies not only to satisfiers and annoyers but also to the nature of the responses that will be emitted by a person. There are culturally determined ways of dealing with a wide variety of problems. For example, many Earth cultures find it generally acceptable to react to aggression with aggression; however, these cultures also have decreed that the outcome of physical aggression will be a satisfying state of affairs for the victor and an annoying state of affairs for the vanquished.

3. *Prepotency of Elements.* Thorndike suggested that it is possible for a learner to react to only the significant (prepotent) elements in a problem situation and be undistracted by irrelevant aspects of the situation.

4. *Response by Analogy.* This fourth principle recognizes the fact that a man placed in a novel situation may react with responses that he would employ for other situations with some identical elements. In other words, the *transfer* of responses from one situation to another will be based upon the similarity of the two situations. This principle, Thorndike's theory of transfer, is sometimes referred to as the theory of *identical elements*.

5. *Associative Shifting.* The last of the five subsidiary principles is closely related to *stimulus substitution*. It is simply an admission that it is possible to shift any response from one stimulus to another. Thorndike illustrates this process by training a cat to stand. Initially the cat stands because the experimenter is holding a piece of fish in his hand. Gradually the amount of fish is decreased until the cat stands even when no fish is presented.

Summary of Thorndike's Learning Theory

These five subsidiary laws, together with the two major laws that have been described (there is a third major law, the Law of Readiness [see Hilgard, 1966], which is not of crucial importance to the system), present a relatively clear, although simplified, picture of Thorndike's views on learning. For him, learning consists of the formation of physiological bonds or connections between stimuli and responses. These are bonds which are stamped in through use and because of the satisfying nature of their consequences—or, conversely, they are bonds that are weakened or stamped out through disuse or because the responses are associated with unpleasant states of affairs. In addition, humans arrive at appropriate responses largely through trial and error. They may also respond in given ways because of predetermined set or attitude, perhaps determined by culture or by more specific situational modifiers—for example, a hungry person will respond to food in a different way from one who is not hungry. Some responses will be based on behavior learned in other somewhat similar situations (response by analogy) while others may have resulted from a conditioning procedure (associative shifting). In many cases, behavior will be engaged in only in response to the most important aspects of a situation (the most prepotent elements).

Thorndike's Contribution

Thorndike's most important contribution to the development of learning theory is probably the emphasis he placed on the consequences of behavior as determiners of what is learned and what isn't. In addition, he is largely responsible for the introduction of animal studies as a means of verifying predictions made from theory. Despite the considerable deprecation that Earth psychologists have received and continue to receive because of the use of animals for experimental purposes, it remains true that there are many procedures which cannot, for ethical and legal reasons, be used with humans. It is also possible to control and to measure objectively many more variables in animal studies. A third area in which Thorndike has made significant contributions is the application of psychological principles, particularly in the area of teaching. A large number of his writings were devoted specifically to pedagogical problems, sometimes in specific areas—arithmetic (Thorndike, 1922), Latin (Thorndike, 1923), and the psychology of interest (Thorndike, 1935).

Early Behaviorism in Retrospect

It is somewhat amusing to consider that the first fumbling steps of the science of psychology on Earth so closely parallel the small advances made by our Blips several centuries ago. Looking back on early Blip psychology, one observes that there were numerous attempts to

relate primitive conceptions of stimulus-response learning to the everyday behavior of normal Blips — and one also observes that these attempts
generally failed. Interestingly, the reason they failed is not so much because the explanations of behavior and learning advanced by restricted
S-R positions are inaccurate but simply because these explanations are
insufficient. That is, while they suffice to explain *some* behavior, their
generality is extremely limited. Later Blip psychologists were quick to
realize that classical conditioning is a clear explanation for *one* kind of
learning but that other explanations were also needed. The same
progression can be detected in Earth psychology. The theoretical positions of people like Watson, Guthrie, and Thorndike have not yet been
discarded and are generally admitted into contemporary formulations
as explanations for simple types of learning. The next few chapters
will continue our examination of this first phase of the development of
learning theory.

Summary of Chapter 4

This chapter has presented an introduction to the study of theories of
learning. These theories have been described as systematic attempts to explain and predict modifications in human behavior. Three related theoretical
positions have been described: Watson's theory of classical conditioning,
Guthrie's one-shot learning theory, and Thorndike's trial-and-error position.
All three are illustrative of the behavioristic preoccupation with the objectifica-
tion of the science of psychology, and each (as is made evident in succeeding
chapters) contributed to the development of more recent formulations.

1. Learning is defined as behavior change that is due to experience. This is a
   "behavioristic" definition of learning. It is meant to include attitudinal
   changes, since behavior includes not only overt acts but also covert ones.
   This definition of learning does not include the effects of maturation and
   neurological change on behavior, nor does it account for the effects of
   drugs.
2. Behaviorism is the movement in psychology whose followers are primarily concerned with "behaving" rather than with "thinking," "feeling," or
   "knowing." Learning theorists who are more concerned with "knowing,"
   or cognition, and less with observable behavior are sometimes referred to
   as cognitivists.
3. Watson was the originator of the behavioristic movement in psychology.
   His position was a carefully objective reaction to an earlier, more mentalistic psychological orientation. He based much of his theory on the work of
   the Russian physiologist Pavlov.
4. Classical conditioning is the process of acquiring new behavior through
   the repeated pairing of stimuli. The usual illustration of this phenomenon
   is Pavlov's dog, who learned to salivate in response to the sound of a
   buzzer after the buzzer and food had been presented to the dog simultaneously over a number of conditioning trials.

5. The model of classical conditioning is particularly useful for explaining the learning of emotional responses in people. Reactions of fear, love, hate, and so on can often be traced, particularly in young children, to experiences where previously neutral stimuli are associated with emotion-producing stimuli. It is probably through such a procedure that most humans come to dislike the sound of a dentist's drill.

6. Watson was a strong believer in the power of the environment in determining people's behavior. Probably the most often quoted statement attributed to Watson is his claim that he would be able to make anything he wished out of a dozen healthy infants, if he were given a free hand in determining their environments.

7. Guthrie's explanation of learning is referred to as a "one-shot-learning" theory based on contiguity. He maintained that whatever response follows a stimulus will be likely to follow that stimulus again when it is repeated. In addition, the strength of the bond between the stimulus and the response is thought to be fixed and unchangeable after the first pairing.

8. The notion that stimuli and responses occur in temporal contiguity was made plausible by Guthrie through his statement that external stimuli gave rise to movement-produced stimuli (MPS). MPS are really responses that serve as stimuli for other responses in the chain of response events that are maintained between the presentation of a stimulus and the occurrence of a response.

9. Guthrie suggested that there are three ways of breaking habits. These methods are based on the notion that habits are really never forgotten, but they can nonetheless be replaced. The three methods involve repeated presentation of a stimulus (fatigue method), presenting the stimulus so faintly that a response is not elicited (threshold method), and presenting the stimulus when the response cannot occur (method of incompatible stimuli).

10. The two alternative explanations for the formation of relationships between stimuli (S-S), between responses (R-R), or between stimuli and responses (S-R) are contiguity and reinforcement. The contiguity explanation maintains that the co-occurrence of the events in question is sufficient; the reinforcement position takes into consideration the notion that pleasant consequences of behavior will have a facilitating effect on learning, whereas unpleasant consequences will be detrimental. Watson and Guthrie are contiguity theorists. Thorndike is not.

11. Thorndike described learning as involving the formation of bonds between neural events corresponding to stimuli and responses. Learning involves "stamping in" bonds; forgetting involves "stamping out" bonds.

12. Thorndike's major contribution is his Law of Effect, which specifies that the effect of a response will be instrumental in determining whether it will be stamped in or out. He believed that pleasure is much more effective in stamping in responses than pain is in stamping them out.

13. Five subsidiary laws also form part of Thorndike's system. The most important is the law of multiple response, which states that the learning of an appropriate response is achieved through trial and error. In addition to this law, Thorndike had others that stated that behavior is generalizable (response by analogy), that culture and attitude affect behavior, that man is selective in responding (prepotency of elements), and that stimulus substitution (classical conditioning) occurs.

5

Skinner and Operant Conditioning

To be sent to a distant planet in order to explore the species that inhabit other worlds is the ambition of every Koron behavioral scientist. Not, mind you, that there is ever any display of emotion, one way or another, when the public draws are made. Usually, a Blip is asked to select several candidates for the next venture of the Koron Space-Exploration Department. An electronic diobol could do the job as well, of course, but no better. In fact the choice is purely arbitrary, since all behavioral scientists are of the same genetic series, namely LVKX4, and all are therefore equally capable. Some, like me, are considered to be mutations, but are really identical—as far as it is possible to tell—to all other Korons with the same series number.

The draw was made approximately 12 Earth months ago. My own Blip, Can, was chosen to select two scientists: one to proceed to a planet in the Hebros system, the other to come to Earth.

I think Can was grinning a wee bit when he pointed his finger at me and said "You."

Before coming to your planet, I was given all of the geographical and meteorological information that we had about Earth. In addition, I was told what we knew about human behavior. Nothing!

In the course of reviewing behavioristic theories, however, I have uncovered a giant of a behaviorist named B. F. Skinner. His theory of operant conditioning is the subject of this chapter.

Skinner's Theoretical Orientation

It may appear to be a contradiction to state at the outset that Skinner's theoretical orientation is antitheoretical, but the statement is only superficially contradictory. Skinner's views on theorizing are summarized in his declaration that theory, while it can be amusing to its creators, will be of little practical value (Skinner, 1961). His system is not intended to be a systematization into principles and laws of what is known about behavior but simply a description of the observations that he has made. Interestingly enough, it is precisely because Skinner's work has taken a clearly objective, descriptive form and not a more inferential, speculative one that his most basic work remains relatively free from sound invalidating criticism. The main critics are those who interpret Skinner's system as implying that principles of operant conditioning can eventually be used to explain and control *all* human behavior. However, their criticism is aimed more at the application of the system than at the system itself.

For the sake of simplicity, Skinner's observations can be divided into those concerned with independent variables (factors that can be directly manipulated experimentally) and those concerned with dependent variables (variables not manipulated by the experimenter that are thought to be affected by the independent variables). In addition, he is very much concerned with discovering the specific relationships that exist between dependent and independent variables, with the explicit goal of increasing and refining control over dependent variables. The essential elements of the system, viewed in terms of dependent and independent variables, are summarized in Table 1.

Table 1. *Skinner's System*

Independent Variables	Dependent Variables
Type of Reinforcement Schedules of Reinforcement	Acquisition Rate Rate of Responding Extinction Rate

The central question that Skinner's system is intended to answer is how do the independent variables—reinforcement types and schedules—affect learning?

Two Types of Learning

In his attempts to explain learning, Skinner had available to him the explanation that had already been advanced by Pavlov and elaborated by people like Watson and Guthrie. It appeared to him, however, that the classical-conditioning explanation explained only a very limited variety of human and animal behavior. Specifically, he maintained that these earlier theoretical formulations could be used to explain the acquisition of behaviors *only* where the initial response could be elicited by a known stimulus. The learning that would then occur would result from pairing this stimulus with another over a number of trials.

While Skinner accepted this model as accurate for explaining some behavior, he declared that the majority of the responses that people manifest do not result from obvious stimuli. He further maintained that, in any case, the stimuli, observable or not, are really not central to an accurate and useful explanation of the learning.

Responses elicited by a stimulus are labeled *respondents;* those responses simply emitted by an organism are labeled *operants.* In other words, in respondent behavior the organism reacts *to* the environment, while in operant behavior it acts *upon* the environment. Classical conditioning can be employed to explain learning based upon respondent behavior. Skinner called this type of learning *Type S* conditioning. He advanced a different model to explain learning based on operant behavior: the model of operant or instrumental conditioning, also referred to as *Type R* conditioning. The distinctions between these two forms of learning are detailed in Table 2.

It was Skinner's (1938) contention that most significant behaviors people engage in are operant. Walking to school, drinking Bacardi

Table 2. *Classical and Operant Conditioning*

Classical	*Operant*
Deals with *respondents* that are *elicited* as responses to *stimuli* Type S (stimuli)	Deals with *operants* that are *emitted* as *instrumental* acts Type R (reinforcement)
Pavlov	*Skinner*

white rum, writing a letter or a textbook, answering a question, smiling at a stranger, drinking Bacardi white rum, fondling a rat, fishing, drinking Bacardi white rum, shoveling snow, skiing, reading, drinking Bacardi white rum, and drinking Bacardi white rum are all examples of operant behavior.* While it could be argued that there are known and observable stimuli that readily and reliably lead to some of these behaviors (that is, thirst readily and reliably leads to drinking Bacardi white rum), the real point is that the stimuli that can lead to these responses are not central in the learning that takes place.

Stated very simply, the model of operant conditioning says that when a response—regardless of the conditions that might or might not have led to its emission—is followed by a reinforcer, the result will be an increase in the probability that this response will occur again under similar circumstances. Further, the model states that the reinforcer, together with the circumstances surrounding its administration, is a stimulus that can come to have control over that response through repeated presentation. A simplified presentation of a model of operant conditioning and a classical-conditioning paradigm are presented in Figure 1.

Essentially any behavior that is acquired as a result of reinforcement can be interpreted as an illustration of operant conditioning.

A. *Operant conditioning*

S ← (desire to catch a fish)
- → R₁ (grey hackle) ———→ no bites
- → R₂ (royal coachman) ———→ two trout
- → R₃ (Idaho nymph) ———→ one nibble
- → R₄ (Lefrancois nymph) ———→ nothing

How Lefrancois Learned to Use a Royal Coachman Fly

B. *Classical conditioning*

UCS ————————————→ UCR ("Ouch," three French
(fly in ear)   swear words, and with-
                                          drawal behavior)

CS – – – – – – – – – – – – –→   CR (avoidance behavior)
(color of fly, its name, etc.)

How Lefrancois Learned to Avoid a Lefrancois Nymph

Figure 1

*Kongor really did not drink much white rum; he simply thought this would be clever (GRL).

Figure 1 shows one example — a fly fisherman who becomes conditioned to using a certain type of fly because he has been reinforced for using it in the past.

The extent of the applicability of this model to human behavior will be made more evident as we proceed to a discussion of the variables involved.

Reinforcement

Skinner's explanation of learning through operant conditioning is based on the somewhat hedonistic notion that we tend to behave in such a way as to increase pleasure and decrease pain. However, subjective terms like pain and pleasure do not have an important role in a position so clearly and explicitly objective as Skinner's. Accordingly, reinforcement is defined in a rather operational, if somewhat circular, manner. Reinforcement includes *any and all stimuli that increase the probability of a response occurring;* therefore, it is *not* necessarily a pleasant stimulus in any universal sense. Nor is a stimulus that is reinforcing for one situation necessarily reinforcing in another, even though the same person is involved. In addition, what is reinforcing for one person is not necessarily reinforcing for another.

To illustrate these comments, let us consider the case of Henry, a buck-toothed, freckle-faced, lovable little school child of ten. Henry took a spelling test, for which he studied very hard, using a number of mnemonic devices. For example, in order to remember how to spell "separate" he talked himself into remembering that there is "a rat" in "separate." He gets his results back — 95%. This knowledge of results serves as a reinforcer; it increases the probability that the response of studying hard and using mnemonics will occur again.

Consider, on the other hand, Agnes. Agnes is a bright little girl. She always gets 100% in spelling. This time she has studied differently — she has used the same mnemonic device Henry used. Unlike Henry, however, she became confused on the test and thought there was "erat" in separate. She also received a grade of 95%. However, this same stimulus is not a reinforcer for Agnes and will probably have the opposite effect on her behavior.

Types of Reinforcement

Skinner distinguishes between two types of reinforcement: positive and negative. A *positive reinforcer* is a stimulus which, when *added to* a situation, increases the probability of the response occurring again in similar circumstances. A *negative reinforcer* is a stimulus which, when *taken away from* a situation, increases the probability of a response occurring. It is important to note that the effect of both positive and negative reinforcers is to *increase* the probability of a response occurring. It is also important to note that the effect of the stimulus on a response—not the nature of the stimulus itself—determines whether or not it is a reinforcer.

Punishment

Punishment, like reinforcement, is also defined in terms of its effects. In this case, however, the effect is not a strengthening of the behavior but rather a suppression of it. The same considerations need to be applied to punishment as were applied to reinforcement. That is, some stimuli may be punishing in some circumstances but not in others; some stimuli may be punishing for some people but not for others.

Punishment and Negative Reinforcement

An error in definition prevalent in textbooks of psychology and educational psychology is the confounding of punishment with negative reinforcement. It is very common to read such declarations as "punishment is a negative reinforcer . . ." immediately following definitions specifying that reinforcement, whether positive or negative, increases the probability of a response occurring while punishment does not. How, then, can punishment be a negative reinforcer?

The confusion can easily be clarified by reference to Table 3,

Table 3. *Reinforcement and Punishment*

Stimulus

	Pleasant	*Noxious*
Added to a situation after a response	Positive Reinforcement (1)	Punishment (2)
Taken away from a situation after a response	Punishment (3)	Negative Reinforcement (4)

which shows the four possibilities involved in presenting or removing pleasant or unpleasant stimuli. The effects of each of these four activities define positive (1) and negative (4) reinforcement on the one hand and the two types of punishment (2 and 3) on the other. Each possibility is illustrated below with a rat and then with a person.

Rat Illustration. Skinner has made extensive use of rats in investigating the effects of types and schedules of reinforcement on learning. Typically the apparatus used consists of what is known as a Skinner box, a cagelike structure that can be equipped with a bar, a light, a food tray, a food-releasing mechanism, and perhaps an electric grid through the floor (see Figure 2). The object of a typical experiment might be to condition a rat to press the lever whenever he is placed in the cage. A number of experimental variations can be employed to illustrate punishment and reinforcement.

(a) light   (b) food tray   (c) bar or lever   (d) electric grid

Figure 2. *A Skinner Box*

Positive Reinforcement (1).* If, when the rat depresses the lever, the food mechanism releases a pellet of food into the tray, the effect may be an increase in the probability of the occurrence of bar-pressing behavior. In this case, the food is a positive reinforcer.

Punishment (2). If the rat, who must stand on the electric grid when he depresses the bar, is given a mild shock every time he does so, the rat will probably attempt to avoid the bar in the future. The shock is, in this case, one type of punishment.

Punishment (3). If the rat, who is in the process of eating, stops to lick his chops, and a sadistic experimenter takes away his food, the probability of the rat licking his chops again will decrease. Perhaps if the experimenter continues to remove the food every time the rat licks his chops; the rat may eventually cease licking them altogether. A rat with slovenly table manners is a rarity well worth psychological investigation. In any case, this would be an example of punishment as well.

Negative Reinforcement (4). If the current is turned on continually in the grid, but turned off every time the rat presses the lever, he will probably eventually learn to depress the lever immediately upon entering the cage. The electric current is, in this case, a negative reinforcer.

People Illustration

The following examples of punishment and reinforcement are based on my observations of human behavior. The subject is the Lefrancois' 3-year-old son. His experiences for one day included the following:

Positive Reinforcement (1). Early in the morning the boy offered to kiss his father, claiming that he had "dreamed up" a few kisses. Both parents lavished verbal praise on him for this touching filial behavior. The praise, assuming that its effect was to increase the probability of the reoccurrence of the kissing response, is a positive reinforcer.

Punishment (2). Some time later, the same young hero kicked his sister in the posterior. The sound blow dealt him by this sister probably illustrates the first type of punishment.

---

*The numbers refer to Table 3 (K).

Punishment (3).   At lunchtime, he was given a handful of jelly beans after his dessert. He promptly ate one, licked another and rubbed it on the wall, and hurled a third one at his sister. His mother's taking the candies from him is another illustration of punishment.

Negative Reinforcement (4).   For a more serious misdemeanor, the boy was isolated in his bedroom and made to stay there until he stopped crying, which he eventually did. Allowing him to leave the room as a consequence of stopping crying is an example of negative reinforcement.

Sources of Reinforcement

In addition to distinguishing between two types of reinforcement, Skinner describes three sources of positive or negative reinforcement — primary, secondary, and generalized — that are identifiable in terms of their generality and in terms of the learning that occurs as stimuli become reinforcers.

Primary reinforcement includes stimuli that are initially reinforcing for an organism. In other words, a primary reinforcer serves as a reinforcer without any learning taking place. Examples of primary reinforcement are stimuli like food, water, and sex, which satisfy basic, unlearned needs (primary needs).

Secondary reinforcement describes a stimulus that is not reinforcing to begin with but becomes reinforcing as a result of being paired with a primary reinforcer. The light in the Skinner box is sometimes used as a secondary reinforcer. Over a succession of trials, it is turned on every time the animal is fed (given a primary reinforcer). Eventually the animal will respond simply in order to have the light go on. At this point, the light has acquired secondary reinforcing properties.

Generalized reinforcement includes the multitude of stimuli that come to be generally reinforcing for a wide range of behaviors through repeated pairing with primary and/or secondary reinforcers. A great variety of generalized reinforcers are culturally determined. For example, prestige, social status, power, wealth, fame, strength, and intelligence are all culturally prized attributes. The external symbols of these attributes constitute generalized reinforcers that are extremely powerful in determining human behavior.

Extinction and Forgetting

Forgetting is a topic of considerable interest to teachers, since it is one of the most common activities of human students. In fact, one could perhaps describe the process of teaching as an attempt to bring the rate of learning somewhere above the rate of forgetting. One could arrive at an index of a teacher's effectiveness by computing the difference between these two rates.

In the context of Skinner's system, the terms *extinction* and *forgetting* are not identical. Extinction is often, although not always, the result of an experimental or contrived process, whereas forgetting is the result of a natural process. Extinction occurs when an animal or person

Forgetting: One of the Most Common Activities of Students

who has been reinforced for engaging in a behavior ceases to be reinforced; the outcome will be a relatively rapid cessation of the behavior in question. Forgetting, on the other hand, is a much slower process that also results in the cessation of a response but not as a function of withdrawal of reinforcement. Forgetting occurs simply as a result of the passage of time with no repetition of the behavior during this time.

It is quite simple to condition a pigeon to peck at a colored disc. If food is used as the reinforcer for this response, and this reinforcement is suddenly withdrawn completely, the pigeon will in all likelihood continue to peck at the disc sporadically for some time. However, in a relatively short time he will cease pecking entirely, at which point extinction will have occurred.

Not infrequently, a behavior that has been extinguished through withdrawal of reinforcement will reappear without any further conditioning; this phenomenon is referred to as *spontaneous recovery*. The second extinction period will almost invariably be much shorter than the first.

Assume that the pigeon that has been conditioned to peck at a disc is taken out of the cage and not allowed to return to it for a very long period of time. If it does not peck at the disc when it is reintroduced into the cage, one can say that forgetting has occurred. Skinner reported the case of at least one pigeon that had still not forgotten the disc-pecking response after 6 years. He also reported one instance of a pigeon that emitted 10,000 pecks prior to extinction.

Schedules of Reinforcement in Experiments

Skinner's observations and experiments are largely directed toward the elaboration and clarification of the effect of such variables as reinforcement types and schedules on measures of learning—including extinction rate, acquisition rate, and rate of responding. Probably the most easily manipulated and most effective variable in operant conditioning is the manner in which rewards are administered. In a carefully controlled laboratory situation, the experimenter can determine precisely what reinforcements he will use and how and when he will use them. In other words, he is in complete control of schedules of reinforcement. Basically, he has two choices: he can reinforce the animal every time it emits the desired response—that is, he can reinforce *continuously*; or he can reinforce the animal only part of the time, or *intermittently*. If he reinforces the animal continuously, he has no further choices to make. Every trial (correct response) will be rewarded in the same fashion. (Note: It is entirely possible, however, to use a combination of continuous and intermittent reinforcement schedules. This type of arrangement is sometimes referred to as a combined schedule.) On the other hand, if the experimenter employs an intermittent (sometimes called partial) schedule of reinforcement, he can make one of two further choices. The intermittent schedule can be based on a proportion of trials or on a time interval. That is, the experimenter can decide to give reinforcement intermittently but in accordance with a predetermined pattern based on time or on trials. He might, for example, decide that the ratio of reinforced to non-reinforced responses will be 1 to 5, in which case he will reinforce one out of five correct responses. This schedule is an intermittent *ratio* schedule of reinforcement. On the other hand, he might decide to reinforce the animal once every 5 minutes, providing it emits at least one correct response prior to reinforcement. This alternative is an intermittent *interval* schedule of reinforcement.

The experimenter would further have to decide whether the reinforcement would be administered in a fixed or in a random (variable) manner. A fixed schedule is one in which the experimenter predetermines the time or the trial of reinforcement. For example, he decides that in the case of a fixed-ratio schedule, reinforcement will occur on every fifth trial. In other words, he decides that reinforcement will occur, for example, at the very beginning of each 5-minute interval but only immediately after a correct response.

The second alternative would be to administer reinforcement at random. The same ratio or interval could be used, but the reinforcement would not always occur at the same time or on the same trial. A random ratio schedule of reinforcement based on a one-reinforcement to five-trial proportion might involve reinforcing the first four trials, not reinforcing the next sixteen, reinforcing numbers seventeen and eighteen, and so on. After one hundred trials, twenty reinforcers would have been administered.

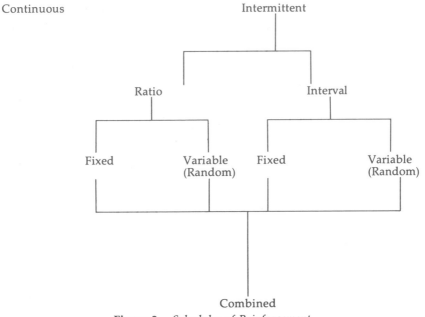

Figure 3. *Schedules of Reinforcement*

In short, the major schedules of reinforcements investigated by Skinner and his followers include continuous reinforcement on the one hand, and fixed-ratio, random-ratio, fixed-interval and random-interval reinforcement on the other. Any combination of these schedules is also possible; the schedules are summarized in Figure 3.

Effects of Different Schedules

The real significance of schedules of reinforcement is not limited to the possible combinations and sequences of schedules or to the number of experimental designs that can be and have been generated by this type of discussion. For teaching, the effects of these schedules on learning are much more crucial.

A word of caution is in order at the outset. Most of the conclusions discussed below are derived from studies of animal learning and are illustrated in terms of these experiments. While it would be highly presumptuous to assume that we can generalize without qualification from animals to man, it would be equally unwise to dismiss all of these findings simply because they cannot easily be illustrated in man.

Effects on Acquisition. It is generally correct to state that initial learning is more rapid if every correct response is reinforced and appears to be haphazard, difficult, and slow if any of the intermittent schedules of reinforcement are utilized. In training rats to press levers or pigeons to peck discs, Skinner typically deprives the animal of food for 24 or more hours (sometimes reducing weight to 80% of normal) in order to increase *drive*. Initial training usually begins with "magazine training," which is training the animal to eat from the food tray and, consequently, to recognize the noise made by the food mechanism as indicative of the imminent presentation of food. After magazine training, all correct responses, and sometimes even responses that merely approximate the desired behavior, are reinforced.

Effects on Extinction. While one measure of learning is the rate with which an animal acquires a new response as a function of reinforcement, another is the rate with which this response becomes extinguished following the withdrawal of reinforcement. Interestingly, while a continuous schedule of reinforcement results in a faster rate of learning than does an intermittent schedule, it also leads to more rapid extinction after withdrawal. In general, the fixed schedules of reinforcement, while they have longer extinction times associated with them than a continuous schedule, also lead to more rapid extinction than the variable ratio schedule of reinforcement. Hence, probably the best training combination for an animal is a continuous schedule initially, followed by a variable-ratio schedule. (Note: The ratio may also be varied over training sessions, with a decreasing ratio of reinforced to nonreinforced trials usually leading to even longer extinction periods.)

Effects on Rate of Responding. A third measure of learning is the rate of responding, which is a dependent variable remarkably sensitive to schedules of reinforcement. A rather interesting observation concerning the relationship between a schedule of reinforcement and the rate of responding can be made. It appears that, in general, an animal

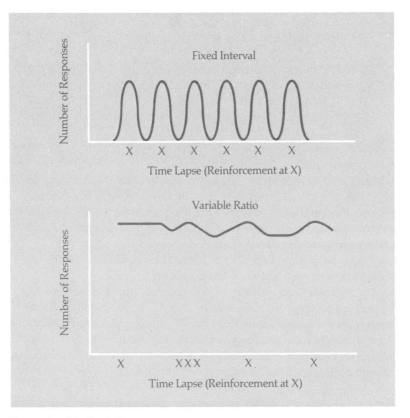

Figure 4. *Idealized Representation of the Effects of Two Schedules of Reinforcement on Rate of Responding*

behaves as one would predict it would behave if it is valid to assume that the animal develops expectations and has some time sense. For example, under variable schedules of reinforcement, when the animal is less likely to develop an expectation of receiving a reward at a given time, rate of responding will be uniformly high and relatively unvarying. If the variable schedule is a ratio schedule rather than an interval one, rate of responding will be higher. Under a fixed-interval schedule of reinforcement, the rate of responding immediately after reinforcement drops dramatically and often ceases altogether. Just prior to the next reinforcement, however, the animal again responds at a high rate (see Figure 4).

Schedules of Reinforcement in Everyday Life

In order to examine the nature of the schedules of reinforcement that affect people's daily lives, it is necessary first of all to determine what is reinforcing for people. Among the answers might be included such commonly accepted reinforcing stimuli as money, praise, satisfaction, and food. Two of these stimuli appear to be on fixed-interval schedules: money and food. For a large number of people, money arrives regularly (at fixed intervals) in the form of a paycheck, and food is taken routinely in the form of meals. For both of these rather important reinforcers, however, there are usually no immediate, simple operants that will predictably result in their presentation. The operants involved in acquiring money have become so complex and so remote from the actual source of reinforcement that it has become difficult to see the relationship between the two. The confusion is further compounded by the fact that the reinforcers themselves are inextricably bound together. That is, money allows one to buy food and, in some cases, praise as well. In addition, the acquisition of money sometimes appears to be a source of satisfaction in itself.

While it may be true that the relationship between behavior and reinforcement is not always simple or obvious, this fact does not necessarily invalidate the notion that a great many human behaviors are affected by reinforcers and their scheduling. It is relatively simple, in fact, to illustrate through a variety of examples how behavior is controlled and modified by reinforcements.

Illustration 1. A fisherman has fished in the same stream for 22 years. Every time he goes fishing he catches at least four fish (continuous reinforcement). Now, at the beginning of this pollution-conscious decade, he suddenly ceases to catch fish (withdrawal of reinforcement).

After four fruitless trips to the stream, he stops going altogether (rapid extinction following continuous reinforcement).

Illustration 2. Another man has also fished in the same stream for 22 years. Sometimes he catches fish and sometimes he doesn't. On occasion he doesn't catch a single fish for an entire season. He has occasionally caught as many as eighteen trout in one day (intermittent reinforcement). Now, also at the beginning of this pollution-conscious decade, he ceases to catch fish (withdrawal of reinforcement). At the end of the decade, he might still be frequenting the same stream (slow extinction following intermittent reinforcement).

Illustration 3. A young child is given his first rattle. A cruel but clever psychologist has removed its innards. The child holds the rattle up, looks at it, shakes it, bites it, strikes his knee with it, drops it, and forgets it. (The unreinforced response of shaking the rattle is not strengthened.)

Illustration 4. The same young child is given a rattle that has been kept away from all psychologists. He looks at it, shakes it, looks at it again, and then proceeds to shake it vigorously for some time (the sound of the rattle serves as a reinforcer and strengthens the operant that causes it).

Shaping

Shaping — one of Skinner's procedures that has received a great deal of attention — is a technique employed to train animals to perform acts that are not ordinarily in their repertoire. (The discussion of operant conditioning presented so far in this chapter has considered only instances of behavior where the operants in question were available to the animal.) It is entirely possible that if one waited long enough beside a Skinner box, the rat in the box would eventually accidentally depress the lever in the course of exploring his environment. This operant could then be slowly conditioned through the use of reinforcement.

However, if the experimenter wanted to train a rat to go to corner *A* of his cage, pick up a marble in that corner, carry it to corner *B*, drop it there, return to the center of the cage, lie down, roll over, get up, return to corner *B*, pick up the marble again, and carry it to corner *C*, the rat would probably die of old age before it emitted the operant.

Stupid Rat Dying of Old Age before Learning Very Much

Nevertheless, it is possible, through *shaping*, to teach a rat to engage in behaviors that are very impressive, if not as complex as the behavior described above. *Shaping* is sometimes referred to as the method of *successive approximations*, or as the method involving the *differential reinforcement of successive approximations* (Skinner, 1951). An experimenter using the technique of shaping reinforces every step that takes the animal closer to the final response, instead of waiting for the final desired response to be emitted. Even a behavior as superficially simple as bar pressing or disc pecking is usually brought about through shaping. The experimenter begins by reinforcing the rat every time it turns toward the bar. Later, only movements that bring it closer to the bar are reinforced. After the rat has learned to approach the bar, he is not reinforced again until he touches it. Eventually his behavior will have been so *shaped* that he will readily press the bar when put in the cage.

Most animal trainers employ techniques that amount to shaping procedures. Lefrancois reports speaking informally to trainers at the Miami Parrot Jungle, at the Seaquarium in Miami, and at the San Diego Zoo. The trainers described procedures based on the careful administration of rewards in *shaping* procedures. All of them had succeeded in training animals to perform in a variety of extremely novel ways. Parrots walked on tightropes, parachuted, played tunes, rode bicycles, and clapped; seals and porpoises jumped incredible heights with military precision in predetermined order; bears in the San Diego Zoo played guitars, danced, rolled somersaults, and also clapped their hands.

One critical requirement for the successful use of *shaping* procedures is that the environment be controlled. For example, the Skinner box is constructed so that the rat cannot perform very many responses other than those which the experimenter wishes to reinforce. Similarly, a professional animal trainer would not attempt to condition a dog when the dog is chasing a rabbit but would first confine the dog and secure its attention. In other words, the environment is arranged so as to facilitate the appearance of the desired response.

Shaping and People

There are probably many more human behaviors that are acquired through shaping than people are aware of. For example, in the course of learning any task involving muscular coordination, a large number of inappropriate or ineffective responses are abandoned, while appropriate (and, consequently, reinforced) responses become more firmly established.

The verbal behavior of people is also susceptible to the effects of reinforcement (Skinner, 1957), a phenomenon that Greenspoon (1955) illustrated experimentally through a technique referred to as *verbal conditioning*. In the study, the experimenter simply interviewed the subject and asked him to say words. The subject, who had no idea what words were required of him, began to verbalize. Each time he said a plural noun, the experimenter reinforced him by saying "mm hm." Over the course of the training session the incidence of plural nouns spoken by the subject increased significantly.

While this type of experimental procedure may, at first glance, appear to be somewhat remote from the realities of everyday life, on closer examination it becomes evident that people engage in many behaviors that are examples of the effects of verbal conditioning. For example, a high-pressure, door-to-door salesman often gets a customer to commit himself by employing a verbal-conditioning technique. First, the salesman suggests that the customer is intelligent. Then he proceeds to reinforce all declarations of intelligence made spontaneously by the customer. Eventually the customer will have admitted either that he is so intelligent that he cannot pass up such a good deal or that, being so intelligent, he is sufficiently concerned for his children to purchase an encyclopedia.

Verbal fluency (sometimes called verbosity in women and verbal ability in men) can sometimes be turned on or off by a skillful listener who reinforces a speaker or withdraws reinforcement through subtle facial expressions and gestures. A rather striking, although sometimes boring, illustration of the power of reinforcement in conversation can easily be provided by almost anyone. The procedure involves simply making the decision that your next conversation will be with someone who talks only about herself. It is quite likely that by making only a minimum number of comments but by expressing great interest in certain personal expressions, you can easily control the substance of your conversation.

Lefrancois reports two attempts to demonstrate for a class the power of reinforcement in shaping the verbal behavior of subjects. In neither case did the demonstration work as planned, but in both instances the outcomes were illustrative of equally striking phenomena.

Demonstration 1. The first demonstration was intended to be a simple replication of the Greenspoon experiment with a number of important variations. The subject was asked to sit in front of a rather large senior undergraduate psychology class of which he was a member. The class had previously had the Greenspoon experiment explained to them and had been instructed to reinforce all plural nouns by paying attention, nodding occasionally but not too obviously, and smiling from time to time. They were asked to appear less interested when the subject said words that were not plural nouns. One member of the class surreptitiously recorded the number of plural nouns emitted during each 2-minute interval of the session.

A number of factors detracted from the experiment and were probably responsible for the fact that it did not work as planned. It appeared that not all members of the class immediately recognized plural nouns. In addition, the subject, being a psychology student, was somewhat suspicious and perhaps overly tense. In any case, the number of plural nouns did not increase significantly over a 20-minute period. What did happen, however, was a clear illustration of verbal conditioning. It appeared (this was verified through an interview afterward) that the subject had, on the previous Saturday night, gone to a country dance and imbibed somewhat too freely. He had then challenged some of the local citizens to display their pugilistic skills for him. As a result he had spent the better part of that night in the local jail.

As this brave subject sat in front of his fellow students the following Monday morning, looking at them through bleary eyes, it was inevitable that he should, in the process of free association, say such sequences of words as "Saturday night, drunk, fight, yippee, . . . police, jail. . . ." The mood of the class was such that each of these words occasioned titters and suppressed laughter. But the subject was a "ham"* — knowing his audience, he repeated some of his words again, sprinkling an odd neutral word here and there. In the end the class laughed openly every time he said a Saturday-night-related word, and the number of such words increased dramatically as the session progressed. The subject's behavior was indeed shaped by the reaction of his audience.

Demonstration 2. A second classroom demonstration was attempted with two other classes which consisted entirely of teachers who had returned to the university for a 6-week summer course. Lefrancois' attempt in these demonstrations was an even bolder one, for the experiment involved trying to change people's attitudes through reinforcement. Two experimental sessions were undertaken — one with each of the two classes. The procedure was to have four people volunteer as panelists for a discussion of the merits of corporal punishment in schools. It was assumed that the topic was sufficiently controversial to be suitable for a good two-sided debate. The panelists were given 5 minutes in which to consult each other and organize their thoughts; none was asked to be for or against punishment. However, the entire class in the first demonstration was instructed to reinforce all statements supporting the use of corporal punishment in the schools. They were allowed to participate in the discussion but were asked to make only pro-punishment statements. The intention was to increase pro-punishment statements on the part of the panelists, both through the effects of reinforcement and perhaps through the effects of group pressure as well.

In the second class, the procedure followed was identical except that statements condemning corporal punishment were reinforced.

The results of both of these demonstrations are rather striking. In neither case was there an increase in the number of reinforced statements given by panelists during the experimental session. It appeared that panelists solidified their views whether or not they were reinforced.

---

*Our language diobols define "ham" as a piece of pig treated so as to be edible. As used here, however, the term refers to talent for acting (K).

One plausible explanation for this behavior is that the panelists probably anticipated receiving reinforcement from the professor for putting up a good argument. It was also clear, after the fact, that panelists saw themselves as debaters, and, as such, would have been violating implicit rules had they changed their minds.

What did change, however, were the attitudes of the entire classes. After each session, subjects were asked to indicate what they really believed about corporal punishment. In the first session, students were overwhelmingly in favor of it; in the second, they were equally overwhelmingly opposed to it.

While "shaping" was probably not involved in this attitude change, perhaps reinforcement was, since every time someone *in the class* made a good point, he or she would be very strongly reinforced by the entire class. Despite the fact that students knew what was going on, the praise of fellow students could easily have affected their behavior.

Fading, Generalization, and Discrimination

Shaping is one technique employed in training animals to perform complex behaviors. Another is *fading*.

Reese (1966) describes a procedure whereby a pigeon is taught to "read" two words: *PECK* and *TURN*. It is assumed that the pigeon has learned to read if it responds appropriately to either of these words when presented in a viewer.

This type of training presents some special problems. While it is relatively simple to train a pigeon either to peck or to turn using a shaping procedure, the bird will then immediately *generalize* the learned response to the other word. For example, if the pigeon is taught to peck in response to the word *peck*, it will also peck in response to the word *turn*. If, however, the two stimuli are made highly different so that the pigeon can easily *discriminate* between the two, he can be taught to respond appropriately to each stimulus through *shaping*. For example, the word *turn* might be printed in large black letters and the word *peck* in small red letters. Pigeons have excellent color vision. Over successive trials, after the pigeon has learned to peck and to turn as instructed, the differences between the stimuli are *faded* out: the large black letters become smaller, and the small red letters become both darker and larger, until finally each word is black and the letters are of uniform size. The pigeon can now *discriminate* between the two.

Generalization and discrimination are of considerable importance in human learning. Generalization involves engaging in previously learned behaviors in response to new situations that resemble those in which the behaviors were first learned. One example is obviously that of a pigeon turning in response to the word *peck* before he has learned to discriminate between *turn* and *peck*. Examples of generalization in human behavior are infinite. Any 5-minute segment of behavior in the life of a normal person is likely to be replete with instances of old behaviors being generalized to new situations. New cars are driven in ways similar to those employed in driving old ones; if someone hits a stranger accidentally, he may apologize; when faced with the problem of adding 27 kangaroos and 28 zebras, a farmer reasons that 27 kangaroos and 28 zebras are as many animals as 27 pigs and 28 horses; people assume that objects fall from mountaintops as they do from treetops; strangers shake hands when introduced; and so on. All of these behaviors can be interpreted as examples of responses to new situations that are based on previous learning; all are examples of generalization. It is precisely because not all, or even most, situations to which a person must react in a lifetime can be covered in schools or in other learning situations that generalization is of such crucial importance. Hence, teaching for generalization (which is really teaching for transfer) is one of the primary functions of schools.

Discrimination is a process that is complementary to generalization in that it involves making distinctions between similar situations in order to respond appropriately to each. The pigeon's learning to respond to the two highly similar situations involved in the presentation of the words *peck* and *turn* is an example of discrimination.

Discrimination learning is probably as important for human behavior, particularly in learning socially appropriate behavior, as is generalization. Children must learn to discriminate at relatively early ages which responses are appropriate to which situations. For example, it is permissible to kiss one's parents but not strangers; sisters should not be punched but neighborhood bullies can be; it is sinful to make noises in quiet churches but permissible to make the same noises in quiet houses; and so on. Accordingly, socially appropriate adult behavior is very much a function of having learned to discriminate between similar situations calling for different types of behavior.

The processes of discrimination and generalization are illustrated in Figure 5.

In the first case, the appropriate response (for a human, but not for a Koron) is to eat any of the five vegetables—in other words, a

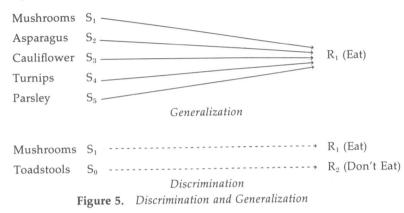

Figure 5. *Discrimination and Generalization*

generalization of the eating response is appropriate. In the second case, the human must discriminate between two stimuli. Generalization here is inappropriate.

Superstitious Behavior

Earlier in this chapter a fixed-interval schedule of reinforcement was defined as the administration of rewards based on a time interval but occurring only *immediately after a correct response.* A *superstitious* schedule — so called because it seems to explain superstition in man and animals — is a slight variation of a fixed-interval schedule of reinforcement.

A superstitious schedule of reinforcement is a fixed-interval schedule without the provision that reinforcement will occur only after a correct response. In other words, the reinforcement will be given at a specified time regardless of the behavior being engaged in at the time. It follows from the law of operant conditioning that any behavior just prior to reinforcement is strengthened. Whether or not the behavior is related to the reinforcement in a causal manner is of no consequence. For both man and animal, temporal contingency alone is sufficient to establish a relationship between reinforcement and behavior.

Numerous examples of superstitious behavior in animals are cited in the literature. In fact, it appears that in most conditioning sequences there are behaviors that accidentally precede reinforcement and temporarily become part of the animal's repertoire. For example, a rat who has just learned to depress a lever may do so with his head always to the right or with his left leg dangling. Both actions are examples of superstitious behavior.

A Superstitious Student

Skinner (1951) reports conditioning six out of eight pigeons using a superstitious schedule of reinforcement. Whatever the birds happened to be doing at the time of reinforcement tended to be learned. One bird turned clockwise prior to each reinforcement. Another tossed its head toward a corner, and two others developed an unnatural pendulum motion of the head and body.

There is no better place to observe superstitious behavior associated with thinking than in a crowded examination room at the end of a university semester. Some people scratch their heads; others frown; some move their lips, hands, legs, or feet; some chew their hair, and others engage in a variety of behaviors not causally related to clear thinking. One year Lefrancois observed a student repeatedly crossing his eyes and looking at his nose as he attempted a multiple-choice test. He failed the test and probably strained an eye muscle in the process.

The Effects of Punishment

Few topics in child rearing and education have received more attention than punishment. It is interesting that much of this attention results from the prevalence of punishment rather than from its effectiveness. Since Thorndike's (1932) early work, it has generally been accepted that punishment is much less effective in eliminating undesirable responses than reinforcement is in bringing about desirable ones.

From a learning-theory point of view, a number of practical and theoretical objections to the use of punishment can be raised. First, the likelihood that punishment will lead to appropriate behavior is often very remote. Essentially punishment serves to draw attention to undesirable behavior but does little to indicate what the desirable behavior should be. Second, punishment does not eliminate behavior but usually only suppresses it. What is affected is the rate of responding. The advantage that nonreinforcement has over punishment is that it, theoretically, leads to the complete extinction of the unreinforced behavior.

Third, punishment can lead to emotional states that will probably not be associated with love or happiness or any other pleasant feeling. These negative emotional states may, through contiguity, become associated with the punisher rather than with the undesirable behavior.

A fourth, more general objection to punishment is that it often does not work. Sears, Maccoby, and Lewin (1957) cite evidence to show that mothers who punish children for toilet accidents are more likely to have children who wet their beds, and parents who punish aggression are more likely to have children who are aggressive.

On the other hand, it is probably true that punishment, in the form of disapproval and withdrawal of reinforcement, is sometimes essential and effective. Completely permissive environments have been shown to be as bad as those in which too much punishment was used (Sears et al., 1957). People, unlike most animals, are often able to interpret causal relationships. If they see clearly that punishment is the consequence of a particular behavior, the behavior may well be permanently suppressed as a result of the punishment, unless other sources of reinforcement attend the behavior. In this context, it is interesting to note that delayed punishment is much less likely to be effective than punishment that immediately follows the transgression.

Operant Conditioning in Schools

If, indeed, most significant human behaviors are operant, the importance of Skinner's observations can hardly be overestimated.

There is some argument, however, about the extent to which behavior is controlled by reinforcement contingencies. Much of this argument centers around the inability of man to decide whether he possesses free will or whether freedom is merely an illusion that accompanies behavior that is actually determined by the unconscious anticipation of reinforcement. I, as a Koron, do not care to attempt to solve this problem.* I think it is sufficient to point out that man often behaves in much the same way as *rattus norvegicus*, except that his Skinner box is somewhat larger and less well controlled. In fact, it is not inappropriate to draw an analogy between a classroom and a Skinner box. In this analogy, the teacher is the experimenter—that is, he is the administrator of rewards and punishments. The students, on the other hand, are analogous to the Skinnerian rats. As the experimenter, the teacher can profit from knowing that reinforcement is effective in bringing about changes in behavior, that schedules of reinforcement may be varied to good advantage, that punishment is not very effective for learning, and that some reinforcers are more powerful than others. He might profit from greater knowledge about *sources* of reinforcement. For example, Bijou and Sturges (1959) classify reinforcers in five categories: consumables (such as candy); manipulatables (like toys); visual and auditory stimuli (for example, a bell signal that means "good work"); social stimuli (like praise); and tokens (such as discs that can be exchanged for other reinforcers). To this list can be added the Premack Principle (Premack, 1965), which states that behavior that occurs frequently and naturally (and that must therefore be pleasant) can be used to reinforce less frequent behavior. For example, a child who reads a great deal but dislikes arithmetic could be told that he will be allowed to read if he does an arithmetic assignment. Each of these classes of reinforcers may be employed effectively by a teacher. Indeed, there are numerous illustrations of their use in psychological literature (for example, Birnbrauer & Lawler, 1964; Brinbrauer et al., 1965; O'Leary & Becker, 1967).

Skinner's Position in Retrospect

Skinner stands out in the history of psychological thinking as one of its great system builders. Although behaviorism was originated and defined by Watson and although many other theorists have contributed significantly to its development, it is Skinner's name that is most frequently brought to mind when one thinks of behavioristic psychology.

*Kongor actually *could not* solve it, although he chose not to admit it (GRL).

Probably his greatest contribution to the understanding of human behavior is his description of the effects of reinforcement on responding. In addition, Skinner has attempted to relate these findings not only to individuals but also to social groups (see, for example, *Science and Human Behavior,* 1953). Since the inception of Skinner's work, numerous theorists have incorporated large portions of his system into their own positions (see, for example, Bijou & Baer, 1961; Bandura, 1969; Hewett, 1968).

One of the tangible applications of Skinner's work has taken the form of programed instruction, which is a teaching technique premised specifically on principles of operant conditioning. Essentially, a program consists of a series of related statements (frames) that require the student to emit a response (operant) and attempt to reinforce him by telling him that he has answered correctly. (For a discussion of programed instruction, see DeCecco [1968], Holland & Skinner [1961], or Lefrancois [1972].)

Summary of Chapter 5

This chapter has presented an account of the work of B. F. Skinner. A description of *rattus norvegicus* was given, as well as a number of illustrations of his usefulness in Skinner's laboratory. The principles of operant conditioning discovered by Skinner were discussed and related to animal and human behavior.

Operant conditioning is largely irrelevant for Koron behavior but retains some meaning for the behavior of Blips.

1. *Rattus norvegicus* is a useful subject in the psychological laboratory. He, along with pigeons, has served as Skinner's main subject.
2. Skinner observed and described the relationship between independent variables (reinforcement types and schedules) and dependent variables (rate of acquisition, rate of responding, and extinction rate). He did little theorizing in the form of deriving laws from his observations and basing inferences on these laws.
3. Skinner identified two major types of learning: that involving stimulus-elicited responses (respondents) and that involving emitted instrumental acts (operants). A classical-conditioning model (Type S) explains respondent learning; an operant-conditioning model (Type R) explains operant learning. Skinner's system deals almost exclusively with operant learning.
4. One of the most important variables in the Skinnerian system is *reinforcement*. A reinforcer is a stimulus that increases the probability of a response occurring. It can be positive (effective through its presentation) or negative (effective through its removal). A negative reinforcer is not the same thing as punishment. Punishment does not increase the probability of a response occurring.

5. Reinforcement can be primary, secondary, or generalized. That is, it can satisfy basic needs (such as food), or it can become reinforcing through association with a primary reinforcer (dish), or it can become reinforcing for many behaviors through learning (money).

6. *Extinction* is the elimination of a behavior through the withdrawal of reinforcement. *Forgetting* is the elimination of behavior through the passage of time. Extinction is a relatively rapid process, whereas forgetting occurs more slowly.

7. *Scheduling of reinforcement* refers to the manner in which an organism receives reinforcement. Two broad categories of schedules exist: continuous and intermittent. Intermittent schedules of reinforcement can be based on proportion of trials (ratio) or on time lapse (interval). Both ratio- and interval-based schedules can be either fixed (unvarying) or random (variable).

8. Continuous schedules of reinforcement typically lead to rapid acquisition and also rapid extinction. Intermittent schedules have longer extinction times associated with them but are less efficient for early training. As one would predict, rate of responding is typically based on the expectations of reward an animal or person is likely to develop during training. High rates of responding usually occur where reinforcement is dependent upon the number of responses emitted. Varying rates occur for a fixed-interval schedule with high response rates preceding reinforcement and a virtual cessation of responding just after reinforcement.

9. *Shaping,* or the differential reinforcement of successive approximations, is a technique used to bring about novel behavior in animals. It involves reinforcing responses that move in the desired direction until the final response has been conditioned.

10. *Verbal conditioning* is a procedure employed to condition people to emit predetermined verbal responses. It is a technique often used, consciously and unconsciously, in controlling conversations. The procedure simply involves reinforcing, often through nonverbal signs of approval, certain verbal behaviors in the subject.

11. *Fading* is sometimes employed to bring about discrimination learning. Where an animal is to be trained to make different responses to two highly similar stimuli, the differences between the stimuli can be exaggerated for the initial training. As learning becomes more established, the differences are faded out until the animal can respond differentially to the two original stimuli.

12. *Generalization* and *discrimination* are of considerable importance for learning. The former involves transferring one response to other stimuli; the latter involves making different responses for highly similar stimuli.

13. *Superstitious behavior* is incidental behavior that becomes learned when it is present at the time of reinforcement. It is behavior which has no real relationship to reinforcement but which is engaged in as though it had.

14. *Punishment,* while prevalent, is often not very successful. It is claimed that punishment does not tell the offender what to do, but merely what not to do. In addition, it may have some undesirable emotional side effects.

15. Korons are so rational and so unmoved by reinforcement that Skinner's observations are largely irrelevant for us.

6

Neobehaviorism: Hull and Spence

There is a word in this chapter which, I am told, may profoundly shock some human readers—however, I make no apology whatsoever for it.* After all, the report was written for Korons. It is being left on Earth only because of the kindness which the good Dr. Lefrancois and his family have bestowed upon me. Besides, the WORD appears in the Earth edition (which, incidentally, is virtually identical to the Koron version) as a pedagogical device. Judging from my own observations of the limited powers of the human mind and based on reports given to me by Lefrancois, it appears obvious that the theoretical position of Clark Hull may prove somewhat difficult for the average Earth reader, even in the simplified form presented here. Hence, the need for this pedagogical device.

I find it highly amusing that what was included in the Koron version as a piece of humor (on Koros the absurd *is* comic) should become an essential instructional device on Earth. Of course, we have no

*One of the few editorial changes made in Kongor's report was the deletion of the WORD and the substitution of a more acceptable expression in its place (GRL).

122

"bulls" on Koros; the WORD is therefore slightly different in the Koron version.

Hull's position has been classified as a neobehavioristic one (see Marx & Hillix, 1963). He is more behavioristic than neo; as shall become evident later, Hebb and Osgood are probably more neo than behavioristic. (It is possible that the meaning of this paragraph will never be clarified on Earth.)

Clark L. Hull (1884–1952)

Hull was among the most ambitious of the behavior theorists. The final system he developed is of such complexity and scope that only a brief glimpse of it can be given here. A complete account of the system is found in Hull's (1943, 1951, 1952) own books. Summaries are provided in numerous psychology textbooks (for example, Hilgard & Bower, 1966; Hill, 1963).

The development of the system consisted essentially of the elaboration of 17 postulates (Hull, 1943), which were meant to be statements descriptive of human behavior. From these postulates, 133 specific theorems and numerous corollaries were derived (Hull, 1952). A third book describing the application of this system to behavior in social interactions was to be written. Unfortunately, Hull died shortly after finishing the second book, and the third was never begun.

Nature of the System

Hull's explicitly behavioristic system is marked by all of the behaviorist's concerns for objectivity, precision, and rigor. It is referred to as a hypothetico-deductive system in recognition of his attempt to derive hypotheses — in the form of theorems and corollaries — from the postulates he had advanced. However, his work went much further, for he was not content simply to derive theorems but also attempted to verify them in laboratory situations. As one can see from an examination of the system, this was a monumental task — consequently, Hull was only partially successful.

True to the behavioristic approach, Hull looked at human behavior in terms of stimuli and responses. However, he dealt with them in considerably more detail than had most of his contemporaries. For Hull, stimuli consist of a large number of antecedent conditions that affect the organism but that might or might not lead to behavior;

he referred to these antecedent conditions as *input* variables. Accordingly, responses are described in terms of a number of variables referred to as *output* variables. A number of his postulates are devoted to explaining the nature of input and output variables as well as the relationships that exist between the two. A third set of behavior variables that form a central part of Hull's system are referred to as *intervening* variables. They provide the link between input and output variables. They also provide the link between Hull's behavioristic system and neobehavioristic approaches.

Hull was greatly impressed by Pavlov's work on reflexive behavior and classical conditioning. This Pavlovian influence is reflected in part by the fact that the cornerstone of Hull's system is his belief that all behavior consists of S-R connections. The central concept in behavior is that of *habit*, and a habit is an S-R connection or a collection of such connections, which Hull terms a *habit family hierarchy*. Another source of profound influence on Hull was the work of Thorndike, particularly his Law of Effect. The influence of reward on learning became the main explanatory notion in the final system.

Summary of Hull's System

It may appear somewhat presumptuous to begin a discussion with a summary. However, in this case the summary is as much an outline of the following pages as it is a recapitulation of their content.

The system is replete with symbols and mathematical terms and values. While the mathematical terms are not essential to this discussion, the symbols simplify the presentation of the theory — although they do impose some strain on memory. On several occasions, Lefrancois had to take special precautions to prevent "symbol shock" from occurring in undergraduate classes being exposed to Hull's theory for the first time. These precautions consist largely of indelicate stories (told in a delicate manner so as not to offend) interspersed with good Hullian terminology. Symptoms of symbol shock include lower respiration rate, some lowering of body temperature, a change in EEG pattern from Beta to Alpha waves, and closed eyelids. On occasion, some sufferers make strange noises through their mouths. These students are probably in more extreme states of shock.

Figure 1 is a summary, in symbolic form, of the major variables in Hull's system.

Symbol Shock

Input Variables

The presentation of Hull's system in this highly symbolic form may make it appear much more difficult to understand than it really is. While it is extremely complex in scope and detail, it is not nearly so complex in terms of difficulty.

The first point to be made is that the model in Figure 1 is much simpler to understand when interpreted not as a general description of human behavior but only as the representation of one specific behavior for one person at a given point in time. Understanding how the system works in this connection makes it easier to interpret it in a wider sense.

Hull was primarily concerned with developing a system that would enable him to predict a person's behavior, given knowledge

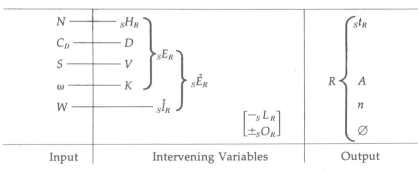

Input	Intervening Variables	Output

Input Variables

N = number of prior reinforcements
C_D = drive condition
S = stimulus intensity
ω = amount of reward (weight)
W = work involved in responding

Intervening Variables

$_sH_R$ = habit strength
D = drive
V = stimulus-intensity dynamism
K = incentive motivation
$_sE_R$ = reaction potential
$_s\mathring{I}_R$ = aggregate inhibitory potential
$_s\mathring{E}_R$ = net reaction potential
$_sL_R$ = reaction threshold
$_sO_R$ = oscillation of reaction potential

Output Variables

R = the occurrence of a response, measured in terms of $_st_R$, A, and n
$_st_R$ = response latency
A = reaction amplitude
n = number of nonreinforced trials to extinction
$\varnothing$ = no response (not used as a symbol by Hull)

Figure 1. *The Hullian System.* (Adapted from Hilgard and Bower, 1966, p. 164, by permission of the publisher, Appleton-Century-Crofts.)

about the stimulus. One of the real difficulties in the application of this system to behavior is that a great deal of knowledge about the subject's past experiences is necessary. The input or stimulus variables are the predictors; the output or response variables are predicted. In different terms, the stimulus variables are *independent* variables, and the response variables are *dependent* variables. When one examines Figure 1, it becomes clear that complete knowledge of input requires knowing how many times in the past the S-R bond in question has been reinforced (N). This variable, combined with knowledge about the physical intensity of the stimulus (*S*); the drive conditions of the organism (*C_D*); the reward attached to responding (*ω*); and the amount of work required in responding (*W*) would theoretically allow prediction of the output variables.

Intervening Variables

While the input and output variables are the only directly observable and measurable events described in the system, the intervening variables are probably more crucial for understanding what Hull's theory is really about. These variables have direct links with the external variables in that they intervene between stimulus and response events in such a way as to determine whether or not a response will occur for a stimulus. However, it is important to note that the power of intervening variables in determining responses is, theoretically, completely determined and controlled by input variables. Thus, the intervening variables are nothing more than explanations of observed S-R relationships. For each stimulus variable there is a specific corresponding intervening variable, which can be interpreted as the effect that an input variable (a feature of the environment) has on an individual. Viewed in this way, intervening variables are relatively easy to interpret. Each variable is described in turn in the following section.

1. $_SH_R$. The most important intervening variable, habit strength, is a behavioristic concept defined in terms of the strength of the bond between a specific stimulus and response. For Hull, habit strength was determined largely by the number of previous pairings of a stimulus with a response, provided that reinforcement occurred on every trial. He introduced specific numerical functions to illustrate the precise relationship between number of pairings and habit strength (which are of much more academic than practical interest). While at first glance it might appear that habit strength would be most influential in determining behavior, such an assumption is not accurate. In effect, it appears that habit strength is but one of a number of variables that affect behavior.

2. *D*. Because of its connection with reinforcement, drive is a central concept in Hull's learning theory. He saw learning as the process of responses becoming connected with stimuli when they lead to a reduction in drive or, more precisely, when they lead to the removal or reduction in number or intensity of stimuli associated with drive.

Drive can be primary or secondary (as can reinforcement since it involves reducing drive). Primary drives are those associated with tissue needs; secondary drives are conditioned to primary drives through contiguity. Drive, as an intervening variable, corresponds to the input variable *drive condition*, which is defined in terms of number of hours of deprivation. Hull identified two components of drive: the *drive proper* increases as a direct function of the number of hours of deprivation, and the *inanition component* is recognition of the fact that drive decreases if number of hours of deprivation (starvation) is too long.

Decreased Drive after Too Many Hours of Deprivation

Drive assumes three central functions in Hull's theory. (1) It provides for reinforcement without which learning would not occur; (2) it activates habit strength — meaning that, without drive, behavior will not take place even if there is a strong previously established habit $_sH_R$ — and (3) drive stimuli become attached to specific behaviors through learning. Were it not for this distinctiveness of drive stimuli, the behavior engaged in might be totally inappropriate; people might drink when they were hungry, or eat when they were cold, or cover up when thirsty. . . . Essentially, it is this distinctiveness of drive stimuli that determines whether or not a response will be reinforcing.

3. *V.* Stimulus-intensity dynamism is the label applied to the intervening variable that corresponds to the input variable *S*, or stimulus intensity. It is assumed that increasing the physical intensity of a stimulus increases the probability of a response occurring. This effect is manifested in the variable *stimulus-intensity dynamism*, which interacts in a multiplicative fashion with habit strength and drive to determine the probability of a response.

4. *K.* Incentive motivation, which is determined by the amount of reward (ω, as an input variable), is also assumed to interact with other intervening variables in determining the likelihood of a response. It was Hull's belief that the greater the amount of reward (for example, food for a rat), the stronger would be the organism's potential for reacting to a stimulus.

These four intervening variables ($_sH_R$, *D*, *V*, and *K*) comprise the first and most important term in the equation employed by Hull in determining what he called reaction potential ($_sE_R$): $_sE_R = {}_sH_R \times D \times V \times K$. It is interesting and revealing to note that since reaction potential is a multiplicative function of these variables, if the value for any of them is zero, reaction potential will also be zero. In other words, in the absence of drive, it makes no difference how intense the stimulation, how great the reward, or how strong the habit, the response will not occur; in the absence of the appropriate stimulus at sufficient intensity, R will not occur; in the absence of reward, there will be no response, and in the absence of a previously learned habit, there will also be no response. Consider the case of a man sitting at a table upon which are set a variety of appetizing dishes. If he has just eaten, he may not touch a single dish, despite the fact that the stimulus, the reward, and the habit are all very strong. In this case, drive would be too low. By way of further illustration, consider the other possibilities: no food ($K = 0$); the man is blind and cannot smell ($V = 0$); or the man has not learned to eat ($_sH_R = 0$). In no case will the response occur.

5. $_sE_R$. This intervening variable is not tied as directly to input variables as it is to other intervening variables or to output variables. Reaction potential, sometimes called excitatory potential, is a measure of the potential that a stimulus has for eliciting a specific response. This potential will depend on how many times the stimulus has been paired with the response and reinforcement, how intense it is, how great the reward, and how strong the drive. In other words, $_sE_R = {}_sH_R \times D \times V \times K!$

The significance of the magnitude of reaction potential in this system is that a minimum amount of potential is required before behavior will take place. Increasing reaction potential will be reflected in shorter response latency ($_st_R$), more response amplitude (A), and longer extinction time (n).

~~BULLSHIT~~*   PSHAW*

6. $_sE_R$. The use of two symbols denoting reaction potential might appear to be somewhat confusing. Actually, Hull used three symbols for reaction potential, the third one being based on the potential for responding that is carried over (generalized) from related behaviors. This second symbol refers to net reaction potential, so called because it is the reaction potential that results from summing the generalized potential with the ordinary reaction potential that results from drive, habit strength, stimulus intensity dynamism, and incentive motivation (and then subtracting inhibitory potential, $_sI_R$).

7. $_s\mathring{I}_R$. Aggregate inhibitory potential (reactive inhibition) results from two input variables: the amount of work involved in responding (W) and any habits of not responding that might have been acquired by the organism. The assumption is that those responses requiring a high expenditure of physical energy are less likely to be engaged in. With continued repetition of a response, this inhibitory potential summates. Its effect is to lower the net reaction potential until eventually the response no longer occurs. Inhibitory potential dissipates quickly so that the response might reoccur very soon.

8. $_sL_R$. The reaction threshold is the magnitude that net reaction potential must exceed before a response will occur (if $_s\mathring{E}_R > {_sL_R}$, R occurs; if $_s\mathring{E}_R < {_sL_R}$, $\varnothing$ occurs).

9. $_sO_R$. Behavioral oscillation is the variable that accounts for the fact that, given relatively complete information about input variables, predictions are not always accurate. Guthrie's answer for this problem had been simply that the stimulus situation had changed. Hull's answer is that reaction potential is not exactly fixed, that it varies around a central value. This variation he labeled behavioral oscillation ($_sO_R$).

Intervening variables and their interaction in Hull's system are summarized after a brief discussion of *output* variables.

---

*The indelicate expression (delicately crossed out) is not intended as a description of content but simply as an antidote to the "symbol shock" that might, by now, have overcome an assiduous reader (K).

Output Variables

The response variables of concern to Hull include the time lapse between the presentation of the stimulus and the appearance of the response (response latency, $_st_R$), the amplitude of the response in a physical sense (A), and the number of unreinforced responses that would occur before extinction (n). Hull postulated that response latency would decrease with increasing reaction potential, whereas both resistance to extinction and amplitude of response would increase.

Two additional symbols standing simply for the occurrence of a response (R) or its nonoccurrence ($\emptyset$) have been included in Figure 1. A summary of the contents of that figure can be given as follows:

$$\text{if } [_s\mathring{E}_R = (_sH_R \times D \times V \times K) - _sI_R > _sL_R], \text{ then } R.$$

This expression reads: if net reaction potential, which is the product of habit strength, drive, stimulus-intensity dynamism and incentive motivation, minus aggregate inhibitory potential, is greater than the threshold, a response will occur.

Two additional concepts arrived at by Hull in the course of deriving theorems and their corollaries are of particular importance here: habit family hierarchies and fractional antedating goal reactions. Both represent significant departures from theoretical formulations that had preceded Hull, and both are relevant for the development of neobehavioristic and cognitive positions.

Fractional Antedating Goal Reactions

It will be recalled that the major explanation for learning advanced by Hull is a reinforcement explanation. More specifically, he maintained that reinforcement consists of drive reduction. The ordinary way of reducing a drive is to attain a goal or to make a *goal reaction*. Goal reactions, as described by Hull, are often consummatory responses, as in the case of food. A fractional antedating goal response (r_G, read "little r G") is a response made by an organism prior to the actual goal reaction. Such responses would include the variety of reactions to environmental stimuli that the organism might make. In the case of a rat who has run through a maze and is approaching food, antedating goal reactions might include licking his chops, sniffing, and turning a last corner, as well as seeing and smelling the maze. These antedating responses are important in that they serve as stimuli (s_G, read "little s G") that maintain behavior toward a goal. In this sense they serve the same purpose as Guthrie's movement-produced stimuli (MPS), but unlike the MPS, r_G-s_G are linked with reinforcement and therefore became rewarding. They are also related to what Hull termed *habit family hierarchies*.

The Habit Family Hierarchy

In the course of acquiring habits (S-R bonds), an individual will learn a number of different responses for the same stimulus; in many cases, each response will lead to the same goal. These alternative responses constitute a *habit family* arranged in hierarchical order. They are referred to as a *family* because they are assumed to be integrated by common *fractional antedating goal reactions* and as a *hierarchy* because there is a preferential ordering based largely on previous reinforcements. In other words, one alternative will usually be preferred over another because it has been rewarded more often in the past; the reaction potential ($_sE_R$) associated with it will therefore be higher.

Both concepts — antedating goal reactions and habit family hierarchy — are employed in somewhat different form by Osgood (see Chapter 8). The introduction of these concepts represents one of Hull's major contributions. Another important contribution from a theoretical point of view is Hull's influence on the design of a wide variety of psychological experiments. This influence has resulted largely from his insistence on precision, rigor, and quantification, as well as his emphasis on logical consistency. This last characteristic of his system most sets Hull apart from other learning theorists. It remains true, however, that Hull's system has failed where he most wanted it to succeed; behavior remains largely unpredictable. His failure has discouraged others from attempting the development of such formal and inclusive systems. Instead, smaller systems dealing with a limited number of aspects of learning are typically advanced.

Kenneth Spence (1907–1967)

The Hullian tradition was continued in the writings of Kenneth Spence, who is considered to be Hull's major follower. Indeed, it is widely accepted that had Hull lived, the further development of his system might well have progressed along lines followed by Spence, as summarized in his two major books (1956, 1960). In his books, Spence continued the development of Hullian neobehaviorism, with a number of important variations from Hull's original system, which are discussed briefly below.

Hull and Spence

While the systems of both Spence and Hull are dedicated to the development of elaborate and formal deductive theories, there is a marked difference in the restraint exercised by each theorist in the development of his work. Whereas Hull was willing to derive theorems, postulates, and corollaries, leaving to others a great deal of the work of experimentally verifying these statements about behavior, Spence was less willing to commit himself to this approach. One manifestation of his caution is inherent in the intended scopes of the two positions. Hull had clearly wanted his system to be sufficient to account for most of the behavior of higher animals and of man. Interestingly, the experimental work incorporated in the system dealt largely with studies of animal behavior or of the conditioned eyeblink in man. Spence, on the other hand, explicitly limited the generality of his system to those situations analogous to the experiments from which he derived his conclusions.

In addition to these rather general distinctions between the theories of Spence and Hull, a number of very specific and very basic changes were made by Spence. Indeed, he was careful to point out these points of distinction between his system and Hull's. The most important of these departures from the original Hullian theory are discussed below.

First, Spence did not accept Hull's concept of need reduction in relation to reinforcement. Hull had maintained that drive stimuli (S_D) give rise to conditions of drive in the organism (C_D) and that the original stimuli are associated with needs. The reinforcement of behavior was assumed to involve the satisfaction of the need and the consequent elimination of the drive condition. Spence's interpretation differed in that he did not give reinforcement any role in the formation of habits. Habit strength was no longer defined in terms of the number of times a response had been paired with a stimulus *and reinforced* but was assumed to be a function solely of the frequency of pairings. Second, Spence saw the reinforcement itself as a result of fractional antedating goal responses (r_G-s_G). The fractional responses define incentive motivation (K) in the Spence system. In other words, reinforcement affects K (incentive motivation) but does not alter habit strength ($_SH_R$ in Hull's system; H in Spence's).

A second distinction between the two systems is Spence's substitution of an additive function for a multiplicative one in the major formula. Hull defined reaction or excitatory potential as a multiplicative function of drive, habit strength, and incentive motivation (in addition to a number of other variables of lesser importance). That is,

$_sE_R = _sH_R \times D \times K$. . . . Spence, on the other hand, defined excitatory potential (E) as a function of the product of habit strength (H) times drive *plus* incentive motivation. In other words, $E = H(D + K)$. The practical difference between these two formulations is that in Hull's expression, if any of the values are at zero, excitatory potential must also be at zero, as illustrated earlier in this chapter by the man sitting at a banquet table. The point made there was that if $H = 0$ (that is, the man does not know how to eat) and so on, behavior would not take place. Spence's reformulation of this equation makes it possible for either D or K to be zero without completely eliminating the possibility of a response. This change obviously takes into account the possibility that where a habit is particularly strong, behavior may take place in the absence of drive or incentive.

Despite the fact that there are these distinctions between Spence and Hull, the points of similarity probably have greater theoretical importance. Both systems are essentially hypothetico-deductive, and both attempt to develop relatively precise formulas for the explanation and prediction of behavior—although, admittedly, Spence's system strives for less precision than does Hull's. In addition, Spence makes use of the same kind of symbolism as does Hull and deals essentially with the same problems of human behavior. His contribution, like Hull's, will only be determined in the wisdom of later years. Early indications are that the Hull-Spence tradition has been a powerful force in shaping the direction of empirical behaviorism in the latter part of psychology's brief history.

It may be of interest to the human reader to know that on Koros a Hullian type of tradition also prevailed among Blip psychologists of ancient times. Contemporary Koron behavioral scientists admit a link, albeit a somewhat remote and tenuous link, between the Hullian movement in ancient Blip psychology and the third of the Eleven Great Laws!

So What?

The human reader, unlike the more rational Koron, often asks the question "So what?"—as if there needed to be an obvious reason for everything. The question is frequently a difficult one, particularly when it refers to such abstract and apparently remote theoretical systems as Hull's. However, one answer is that understanding Hull's theory greatly facilitates the understanding of later theoretical developments. This is not to say that Hull's theorizing is of no immediate practical relevance. Indeed, it may well be of considerable practicality, and the reader is invited to consider possible applications. He is also advised, however, that the relevance of this type of psychological theorizing will be much clearer to him when he has concluded his study of this report.

Summary of Chapter 6

This chapter has presented an introduction to neobehaviorism. The formal theories of Hull and his follower, Spence, were discussed and evaluated as examples of neobehaviorism. The next two chapters discuss two other neobehavioristic positions.

1. *Neobehaviorism* is a term employed to describe learning theories that deal primarily with events that are assumed to take place between the presentation of a stimulus and the appearance of a response. These are essentially S-O-R rather than S-R positions.
2. Hull's behavioristic analysis of behavior can be viewed as an introduction to neobehaviorism. It is a highly formalized attempt to account for behavior in terms of the precise relationships that Hull thought exist between input, intervening, and output variables.
3. A summary of the major Hullian variables and the relationships which exist between them is given by the equation: $_sE_R = {_sH_R} \times D \times V \times K$. It reads: reaction potential is the product of habit strength, drive, stimulus-intensity dynamism, and incentive motivation.
4. Two Hullian concepts that are of special significance in the development of learning theories are "fractional antedating goal response" ($r_G\text{-}s_G$) and "habit family hierarchies." The former is a behavior that precedes the reaching of a goal but becomes associated with the goal through conditioning and hence acquires reinforcing properties. Habit families are hierarchical arrangements of habits that are related by virtue of the fact that they have common goals.
5. Kenneth Spence has continued the Hullian tradition by attempting to modify and to complete Hull's system. It is not unusual to encounter references to the "Hull-Spence" system.
6. Among the major differences between the theories advanced by Hull and Spence are Spence's rejection of drive reduction as a definition of reinforcement, his redefinition of K in terms of $r_G\text{-}s_G$, and his introduction of an additive function in the major formula.

7

Neobehaviorism: Hebb

Making a time jump leaves one with a strange sensation. Obviously, it would be quite impossible to make the long journey from Earth to Androneas without doing several time jumps. One jump is seldom sufficient for a very long trip. Time jumps are executed quite simply by teleporting ships from one space-time dimension to the parallel pure-time dimension and reversing the helix drives. Because there is no *space* in a pure-time dimension, the physical components of the objects being teleported *cease to exist* — only their *souls** remain intact, since souls are immaterial. The strangeness of the sensation results less from the dematerialization than from the sudden and complete *awareness* that the soul acquires as soon as the body disappears. It is then that it is possible to think in pure form — that is, to abstract *thought* completely from all relation to reality. Indeed, it is then impossible to relate thought to any sort of *realness*.

It was while making the second time jump between here and Androneas that I carried out an experiment that my superiors in the

*The word in Koron is Telsig. It does not translate exactly into English, but the concept of *soul* as discussed by Plato is fairly close (K).

Behavioral-Science Division of the Koron Space-Exploration Department detailed for me. It was a fascinating experience, not only because of the sensations attached to it but also because it verified so graphically some of the finer details of the sixth of the Eleven Great Laws. Most of these details would be quite meaningless to you. There is one exception—one small observation that may be of interest to your psychologists.

The experiment involved a reorganization of the soul and body never before attempted. The intention was to separate the soul from body matter in such a way that the rematerializing of the body would not imprison the soul. This feat was to be accomplished by capturing the soul while in the time jump and placing it in a compartment with a variable helix drive. The obvious next step was to accelerate or decelerate the variable helix in order to bring about separate collisions with the space-time dimension. More precisely, it would bring about collisions in the same time dimension in juxtaposed spaces. The technical details of this procedure would undoubtedly boggle the human mind. It suffices that you know that the object of the experiment was to separate my soul and brain so that I could watch my brain function.

Needless to say, the experiment went as planned, and I observed exactly what I knew I would see. Scientific verification is always satisfying.

The precise observations that may be of interest to your psychologists, particularly if they have a neurophysiological orientation (as does D.O. Hebb), are those concerned with neurological functioning. Amazing as it might seem, the actual functioning of the Koron brain is virtually identical to that of the human brain—except, of course, in terms of the absolute amount, complexity, and sophistication of transmission. In all of these characteristics, the Koron brain is vastly superior.

And so, at the thirty-first hexalog of the sixth time cube, I became the first Koron to watch his own brain in operation—in all of the detail made possible by sonar magnification. What an impressive display of electrochemical activity (see Figure 1)—millions of cells firing in synchrony, in complete correspondence with the stream of thought flowing through my soul.

The small observation that may be of interest to Earth psychologists is that neural transmission is invariably accompanied by *blue* electrical activity.*

---

*One of the most annoying features of Kongor's intended humor is its patronizing tone. In any case, his observation is completely irrelevant (GRL).

Figure 1

Reflecting back on the experience, I can easily see that the neurologically based position advanced on Earth by D.O. Hebb is, in some ways, a global description of my earlier observations.

D. O. Hebb (1904–   )

D. O. Hebb, an eminent professor of psychology at McGill University, has developed a position based heavily on physiological and neurological fact and hypothesis. Although he has at times been classified as a behaviorist (Chaplin & Krawiec, 1960), he makes extensive use of mediational constructs. He describes his system as a pseudo-behavioristic one (Hebb, 1960) and admits that his preoccupation is chiefly explaining thought processes and perception, which are topics not often within the scope of rigidly behavioristic positions. He cautions, however, against viewing his writings as comprising a theory;

rather, he lays claim only to having advanced a *proposal* for a theory. His proposal is, to begin with, concerned with *higher mental processes,* a familiar term in contemporary psychological theorizing.

Higher Mental Processes

When a man comes face to face with his first saber-toothed tiger, as he inevitably must, he will turn immediately and run as though the very devil were after him. When the same man comes to a stream with the intention of crossing it and finds that the stone he had laid there for that purpose is gone, he will stop; perhaps he will sit on the bank with his chin in his hands. Later he may decide to get another stone to replace the first.

Meeting One's First Sabertooth

In addition to the obvious lack of similarity between a man running from a sabertooth and one sitting on a river bank, there is a fundamental distinction to be made between these two behaviors. The first behavior can be interpreted in terms of the now familiar S-R model: the tiger serves as the stimulus; running is the response. The second could perhaps also be considered within an S-R framework: the missing stone is the stimulus, and the act of leaving to get a replacement is a response. The problem with this last interpretation, however, is that there might be a delay of several minutes, or even hours, between the presentation of the stimulus and the response. Because of this delay, the S-R model is less than adequate.

The central question here is: what occurs during the lapse of time between a stimulus and a response? It is probable that something related to the stimulus and response must be occurring at least part of the time, since the eventual behavior is made in response to the stimulus that was present much earlier. One phrase used to describe what goes on between the stimulus and response is *higher mental processes*— in layman's terms, *thinking*, or thought processes. In Hebbian terms, this phrase refers to the occurrence of "processes which, themselves independent of immediate sensory input, collaborate with that input to determine which of the various possible responses will be made, and when" (Hebb, 1958, p. 101). In other words, higher mental processes are activities that mediate responses; in a neobehavioristic sense, they are mediating processes.

Because Hebb's theory (or proposal for a theory) is largely neurologically based, a brief account of human neurological functioning should be given first. This account is based largely on Hebb's summary of this process (1966).

The Conceptual Nervous System

The human nervous system consists of billions of cells called *neurons* (approximately 10 billion), which are located in the brain, in the spinal column, in the brain stem that joins the spinal column to the brain, and throughout the body in the form of complex neural pathways and branches. A neuron is an elongated cell whose function is to transmit impulses in the form of electrical and chemical changes. Neurons form the link between receptors (for example, sense organs) and effectors (muscle systems) and thereby assure that the responses made by an organism will be related to the stimulation it receives. Bundles of neurons form nerves, comprising the nervous system.

The simplest unit in the nervous system is, then, the neuron. While it can vary considerably in size and shape, it is microscopic. Neurons are composed of a *cell body*; the *axon*, which is an elongated part sometimes having many branches; hairlike protrusions from the

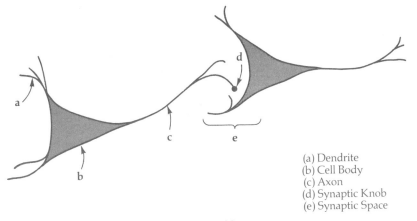

(a) Dendrite
(b) Cell Body
(c) Axon
(d) Synaptic Knob
(e) Synaptic Space

Figure 2. *A Neuron*

cell body called *dendrites;* and *synaptic knobs,* which are enlargements of axon ends. The space between the axon ends and the dendrites of two adjacent neurons is called a *synapse* (see Figure 2). The transmission of impulses in a neuron is from the cell body outward along the axon and across the synaptic space between the axon end of one cell and the dendrites of the next. The receiving extensions of the neurons are the dendrites, while the transmitting ends are the axons. It is believed that repeated transmission of impulses between two cells leads to permanent facilitation of further transmission of impulses between these cells. This facilitative property of neurons is central to Hebb's explanation of learning.

The transmission of a neural impulse probably involves both electrical and chemical changes in cells. The exact nature of these changes or of their transmission across synapses is not known. However, it is known that cells can activate each other in sequence, that they can be activated by stimulation, and that they can transmit impulses that cause glands to secrete or muscles to contract. In addition, it is suspected that cells do not always fire only in sequence but that frequently one cell in a sequence can reactivate another that had fired previously. When this refiring occurs, the reactivated neuron may cause the firing of the cell that reactivated it. In this case, it may be activated again (see Figure 3). The resulting circular pattern of firing is called a *reverberatory loop*. It is highly probable that series of such closed circuits can activate each other to form assemblies comprising thousands of neurons. These hypothetical assemblies are labeled *cell assemblies*.

Figure 3. *A Reverberatory Loop*

The activation of a number of related cell assemblies can also result in the formation of a third hypothetical structure—the *phase sequence* (see Figure 4). These units—the reverberatory loop, the cell assembly, and the phase sequence—play important roles in Hebb's proposal for a theory of learning.

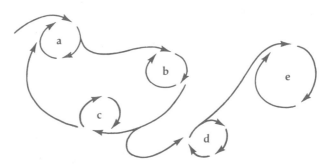

Figure 4. Schematic representation of a phase sequence: **a, b, c,** and **d** can be thought of as cell assemblies, each of which comprises several reverberatory loops (Figure 3).

From a physiological point of view, each cell assembly corresponds to what Hebb refers to as "relatively simple sensory input." Hence, the recognition of even very simple objects will involve the activation of a large number of such cell assemblies or phase sequences. The role assigned to these units in Hebb's explanation of higher mental processes is discussed in the following section.

The human Reader whose loops and sequences have been boggling in reaction to the neurological terminology of the previous section should now turn to the Appendix to this chapter, which contains a 64-frame linear program by H. C. Fricker on Hebb's theory. The program is an effective antidote for human mind boggling.* Readers more familiar with neurology and Korons can proceed directly to the next section.

Learning

This brief introduction to the anatomy and functioning of the human nervous system is essential to an understanding of Hebb's explanation of learning processes. It is important to keep in mind, however, that the neurological units discussed in this and in the previous section are largely hypothetical. While behavioral and anatomical evidence would suggest that something like cell assemblies or phase sequences probably exists, there remains the possibility that this

Reactivity

* Korons need not read the program — for obvious reasons (K).

interpretation is not an accurate one.* Nevertheless, it provides a relatively parsimonious and useful account of human behavior.

In Hebb's theory, as in most other accounts of learning, two properties of the human organism play a central role: reactivity and plasticity. *Reactivity* refers to the capacity of the organism to react to external stimuli. *Plasticity* is the property of the organism that allows it to change as a function of repeated stimulation. A simple demonstration can be used to illustrate these two properties. The procedure involves placing a human subject (preferably male) 2 or 3 feet in front of the experimenter with his back to him. The experimenter then, without warning, kicks the subject squarely and soundly in the seat of the pants. The subject's immediate behavior is an example of *reactivity*. His subsequent refusal to repeat the experiment is an example of *plasticity*.

Within behavioristic or neobehavioristic positions, reactivity is interpreted as involving the emission of responses, while plasticity is manifested when behavior is modified. The interpretation of these events in Hebbian theory takes the form of an attempt to account for behavior in terms of neurological events. For Hebb, plasticity and reactivity are properties of the CNS that account for behavior rather than properties of behavior.

Mediating Processes

One of Hebb's primary concerns is to explain "higher mental processes," or *thought*. In an attempt to arrive at some understanding of these processes, he offers a basic hypothesis and makes a number of assumptions. The previous section lays the groundwork for interpreting these assumptions since they deal with the physiology of the nervous system.

The first and most basic hypothesis, which has already been described, is simply that mediation consists of "activity in a group of neurons, arranged as a set of closed pathways which will be referred to as a *cell assembly*, or of a series of such activities, which will be referred to as a *phase sequence*" (Hebb, 1958, p. 103). In addition, Hebb (1966) makes a number of assumptions about the formation of the *cell assembly*.

---

*Jerzy Konorski (1967) has recently advanced an alternative hypothesis: that the representation of perceptions does not take the form of *assemblies* of *cells* but of single units referred to as *gnostic units*. In addition he renames the *association* area of the cortex the *gnostic* area. His position is somewhat similar to Hebb's in many respects, although it is much more detailed in its application to various types of learning (K).

Assumption 1. A cell assembly (or mediating process) is established as the result of the repeated firing of cells. It arises as a function of the repetition of a particular kind of sensory event. In other words, the repeated presentation of a specific stimulus will tend to reactivate the same assemblies each time, serving to facilitate transmission of impulses across the synaptic spaces between the neurons involved. Hence, repetition has a facilitating effect on further neural activity. Behavioral evidence of this effect is provided by the fact that it is considerably easier to multiply two numbers if they have been multiplied many times previously. Or, more simply, it is easier to recognize a simple object if it has been presented frequently than if it is being seen for the second time. This property of neural transmission defines in part what is meant by *plasticity* of the conceptual nervous system.

Assumption 2. If two cell assemblies are repeatedly active at the same time, an association between the two of them will tend to form. In other words, if cell assembly *A* is always (or often) active when *B* is active, the two will tend to become associated neurologically. That is, the firing of cell assembly *A* may lead to firing in *B* and vice versa. The result will be the formation of *phase sequences.*

A closer examination of the implications of this assumption reveals that it can serve as an explanation for conditioning through contiguity. If cell assembly *A* corresponds to one specific sensory event, and *B* does also, and if, further, *A* and *B* *do* represent the components of thought (mediation), then the establishment of a functional relationship between *A* and *B* simply means that presentation of the event associated with *A* may *remind* one of the event associated with *B*. There is considerable intuitive evidence that this process does indeed occur. For example, if a man is always seen with a cigar, then it is highly probable that anything that reminds one of the man will also bring the cigar to mind. The smell of woodsmoke makes a person think of fire; lilacs go with spring; fish mean water or restaurants; the letter *q* in a word means *u* is next; and motherhood is a good thing.*

Thus, the first purpose of this assumption is to explain learning by contiguity. A second achievement of the assumption is to explain the perception of objects when incomplete sensory data are available. The lines in Figure 5 are almost always perceived as a triangle, although they really are not. (This phenomenon is sometimes referred to as closure in Gestalt psychology — see Chapter 9.) For the sake of simplicity, the cell assemblies associated with triangularity can be said to comprise units representing each of the corners *A, B,* and *C* of the tri-

---

* A phrase Kongor often parroted but did not really understand (GRL).

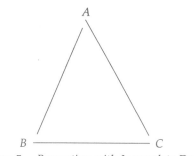

Figure 5. *Perception with Incomplete Data*

angle, as well as each of the sides. Because these features of triangles have been present in contiguity many times, associations have been formed between the cell assemblies that represent them. It is now sufficient to present only limited sensory input (that is, only three sides of a triangle but no corners) in order to evoke activity in the entire sequence of assemblies corresponding to "triangle."

Assumption 3.   An assembly that is active at the same time as an efferent pathway (a neural pathway leading outward from the C.N.S.) will tend to form an association with it. This assumption, like assumption 2, allows Hebb to explain the formation of associations between events that are in temporal contiguity. Activity in an efferent pathway may result in some sort of motor activity. Hence, the associations that are explained by this assumption involve behavioral events and mediation — in other words, thought and behavior. Again there is ample intuitive evidence that such associations are very much a part of human learning. Particular sights, sounds, or smells, for example, become associated with a specific motor activity so that engaging in the activity recalls the sensory impression. The reverse is also true. Activity in assemblies that have often been active during some motor response would tend to elicit the same response. This interpretation is obviously a simple neurologically based explanation for the Pavlovian model of classical conditioning. The assemblies relating to the sounding of a buzzer are always present at the time of salivation and are eventually sufficient to elicit salivation.

Assumption 4.   Each assembly corresponds to relatively simple sensory input. This property of the cell assembly makes it necessary to involve large groups of such assemblies (phase sequences) in explaining the perception of even relatively simple physical objects.

Summary of Assumptions

The four assumptions described above can be summarized by describing what *learning* and *thinking* appear to be for Hebb, since the assumptions are made in order to enable Hebb to make those descriptions. Essentially, the term *thinking* is equivalent to *mediation*. Mediation consists of activity in assemblies of neurons, and the nature of the mediation (or of the thought) is determined by the specific assemblies involved. Hebb's contention is that it is clearly the activated area of the cortex that determines the subjective experience of the organism and not the nature of the neural activity itself. For example, it is possible to stimulate the optic nerve electrically or by using pressure. In either case, the effect is the same: the subject sees light (Hebb, 1966, p. 267). On the other hand, the activation of specific receptors will always affect the same area of the cortex (and presumably the same cell assemblies). Hence, it is possible to "feel" the same reaction for the same stimulation on different occasions. If this were not true, of course, human awareness, as it is now known, would not exist.

The acquisition of learned mediating processes results from the repetition of the same sensory event leading to the formation of associated assemblies. Thus, learning consists of the "permanent facilitation" of conduction among neural units. Essentially, a phase sequence is a neurological unit where the transmission of impulses has become so easy that the activation of one part of the sequence is sufficient to activate the entire organization. In Hebb's earlier writings (1949), he maintained that activity, once begun, is almost autonomous — that is, almost self-sustaining — but in the light of more recent physiological discoveries, he has revised this notion (Hebb, 1958, 1966). He now considers the system semiautonomous, taking into account that some degree of external stimulation is necessary for continued cortical functioning. The evidence for this hypothesis comes from findings about the reticular formation and its functions. Many of these findings are incorporated in Hebb's account of motivation, which is discussed later in this chapter (see Chapter 3 also).

Hebb's neurologically based explanation for learning accounts for the formation of stimulus and response associations in terms of connections that are formed between their corresponding neurological counterparts (active cell assemblies or phase sequences). Assumptions 2 and 3 deal with this type of learning. Higher processes involved in learning (insightful problem solving, for example) are assumed to involve the combination of phase sequences (sometimes through chance) in higher-order organizational units — supraordinate phase sequences. Again, these sequences are hypothetical constructs and not necessarily "real." Two additional concepts—*set* and *attention*—are discussed by Hebb, both as evidence of mediation and as illustrations of significant phenomena in human functioning.

Set and Attention

When a starter at a race tells the contestants that he will fire his pistol a few seconds after saying "On your mark" and that they can then proceed to run like scared rabbits over the dirty cinders, he is attempting to establish *set*. If he succeeds, the contestants will sprint forward when the pistol sounds. (It would be interesting to see what the effect on the starter would be if all contestants had agreed beforehand to relax when the pistol was fired.)

A superficial and incorrect behavioristic interpretation of this situation might be that the sound of the pistol was the stimulus that led to the response of running. On the other hand, consider what might have happened if the starter had said, "I'm going to fire this pistol to see if my blanks are any good. Just relax." If he then fired the pistol, and no one ran, it would be quite obvious that the pistol alone was not the stimulus that led to the running response, but that the initial instructions were also involved. In other words the "set" given to the contestants *together with* the stimulus is responsible for the behavior.

Consider, further, what would happen if an attractive, bikini-clad co-ed strolled along the track just prior to the sounding of the gun (the contestants are all male). Would *GSR* (galvanic skin response) increase? Would blood pressure and heart rate go up? Would temperature jump? Probably not. If, on the other hand, these same contestants had already finished the race and were lounging around recuperating when the girl walked by, the phase sequences activated might be quite different. These two examples are illustrations of the effect of *attention* on behavior. Set refers to selectivity among responses; attention refers to selectivity among input. Both characteristics are assumed to be largely a function of the preactivation of specific cell assemblies. When the racer is told to get ready to run, he is "set" to respond by running when he hears a bang. When he is "attending" to the imminent sound, he is less likely to attend to other distracting stimuli.

Both these characteristics of human behavior are particularly relevant for teachers. Set is intimately involved in choosing appropriate responses, attention is essential for learning, and each is obviously affected by the other. In addition, both attention and set are closely related to arousal, a concept which is central to Hebb's theory of motivation.

Motivation

Not only is arousal a key concept in Hebb's theory of motivation, but it is also central to his learning theory. Actually, it is misleading to speak of learning and motivation as different theories for two reasons: first, Hebb does not pretend to advance a theory for either learning or motivation, but only a proposal for a theory; second, for Hebb learning and motivation are "different" only as they relate to different questions but not because different answers are proposed for them. In fact, the same arousal concepts are pertinent for both. It is simpler and clearer, however, to treat the topics in separate sections.

It will be recalled that in Chapter 3 a distinction was made between the two functions of a stimulus: the cue function and the arousal function. This distinction was based on Hebb's (1966) account of motivation. To recapitulate briefly, the *cue* function is the message function; it tells the organism how to feel, think, or react. The *arousal* function, on the other hand, is defined by the general activating or arousing effect of stimuli. The full significance of these two properties can now be made much clearer in the light of the neurological hypothesizing that has been described in this chapter. The cue, or message, of a stimulus will, within the context of Hebb's theory, involve the activation of the specific assemblies corresponding to the stimulation. The arousal function, however, will involve a larger number of cell assemblies. This preactivation is thought to be effected through the reticular formation (see Chapter 3) and is also considered to be essential for the "cue" to have its effect. It is in this sense that arousal is so intimately involved in learning, since learning is concerned with the cue or message component of stimulation.

Hebb's theory of motivation is known as a single-drive theory. The drive is defined in terms of generalized arousal, a concept that is interpreted by Hebb in much the same way as it is described in Chapter 3. For example, Hebb makes the assumption that there is an optimal level of arousal, above and below which behavior will not be maximally effective. He also makes the related assumption that humans behave so as to maintain arousal at or near the optimal level. This assumption implies that there is a *need* for maintaining a moderate level of arousal.

Indeed, this assumed need is the reason arousal theories are referred to as *drive* theories. (It will be recalled that drives are related to needs in that they are the tendencies for activity that are induced by needs.) The question of whether or not there is a *need* for arousal has been indirectly examined through an investigation of the effects of prolonged reductions in arousal on the behavior of humans.

The Need for Stimulation

The original experiments in a long sequence of related investigations in this area were conducted at McGill University under the direction of Hebb. His collaborators, Bexton, Heron, and Scott, reported the results of the initial studies in 1954 and 1956. (Since then numerous investigators have replicated their early findings [see, for example, Schultz, 1965, or Zubek, 1969].)

The first experiment (Heron, 1957), referred to as a sensory-deprivation or perceptual-isolation* study, employed a group of male college students who had volunteered for an experiment where they would not be asked to *do* anything and for which they would be paid twenty dollars per day. In actuality, not only were they not *asked* to do anything, but they were not allowed to do anything. Instead, they were made to lie on cots for most of the 24 hours a day, getting up only for toilet duties or to eat. Meals were served to subjects as they sat on the edges of their beds. Each cot was isolated in a soundproof cubicle, and subjects wore translucent visors that did not allow them to see but permitted diffuse light to enter. Over their ears they wore U-shaped foam pillows that were designed to prevent hearing. As a further precaution against the perception of sounds, air-conditioning equipment hummed ceaselessly and monotonously. Subjects wore cotton gloves and had cardboard cuffs that extended over their fingertips in order to discourage tactile sensation. In short, the experimenters attempted to ensure that a minimum of sensory stimulation would be experienced by the subjects for as long as they wished to remain in isolation. Interestingly, none of the subjects wished to remain for more than 2 days. In some later experiments where conditions of deprivation were more severe (for example, complete darkness, no sound, body immersed in water to simulate weightlessness), subjects often did not last more than a few hours (see, for example, Shurley, 1966; Barnard et al., 1962).

*Zubek (1969) distinguishes between sensory and perceptual deprivation. The former is assumed to involve conditions of darkness or silence, whereas the latter indicates an unvarying stimulus field, such as in the Hebb experiments (K).

Since the chief source of cortical activation (arousal) is sensation, perceptual deprivation should result in a lowering of arousal. This assumption has been confirmed through EEG ratings of subjects before, during, and after isolation (Heron, 1957; Zubek & Wilgosh, 1963). After prolonged isolation, it is not uncommon for the cortical activity of subjects who are awake to approximate that of a normal *sleeping* human.

Among the effects of sensory deprivation is impairment in perceptual and cognitive functioning as evidenced in post-isolation performance on simple numerical or visual tasks (Heron, 1957). In addition, subjects often become irritable, easily amused or annoyed, and almost childish in their reaction to limited contact with experimenters. For example, they often attempt desperately to engage the experimenter in conversation, acting in much the same way a child does when trying to gain the attention of a preoccupied parent.

Another striking finding of sensory-deprivation studies is that subjects frequently report experiencing illusions of various kinds—in some cases, hallucinations—after prolonged isolation. Numerous studies have since investigated the conditions under which hallucinations are most likely to occur (see, for example, Zuckerman, in Zubek, 1969). One general conclusion that can be derived from these studies is that hallucinations *do* in fact result from sensory deprivation but are somewhat infrequent and markedly affected by the subject's pre-isolation attitudes.or set.

These studies of sensory deprivation tend to add further support to arousal-based explanations of human behavior. There seems to be little question that behavior is more nearly optimal under conditions of moderate arousal. In addition, it appears that humans do endeavor to maintain arousal at that level. For example, subjects in isolation often talk to themselves, whistle, recite poetry, or attempt to draw the experimenters into conversation. Such behavior has led Schultz (1965) to hypothesize that the need for arousal is really a need for stimulation. In this connection he proposes a *sensoristatic* model of behavior—a kind of homeostatic model in which *sensation* is the dependent variable. Quite simply, the Schultz sensoristatic model is based on the contention that individuals seek sensory variation. Thus, this model is in effect, if not in terminology, identical to an arousal model.

Hebb's explanation of motivation is essentially premised on the assumption that arousal is a central variable in human learning and behavior and therefore is similar to the motivational positions adopted by Berlyne, Osgood, and Bruner, among others.

In summary, it bears repeating that Hebb does not view his writings as comprising a theory but only as a proposal for one. It is interesting, however, that he is one of the few neurologically and physiologically oriented theorists to whom much attention has been paid. Indeed, it should become quite clear in Chapter 10 that both Bruner's and Ausubel's positions can easily be supported by Hebb's neurologizing. Bruner specifically states that the neurological mechanisms that must underlie his explanation of behavior will need to be very similar to Hebb's. For example, the concept of cell assemblies and phase sequences is particularly useful in both of these systems. Further evaluation of the "theory" must await experimental investigation of its constructs.

Summary of Chapter 7

This chapter has presented a description of D. O. Hebb's explanation for human behavior. A short program detailing Hebb's notions regarding neurological functioning was included. In addition, sensory-deprivation studies were discussed in relation to arousal theory.

1. Hebb, a Canadian psychologist, has advanced a neobehavioristic model based largely on neurological and physiological knowledge and hypotheses. He claims to have described only a proposal for a theory, not a complete theory.
2. The human nervous system is made up of cells called *neurons*, which consist of a *cell body*, receiving extensions called *dendrites*, and an elongated part called an *axon*. Transmission among neurons is from axon ends (sometimes enlarged and then labeled *synaptic knobs*) across the *synaptic* space, which is the separation between the axon end and the dendrites of an adjacent cell.
3. Hebb attempts to explain *higher mental processes* in terms of activity in neural assemblies. He reasons that this activity must take the form of reverberatory loops, which are neurons arranged in such a way that they can keep reactivating each other.
4. Arrangements of related cell assemblies are called *phase sequences*. Both cell assemblies and phase sequences are hypothetical constructs that are employed to explain learning. Mediation (thinking) is defined in terms of activity in cell assemblies or phase sequences.
5. Hebb makes a number of important assumptions. First, he suggests that cell assemblies result from the repeated presentation of similar stimulus patterns and therefore the repeated activation of the same neurons. The second assumption is that if two assemblies are often active at the same time, they will tend to form associations with each other. This last assumption can be used to explain conditioning.
6. A third assumption made by Hebb is that motor activity will become associated with the assemblies that are often active with it. This assumption explains the formation of motor habits. A fourth assumption is that each cell assembly corresponds to relatively simple sensory data.
7. *Set* and *attention* are central processes in learning and perception. Set refers to selectivity among motor responses, whereas attention refers to selectivity among input.
8. Hebb's *theory of motivation* is based on a concept of arousal similar to

that discussed in Chapter 3. It centers around the assumption that there is an optimum level of arousal for maximally effective behavior and that people will behave so as to maintain that level.

9. Studies of *sensory deprivation* tend to support the contention that there is a need in humans for a variety of sensory stimulation.

10. Electrical activity in the cortex appears *blue* under sonar magnification.

Appendix to Chapter 7

(The following is a revision of an unpublished program written by H. C. Fricker. Used with permission.)

D. O. Hebb's Neurological Theory

Objectives. When you have completed this program you should be able to do the following:

1. Define:
   a. central nervous system
   b. neuron
   c. dendrite
   d. axon
   e. synapse
   f. synaptic knob
2. Explain:
   a. the formation of a cell assembly
   b. the formation of a phase sequence
   c. mediation
   d. reverberation

Directions: The following is a 64-frame program. Most of the frames have one blank. On the right are the correct responses for each of the blanks. Fold a sheet of paper or make a strip of cardboard to cover these responses. With the correct answers covered, begin by reading the first frame. WRITE your response in the book or on a separate sheet of paper. As you move to each successive frame, lower the paper or cardboard so as to check your answer. The program can be completed easily at one sitting. You may wish to measure your learning by taking the short test which is included at the end. If you make many errors, the program is not a good one. If you make no errors, you are very intelligent. Good luck.

1. The brain and spinal cord are together called the "Central Nervous System" because of their function as a "switchboard" or "telephone

exchange" between the receptors and effectors of the body. The basic element of the Central Nervous System is the NEURON. The C.N.S. contains billions of these _____.

2. The Central Nervous System consists of a network of neurons in the brain and spinal cord. The basic element of the C.N.S. is the _____.

neurons

3. "C.N.S." is an abbreviation for <u>Central</u> _____ _____.

neuron

4. Impulses are transmitted over this vast system in the form of tiny electrical charges moving from one neuron or group of neurons to the next. In this way, "signals" picked up by the sense organs pass to the brain, and "instructions" are sent to the muscles of the body. This intricate system is known as the <u>c</u>_____ <u>n</u>_____ <u>s</u>_____.

nervous system

5. Neurons vary widely in shape, but basically each consists of a cell body with several hairlike extensions through which electricalchemical impulses are received and passed on to other neurons. Below is a sketch of a _____.

central nervous system

6. The impulses that pass through the C.N.S. are in the form of tiny _____ charges.

neuron

7. The senses receive millions of stimuli every waking hour (somewhat fewer during sleep). Most of these are of insufficient strength to set up impulses in the neurons associated with

electrochemical (electric)

them. Of those that do, only the strongest reach the brain and are acted upon. This is one way in which the C.N.S. "mediates," or modifies, the S-R process. Of all the impulses received by the senses, what proportion reach the brain? ___ (all, most, few, none)

8. "Mediation" refers to any resistance or interruption or modification to the passage of an impulse through the C.N.S. Suppose you are about to swear, but the presence of certain people, plus your past experience, lead you to choose a different word. This is an example of m_____ .

few

9. You could not possibly respond to every detail of everything you see, hear, feel, etc. Hence, only the most intense impulses pass through the C.N.S.; the others are stopped, or _____ .

mediation

10. If you have an urge to scratch your nose (not now, silly!), you may assume that the itch stimulus was a relatively persistent one, such that an impulse traveled the neuron path to your brain, where it excited a response path terminating in the muscles of your arm and hand. The C.N.S. provided a neuron path from the *stimulus* of the itch to the _____ of scratching.

mediated (or similar word)

11. The receiving extensions of neurons are called DENDRITES. Say the word. Write the word: _____ .

response

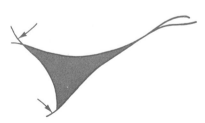

12. Dendrites receive impulses from the senses or from other neurons and pass them into the

dendrites

cell body. Impulses enter the neuron via the
_____ .

13. Dendrites are the extensions through which   *dendrite(s)*
neurons _____ (receive, pass on) impulses.

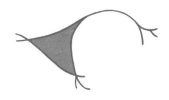

14. There may be one, two, or more dendrites on   *receive*
the neuron. If these lie close enough to other
neurons, and the other neurons contain a sufficiently strong electrical charge, an impulse
will pass between. Receiving extensions of
neurons are called _____ .

15. Each time an impulse passes from neuron *A* to   *dendrites*
neuron *B* it becomes easier to repeat in the
future. This is the learning process, as we shall
see later. Therefore, let's do it once more: when
you think of the receiving extensions of neurons, you think of the name _____ .

16. An extension of the neuron through which   *dendrites*
impulses are passed on to a following neuron
is called an AXON.

Say and write the word: _____

17. The dendrites of one neuron receive impulses   *axon*
    from the _____ of another.

18. A neuron consists of a cell body and hairlike   *axon(s)*
    extensions called _____ s and _____ s.

19. The end of the axon may or may not touch the   *dendrites*
    dendrite of another neuron. The point of con-   *axons*
    tact or near contact is known as a SYNAPSE,
    and the impulse must jump this point in order
    to excite the next neuron. Dendrites and axons
    meet at a s_____;

20. A weak impulse may be unable to jump the _____ to the next neuron. *synapse*

21. As successive impulses discharge across a synapse a change takes place. Transmission becomes easier. The more frequent the transmission, the greater the ease with which impulses pass. In this way, learning takes place. In a learned S-R sequence, impulses pass easily from a____ to d_____ across the s_____ . *synapse*

22. The enlarged end of an axon is called a synaptic _____. *axon* *dendrite* *synapse*

23. Sometimes a synapse occurs directly between an axon and the cell body of the following neuron. Such an arrangement bypasses the _____ . *knob*

24. If a stimulating impulse entering the C.N.S. fails to produce the usual response, the S-R sequence has been interfered with. The interference is known as med_____ ; *dendrite*

25. Sometimes the mediation is due to other dis-   *mediation*
    tracting stimuli. In this case, the distracting
    stimuli would be referred to as _____ ing
    stimuli.

26. Fill in the labels for this diagram.   *mediating*
       (a) _____
       (b) _____
       (c) _____
       (d) _____

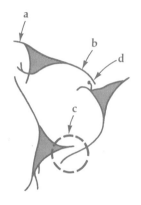

27. We will now discuss the "cell assembly." As   *dendrite*
    the name implies, the cell assembly is an asso-   *axon*
                                                          synapse
                                                          synaptic knob

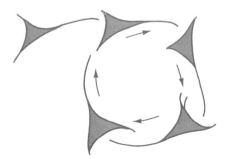

ciation of neurons. You know now how one neuron "fires" or excites another, and how an impulse passes along a chain of neurons. Consider what happens when one of the later neurons lies near enough to fire one of the early ones. Voilà! Le ring around Rosie, no? This *assembly* of neural *cells* is called a _____ _____.

28. The brain contains millions of cell assemblies, each associated with a particular basic stimulus. Cell assemblies are built up very slowly as learning takes place. Simple learning can be described in terms of the formation of ____ _____s.

cell assembly

29. A cell assembly is a circuit containing, perhaps, thousands of neurons. The whole circuit is excited in response to a particular basic _____ _____.

cell assemblies

30. Each perceptibly different sense stimulus is represented in the brain by a cell assembly. You have one for each of the many different colors and probably thousands for the sounds you know. The more discriminating you are regarding colors, the more _____ _____s you have associated with color.

stimulus

31. An accomplished musician has many very finely developed ____ _____ associated with _____.

cell assemblies

32. Electric charges travel around the cell assembly, jumping from the axon of one neuron to the dendrite of the next. This gap, which is jumped by the electric charge, is called a _____.

cell assemblies
sound (music)

33. Cell assemblies must not be thought of as independent of each other. Indeed there exists a vast network of crossconnections, and the firing of one cell assembly is likely to set off many more. In this way, the smell of cooking can elicit visions, tastes, even feelings in the mouth and stomach. A cell assembly is fired by an _____ charge passing through it.

synapse

34. If the sketch below brings to mind "triangle," *electric*
it is because the cell assemblies associated with
the separate lines fire enough other cell assemblies to complete the triangle in your mind. The
cell assemblies together are known as a PHASE
SEQUENCE. A phase sequence is a group of
associated _____ _____s.

35. A group of associated cell assemblies is known *cell assemblies*
as a ph_____ _____.

36. There may be a dozen cell assemblies associ- *phase sequence*
ated with the mental concept of a simple shape.
Such a collection of cell assemblies is called a
_____ _____.

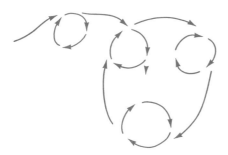

37. A collection of associate neurons is called a *phase sequence*
____ _____; a collection of associated cell
assemblies is called a _____ _____.

38. A phase sequence is a collection of associated *cell assembly*
___ _____s; a cell assembly is a collection *phase sequence*
of associated _____.

39. Every time you see a complete rectangle, all *cell assemblies*

your cell assemblies associated with rectangu-   *neurons*
larity are fired together, and crossconnections
are established among them. Then when some
of them are fired by a visual stimulus like that
on the right, the others are fired also. The abstract concept of rectangularity exists in the
brain as a _____ _____.

40. Do you remember the term used for the point   *phase sequence*
    of contact or near contact between neurons?
    _____

41. Even phase sequences are not independent of   *synapse*
    one another. Crossconnections exist, and this
    accounts for flexibility in thinking. Problem
    solving would be impossible without the
    transfer of impulses among _____ _____.

42. Cell assemblies and phase sequences are *re-*   *phase sequences*
    verberating circuits. For some time after the
    stimulus stops, energy travels round and round
    the circuit. As long as the circuit reverberates
    it can mediate other incoming stimuli. Media-
    tion refers to any interruption or change in
    the connection between a stimulus and a
    _____.

43. A neural circuit that remains active after the   *response*
    stimulus stops is said to re_____ate.

44. As long as a circuit reverberates, it can have a   *reverberate*
    _____ing effect on incoming stimuli.

45. A neural circuit that remains active after the   *mediating*
    stimulus stops is said to _____.

46. You are told to "Add the following numbers."   *reverberate*

This instruction activates its reverberating circuit, which is then ready to mediate the stimuli that follow. Then come the stimuli:

" 5 "

3

Your response is correct because of the mediating effect of a _____ ing circuit.

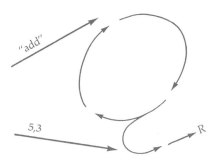

47. Visualize, if you will, the phase sequences that spring to attention in your mind as you hear:

    "Spell the following words."
    "I don't want to scare you, but . . ."
    "Did you hear what happened to Charlie?"
    "We will now discuss sex."

    Instructions and remarks such as these activate appropriate _____ circuits in your brain.   *reverberating*

48. These reverberating circuits then stand ready to _____ incoming material.   *reverberating*

49. A short review, now, before going on. C. N. S. stands for _____ _____ _____.   *mediate*

50. The basic element of the C. N. S. is the neuron. It consists of a cell body, with extensions called _____ s and ___ s.   *central nervous system*

51. Dendrites and axons meet at what is called a _____.   *dendrites*
    axons

52. A "closed circuit" of neurons is called a _____   *synapse*
    _____, which is activated by a particular
    basic _____.

53. A group of cell assemblies associated with a   *cell assembly*
    simple mental concept is called a _____   *stimulus*
    _____.

54. When a neural circuit remains active after the   *phase sequence*
    stimulus stops, it is said to _____.

55. Such reverberating circuits can have _____   *reverberate*
    effects on incoming stimuli.

56. What, then, is the learning process, according   *mediating*
    to Hebb's theory? Several stimuli are received
    together for the first time while the C.N.S. is
    in a state of AROUSAL (alerted, excited, ready).
    This means that there is a background of im-
    pulses passing around the system. As a result,
    several chance firings are made between neu-
    rons, and learning has started.

    When the C. N. S. is excited, alerted, or "at
    attention," it is said to be in a state of _____.

57. With frequent repetition, cell assemblies and   *arousal*
    phase sequences are formed, and *connections*
    among this group of stimuli are learned.
    Learning is, then, the building up of neural
    _____s.

58. If a particular response is made each time these   *connections*
    stimuli are received, it too is learned. For in-
    stance, connections are made between the
    stimuli "add," "two," "five," and the response
    "seven." Two requirements for learning are a
    state of _____ and frequent _____.

59. A background of impulses passing around in   *arousal*
    the C. N. S., which is essential to the formation   *repetition*
    of new neural connections, is known as a state
    of _____.

60. The learning process is essentially the formation   *arousal*
    and strengthening of neural _____s.

61. Once connections have been made, drill serves to build up synaptic knobs, which improves connections. Thus, drill is an aid to learning. This applies, of course, to physical as well as mental learning. "Practice makes perfect" because it improves neural _____.

connections (circuits)

62. The Hebb theory logically supports the principle of distributed practice. Can you see why? What happens within a neural circuit when the external stimuli stop? That's right, the circuit continues to _____.

connections (circuits)

63. If learning continues in a reverberating circuit, consider another principle; that of incubation in creative thinking. The creative thinker finds it effective to go through all the known information regarding a problem, consider all the known avenues of solution—then go to sleep, or otherwise relax. Thus, the external stimuli are cut off and a great many circuits are reverberating. Can you see how a solution often comes unexpectedly in this way? Think about it in the light of what you have learned.

reverberate

64. Finally, bear in mind that Hebb's theory is just that—a theory. It is logical and reasonable and offers an interesting explanation of many things that cannot as yet be proven. But it is important to teachers as a theory of learning in that it suggests practical methods of teaching—which work. Put the theory into practice yourself. Sit back right now and let *your* neural circuits reverberate to reinforce what you have learned from this program.

Short Test for Hebb Linear Program

True–False

1. The brain and spinal column are together called the central nervous system.

2. The receiving end of a neuron is called the axon.
3. Hairlike extensions which protrude from the cell body of a neuron are called synapses.
4. Phase sequences are made up of groups of cell assemblies.
5. Arousal is necessary for the formation of connections between cell assemblies.

Complete:

6. Cell assemblies consist of many _____.

7. The reactivation of a nerve cell by one which it had previously been instrumental in firing forms a(n) _____.

8. The transmission of impulses in the C.N.S. is in the form of _____.

9. The elongated extension of a nerve cell is called a(n) _____.

10. Facilitation of neural transmission is assumed to be caused by _____.

(The answers to this test are provided below.)

Answers to Review Test for the Hebb Linear Program

1. true
2. false
3. false
4. true
5. true
6. neurons or nerve cells
7. reverberatory loop
8. electrochemical impulses
9. axon
10. repeated transmission or firing

8

Neobehaviorism: Osgood

When a young Koron is taken from his glass-lined embryonic chamber for the first time, it is not unusual for him to greet his keeper. He ordinarily does this by saying something like "Greetings."* Some of the higher series numbers may say "Greetings, keeper." On occasion a mutation has been known to say "Greetings, keeper. I am Blurgat M-IV, 712, 648, 311, LVKX4," or some other longish phrase. Invariably, within 2 weeks all young Korons can say whatever they wish. Therefore, it was with some degree of puzzlement that I waited for the young Lefrancois child to say something more intelligent and intelligible than "Hi" when I first met her. Eventually she did say a little more—she said, "Blue, ga, ga, ga, dee." Since I had been assured that most inhabitants of this part of Earth spoke English, I concluded that she must be a mutation. I learned later that human children are like young Blips—*they cannot speak when first born.* Unlike Blips, however, they do not achieve a great deal of facility with their language until several years have gone by—probably because humans have not yet expended much concentrated and systematic effort toward the development of automated language tutors.

*Heh, heh! (GRL)

The prolonged, and sometimes difficult, period of language acquisition undergone by humans provides a great opportunity for psychologists, linguists, and a new breed, psycholinguists, to speculate about the processes that are involved in language learning. Unfortunately, human memory is such an undependable and short-lived phenomenon that once people are mature enough to understand language functions, they no longer remember what it is like to be a human child. Hence, conclusions, principles, and theories must be *inferred* from observations of child behavior. The perennial question is not "Is the observation correct?" or "Is that really a child?" since both can easily be verified. What cannot be confirmed, however, is the inference that since a child behaves in *this* way, he must think, feel, or perceive in *that* way. Obviously, given the penchant of humans for theorizing, the result cannot be anything but a host of speculative theories.

Among the phenomena that these theories attempt to understand are the nature and acquisition of meaning. One example of a contemporary neobehavioristic answer is provided by the theorizing of Charles Osgood. His theorizing is not limited to the area of psycholinguistics but is explicitly intended to serve for all aspects of human performance.

Charles Osgood (1916–   )

The model of behavior presented by Charles Osgood is, in many ways, complementary to Hebb's model. The emphases in each are slightly different, but their basic explanations of human functioning are highly similar. Like Hebb, Osgood attempts to provide a model to explain higher mental processes in behavioristic terms, and also like Hebb, he bases this model extensively on assumptions concerning activity in the C.N.S. Unlike Hebb, however, Osgood does not limit himself to claiming that he is advancing a proposal for a theory but suggests instead that he is advancing a "conception of behavior which at least pretends to be a complete theory in scope although certainly not in detail" (Osgood, 1957). This complete theory is advanced as a two-stage, three-level description of human functioning.

The Model

Figure 1 illustrates the major components of Osgood's system. The two stages are labeled *decoding* and *encoding*, each stage being

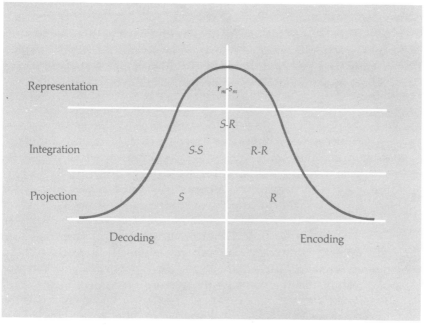

Figure 1. *Illustration of Osgood's Model.*

characterized by three levels of organization: *projection, integration,* and *representation*.

Stages

Decoding and encoding are the two processes involved in interacting with the environment. Decoding is defined as "the total process whereby physical energies in the environment are interpreted by the organism" (Osgood, 1957). Encoding, on the other hand, involves "the total process whereby intentions of an organism are expressed and hence turned again into environmental events" (Osgood, 1957). In simpler terms, decoding involves interpreting the environment (perceiving or sensing physical stimulation), whereas encoding involves behaving. Or, again, decoding involves the stimulus side of the S-R model, and encoding involves the response side. Imagine, if you can, the psychology student whose instructor greets him with a smile and says "Hello, Charlie" when the student's name is really Charlie. The student thinks the professor has been overcome by hard work. That thought is the result of a decoding process. The student then says, "Good afternoon, sir," bowing as he does so. That is encoding.

Levels

The three levels of organization for each of these stages are called the projection level, the integration level, and the representation level. Each is based on both behavioral evidence and speculation relating to the organization and the properties of the nervous system.

Projection

Projection is simply the transmission of neural impulses from receptors to the cortex during the decoding stage and from the cortex to effectors during the encoding stage. It is the least complicated of the three levels of organization, being concerned with transmission and nothing else. That this type of activity exists is obvious; if it were not so, humans would neither behave nor be sensitive to the environment.

Two characteristics of the projection level, termed isomorphism and unmodifiability by Osgood, are of special interest. Isomorphism defines a relationship of one-to-one correspondence between receptors or effectors and the cortex. This isomorphism exists in the sense that activity in a specific area of the cortex always corresponds to activity in the same sensory or muscular area; in other words, transmission is specific and not diffuse. As is evident from the treatment of Hebb's theory, this characteristic is necessary for a stimulus to have a "cue" effect (decoding) as well as for the response to be determined by the stimulus (encoding).

The second characteristic, unmodifiability, is a statement of Osgood's belief that learning does not take place at the projection level. No connections are formed between efferent or afferent neural pathways. Transmission of specific impulses is always along the same pathways. It is important to note that the neural organization in the projection level, while it terminates or originates in the cortex, involves a minimum of cortical activity. Specifically, the assemblies (termed *central neural correlates* by Osgood) that are immediately activated by physical stimulation terminate projection in the decoding stage; those immediately adjacent to pathways leading to the effector systems initiate projection at the encoding stage. The only direct connections between stimulus and response events at this level will therefore be in the form of unlearned reflexive activity.

Integration

This second level of organization is of intermediate complexity. It is the level at which those relationships between stimuli or responses that can serve as explanations for conditioning phenomena are formed. Essentially, an integration is a functional relationship between neural events (what Hebb would label cell assembly or phase sequence). The simplest of these neural events is termed *central neural correlate: central* because it pertains to the cortex rather than to peripheral neural events and *correlate* because activity in this unit is related to activity in a peripheral area and transmitted to the cortex via the projection system.

Integrations, like cell assemblies, are formed as a function of the repeated simultaneous activity of two or more central neural correlates, whether they relate to sensory or to motor signals. The integration is described as a relationship of increased dependence between two central neural correlates, which can be of two types—*predictive* and *evocative.* The latter will result when two environmental stimulus or response events have been paired so often that the activation of the central neural correlates of one is sufficient to activate the central neural correlates of the other. A predictive integration is the relationship between two central neural correlates that results with less frequent pairing of stimuli or responses. In this case, the presentation of one (for example, the activation of the central neural correlates of one) is not sufficient to elicit activity in the central neural correlates of the other but merely serves to *tone* it up. The formation of evocative integrations in the decoding stage is Osgood's explanation for the type of conditioning evidenced by Pavlov's dog. This stage is illustrated in Figure 2. Stimulus S_a (food) activates its central neural correlate a. At the same time S_b (sound of buzzer) activates its own central neural correlate (b). As a result of repeated firing, a and b become linked through the mediation of central neural correlate c (a hypothetical relationship — in actual fact the relationship might be more direct or perhaps much more indirect). Behavioral evidence suggests that eventually the activation of b is sufficient to fire a (that is, the dog eventually salivates in response to the buzzer). Prior to this firing, however, a predictive integration will likely have been set up so that the presentation of food following the sounding of the buzzer will elicit salivation very readily.

Decoding integrations essentially involve stimulus substitution. The establishment of encoding integrations, however, involves *response* substitution. On the encoding side as well, both predictive and evocative integrations are possible, providing a relatively clear explanation for the coordination and direction of motor activity. The many central neural correlates corresponding to muscle movements are, in the case of related acts, firing in contiguity. It follows from both Hebb's and Osgood's explanations that associations are likely to be formed among

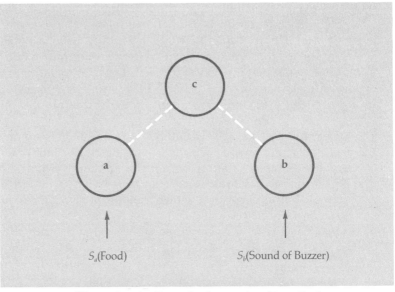

Figure 2.   *An Evocative Integration (Decoding)*

those neural events that are most often simultaneously active. This association would account for the automatic nature of motor habits once they have been acquired and practiced.

Several illustrations of predictive and evocative integrations are given below:

1. A man leaves a controlled intersection while the red light is still on. He does so because the person next to him moved his car forward 2 feet. The poor man gets killed (*evocative integration*).
2. A man follows a familiar tune in a noisy room. He cannot follow an unfamiliar tune in the same room (*predictive integration*).
3. Here is a telephone number: six three three, seven seven two eight. Here is another: six million, three hundred thirty-seven thousand, seven hundred twenty-eight. Why is the second so much more difficult to remember than the first (*predictive integration*)?
4. The first twenty-two steps in a stairway are each 7 inches high. The twenty-third step is only 4 inches high. An experimental subject trips as he is climbing the steps [*evocative integration* (or maybe stupidity)].

The variables that are most directly related to the formation of integrations include temporal contiguity and frequency, both of which are discussed above. In addition, it is Osgood's belief that *spatial propinquity* is also a contributing factor. He suggests that the physical proximity of central neural correlates will affect the formation of integrations. Hence, it follows that those stimuli that are received through one modality (for example, vision) are more likely to form integrations than are those received through different modalities.

Integrations, because of the factors that determine their formation, will necessarily reflect redundancies in the environment. The significance of this for relating to the environment and the cognitive economy that attends the learning of redundancies are discussed at some length in connection with Bruner's theory (Chapter 10). Osgood's treatment of this topic is restricted largely to a consideration of language as an example of redundancy and integrations. He examines the acquisition of meaning (semantic decoding) and the production of meaningful speech sounds (semantic encoding). While both of these processes are partly involved at the integration level of organization, the representation level is probably even more closely concerned with meaning.

Representation

So far, Osgood's theory does not appear to differ substantially from Hebb's or to go any further than to explain learning in terms of the formation of associations. Yet the central purpose of his model is to provide a framework for understanding *higher mental processes.* The bulk of this framework is implicit in Osgood's description of the representation level.

Osgood defines representation rather loosely as the simultaneous termination of decoding and beginning of encoding. In neobehavioristic terms, it is the level of organization at which mediation occurs. This mediation takes the form of fractional responses (r_m-s_m) vaguely similar to Hull's antedating goal reactions but with a number of important differences. They are, to begin with, purely hypothetical; second, they are not *goal* reactions but, instead, any of the many different reactions that might be attached to a stimulus. Hull, of course, did not equate r_G-s_G with meaning but simply assigned them a maintaining and directing function. Meaning for Osgood, however, is a representational mediating process—an r_m-s_m or a combination of these.

In order to clarify the concept of mediating response (r_m) and stimulus (s_m), it is necessary to define two additional terms: *sign* and *significate.* A significate is a stimulus that readily and reliably elicits a response. For example, a red light is a significate, as are food, verbal commands that are understood, kicks in the shin, and French swear words. In other words, any stimulus that readily elicits a response, whether learned or innate, is a significate. A sign, on the other hand, is a stimulus that did not, to begin with, readily and reliably elicit a response but has come to elicit a response through being paired with a significate. The learning process involved is described by Osgood et al. (1957) as follows:

> Whenever a non-significate stimulus is associated with a significate, and this event is accompanied by a reinforcing state of affairs, the non-significate will acquire an increment of association with some fractional portion of the total behavior elicited by the stimulus (pp. 92–93).

The fractional behavior referred to above is defined as a mediating process. The development of such a process is illustrated in Figure 3. This figure represents the hypothetical development of the meaning of the thing *school* and of the word *school*. The significate, for purposes of illustration, is the behavior of a teacher. In this case, the teacher has physically punished the student (keep in mind that this is a hypothetical illustration). The total response (R_t) includes crying, hiding the face, and a number of emotional reactions associated with unpleasant feelings. If the teacher's behavior is repeated a number of times *at school*, the thing *school* may come to have unpleasant connotations for the student. Osgood's theory states that this association will occur as a function of some parts of the response to the teacher becoming attached to the previously neutral stimulus *school* $(r_{m_1}\text{-}s_{m_1})$. These fractions of behavior, described as implicit responses, may lead to an overt reaction (R_x)—perhaps one of attempting to avoid school. It is as though the student comes to anticipate unpleasant consequences in connection with school. Similarly, some of these anticipations $(r_m\text{-}s_m$ processes) can become attached to other stimuli to which they are indirectly assigned. This learning (*assign* learning) involves the assigning of meaning to stimuli. For example, while the student in the illustration learns that school means unpleasant feelings through an associative process, he learns that the printed word *school* means the object school because that is the meaning that is assigned to it (such stimuli are called assigns for obvious reasons). The printed word, however, acquires part of its meaning from $r_m\text{-}s_m$ processes already attached to the object it represents. Hence, a student who dislikes school intensely may feel uncomfortable even when he simply reads the word.

By now the astute Reader may have detected a contradiction in

Significate
(Teacher Behavior)

Total Response
(Student Behavior)

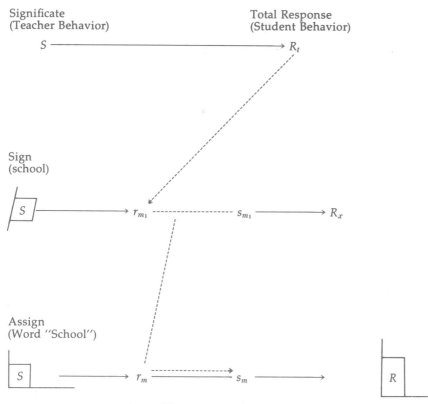

Figure 3. *Mediation*

the last several pages (if not, perhaps he should reread them or consider having a short nap or something before continuing). The illustration employed does not involve reinforcement—in fact, it involves punishment. Osgood et al.'s (1957) explanation for the learning of signs states explicity that the event must be "accompanied by a reinforcing state of affairs." Hence, the contradiction. It is clear that while reinforcement is certainly involved in much human learning, the acquisition of meaning *as described by Osgood* is possible without any reinforcement whatsoever.

Another way of looking at representation is simply to say that it *is* meaning. A thing means whatever mediating processes (r_m-s_m's) it elicits—and it elicits mediating processes that are fractions of behavior often associated with related stimuli. Therefore, meaning is acquired largely as a function of experience.

Consider, for example, why students find psychology so pleasant.* Obviously, if a thing means whatever r_m-s_m processes it has attached to it, then psychology must have r_m-s_m processes that are related to pleasure. To what signs and significates are they related? Below are only several of many possible answers for this question:

1. Finding out that one is sane is surely a significate that evokes pleasure. This is, in fact, one of the rewards of studying insanity and psychology.
2. Good instructors elicit sighs, smiles, and other signs of pleasure.' Psychology is always associated with good instructors.
3. Useful subjects are pleasant. Psychology is useful.

The Semantic Differential

Osgood's notion that meaning consists of representational mediating processes led directly to the construction of one of the few instruments that purports to measure meaning, the semantic differential. It is mentioned only very briefly here. Interested readers might refer to Osgood et al. (1957).

The semantic differential is a bipolar adjectival scale that is designed to elicit a subject's reactions to a word (see Figure 4). It

Good _____ _____ _____ _____ _____ _____ _____ Bad

Ugly _____ _____ _____ _____ _____ _____ _____ Beautiful

Powerful _____ _____ _____ _____ _____ _____ _____ Weak

PSYCHOLOGY

Figure 4. *Example of the Semantic Differential*

usually consists of a series of adjectives that are opposites. The subject is asked to indicate where the meaning for a specific word lies on a scale that represents points between each of the adjectives. An examination of large numbers of responses on these scales has led to the general conclusion that connotative (affective) meaning is definable

*This is Lefrancois' illustration—obviously. Heh, Heh! (K)

in terms of three dimensions (see Figure 5): (1) evaluative — for example, good-bad; beautiful-ugly; kind-cruel; (2) potency — for example, strong-weak; large-small; heavy-light; and (3) activity — for example, fast-slow; active-passive; hot-cold.

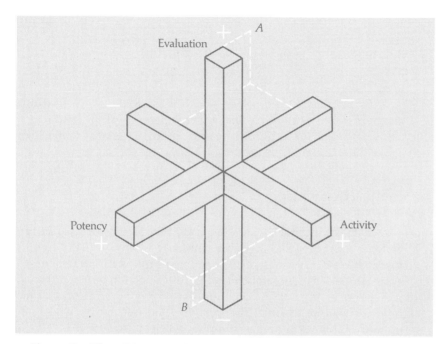

Figure 5. *Three-Dimensional Hypothetical Representation of Meaning of "Psychology" for Two Subjects.* A. Subject *A* sees "psychology" as inactive and impotent, but good. B. Subject *B* sees "psychology" as active and potent, but evaluates it negatively.

For example, a concept such as "psychology" might be evaluated as good, strong, and active; or, less likely, as bad, weak, and passive. (Figure 4 shows only three of the many scales that could be employed here.) The implications of the semantic differential for counseling, for pure research in word meanings, and for advertising and propaganda are rather exciting. A simple illustration of possible uses for each of these areas is described below.

Counseling. A relatively easy, painless, and reliable way of getting a patient's reaction to almost any situation might be to employ a semantic-differential technique. For example, a patient who is suspected of being overly attached to his mother might reveal, when asked to rate both his mother and his wife, that he probably does like his mother better (the rest is up to the counselor).

Word Meaning Research. If an investigator wanted to find out whether words have different connotations for children of different social classes, he could employ a semantic differential. It is highly possible, for example, that *school* means something quite different for a slum-area child than it does for a middle-class child.

Propaganda Studies. One practical use of the semantic differential might involve estimating the effectiveness of propaganda by measuring changes in attitudes toward political parties after exposure to certain campaign techniques.

Associative Hierarchies

One additional Osgoodian construct is that of associative hierarchies, a concept that is highly similar to Hull's notion of habit family hierarchies. An associative hierarchy is simply an arrangement of mediating processes in hierarchical order. In connection with word meanings, for example, it is fairly obvious that many r_m-s_m processes may be involved for one word. However, they are not necessarily all complementary. That is, a single stimulus (such as *school*) may give rise to antagonistic processes. In some respects, school is good; in others, it is not. The immediate affective response to the stimulus is determined by the mediating process that is then dominant.

Osgood's contention is that the order of associative hierarchies is variable. In other words, the response that is dominant now may not be dominant the next time the hierarchy is activated. Three variables—set, context, and drive—are assumed to be instrumental in determining the ordering of alternatives. The effect of each variable with specific reference to the hypothetical hierarchy of mediating processes which an individual has for the *auditory* stimulus "bear" is illustrated in Figure 6.

Set. Set refers to a predisposition to respond or perceive in a given way. If, for example, the individual serving as subject for this illustration had been told to identify all of the words that were animal

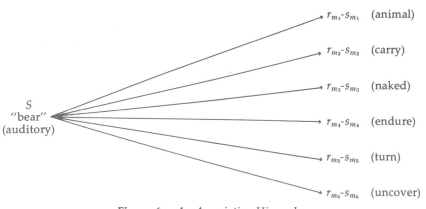

Figure 6. *An Associative Hierarchy*

names in the list *red, green, house, bear, blue* . . . , he would almost certainly select *bear* as meaning animal. He could just as easily have been given a "set," through instructions, to select all verbs in the list, in which case the stimulus would be perceived differently.

Context. Context means the situation in which the stimulus is presented. Referring to the previous illustration, if the subject were read the list *giraffe, horse, bear,* and *deer* and asked what each was, he would respond as though *bear* were an animal. If, on the other hand, he were given the same stimulus in a different context he might respond differently. For example, the sound "bear" in the list *naked, unclothed, nude,* and *stitchless* would elicit a very different response.

Drive. In considering drive, Osgood refers primarily to the effect of specific drive on perception or responding. His contention is that a specific drive can have a direct effect on behavior. The illustration of a man responding to the auditory stimulus "bear" is applicable here as well. The specific drive might be related to hunger and food and, therefore, hunting. An individual in this drive state would be more likely to react as though the stimulus meant animal.

Motivation. In discussing motivation and drive, Osgood accepts Hebb's theorizing without any major modifications. He simply redescribes cue and arousal functions of stimuli and, like Hebb, illustrates how the arousal function is essential to learning. This position is examined in more detail in Chapter 3.

Evaluation of Osgood's System

One of Osgood's main contributions is his explanation of meaning in neobehavioristic terms. As a result, psychologists have been provided with an additional tool, the semantic differential, with which to increase their understanding of human behavior.

The validity of the hypotheses advanced by Osgood about neurological functioning remains unknown. This, of course, is true of Hebb's position as well. In addition, the usefulness of the relatively complex model of behavior advanced by Osgood has not been fully demonstrated. Final evaluation, however, must await further study.

Summary of Chapter 8

This chapter has discussed a last neobehavioristic position — that of Charles Osgood. Details of his theory were related to conditioning phenomena and to the acquisition of word meanings. In addition, a description of the *semantic differential*, together with some illustrations of its potential usefulness, were included.

Lately I have been making a strange noise through my mouth and nose. Humans say it is simply a reflex, but of course we Korons have not retained any reflexes. I fear I am getting ill.* The good doctor Lefrancois has offered to retrieve my chest of medications from the spacecraft, and I have allowed him to do so.

1. Osgood's neobehavioristic analysis of behavior is concerned with two stages of human functioning: *decoding* and *encoding*. The former involves interpreting stimulation, whereas the latter involves reacting.
2. Each stage, decoding and encoding, is made up of three levels of organization: *projection*, or neural transmission; *integration*, or the forming of unconscious associations; and *representation*, the formation of meanings.
3. The label given to the neural units described by Osgood is *central neural correlates*. These correlates lead to the formation of integrations through repeated simultaneous firing.
4. Two types of integration are described: *predictive* and *evocative*. Both result from frequent pairing of activity in central neural correlates. The latter results from high-frequency pairing and is illustrated in conditioning. The former results from less frequent pairings and precedes conditioning.
5. *Representation* involves fractional mediating responses (r_m-s_m) similar to Hull's fractional antedating goal responses (r_G-s_G). Through pairing stimulus events that readily elicit responses (*significates*) with neutral stimuli (*signs*), the neutral stimuli come to represent something similar to the meaning of the non-neutral stimulus. The meaning takes the form of *mediation* (r_m-s_m processes).

---

*The use of the word *fear* is additional evidence that Korons are not free of all emotions — a fact Kongor would not admit, of course (GRL).

6. One of Osgood's contributions to theory and practice is the *semantic differential,* an instrument used to measure connotative meaning. It consists of bipolar adjectival scales (such as hot-cold) on which a subject expresses his reaction to a word. The usefulness of the semantic differential is not limited to the laboratory.

7. *Associative hierarchies* are arrangements of mediating responses (r_m-s_m) in preferential order. This ordering is determined largely by frequency of pairing, but may be altered by *set, context,* or *drive.*

8. Osgood's views on motivation are similar to Hebb's.

3

Learning:
Cognitive
Explanations

9

Gestalt and Cognitive-Field Psychology

I should like to report that I have now recovered from the illness which I mentioned in Chapter 8. As was suspected by the Medical Department of the Koron Space Agency, humans have not yet cleansed their planet of germs. Unfortunately the particular germ that attacked me with such vigor, incapacitating me for the better part of 2 weeks, was quite resistant to all medications I have in my kit. At the height of the illness, I prepared to die — and in the manner of our people, I gave the usual instructions to the good doctor Lefrancois. The poor man was quite shocked — it seems that humans do not practice excumpartation!

I was amazed and made somewhat uncomfortable throughout this long and very serious illness by the seeming unconcern of these people who had formerly appeared to be genuinely fond of me. Even the two young children played carelessly by my sickbox, showing me no sympathy whatsoever. It seemed that everyone excused himself by giving my condition a disparaging label as though that would make it less serious. They would simply shrug wisely and say to each other, "He has a cold, poor Kongor."*

*It wasn't even a very bad cold (GRL).

How much simpler it is on Koros where we have destroyed all agents harmful to Koron life.

As I lay in my sickbox, I reflected on the pages that I have already written. Throughout the first part of this report, I have been concerned primarily with the so-called *behavioristic* explanations for human behavior and learning. These explanations were originally advanced largely as a reaction against the global and imprecise nature of earlier psychological investigations—investigations in which the primary method was the examination of feelings and sensations through introspection. Behaviorism attempted to objectify psychology by reducing it to an analysis of the laws that govern the formation of relationships between stimuli and responses. It is evident that it has not made much progress toward the Eleven Great Laws.

At the same time that behaviorism was being promulgated in the United States, another reaction against the "mentalistic" schools was taking place in Germany. This reaction was not against the subject matter of psychology but rather against its insistence on analyzing behavior into parts. It took the form of *Gestalt** psychology, so named because of its concern with wholes rather than parts. Interestingly, although both the behaviorists and the Gestaltists were reacting against the same tradition, the forms these reactions took were diametrically opposed. Indeed, they were so opposed that Koffka, a Gestaltist, devoted a large portion of his writing to discrediting the claims of Thorndike.

Cognitivism

Largely because of its concern with perception, awareness, and insight, Gestalt psychology is considered to be the forerunner of contemporary cognitive psychology. Cognitivism is an orientation in psychology that is characterized by a relative lack of concern with stimuli and responses. Indeed, there is a tendency on the part of cognitivists to reject much of behaviorism on the grounds that it is overly mechanistic, incomplete, and unsuitable for explaining higher mental processes. In place of what are considered to be overly simplistic notions of human behavior, the cognitivists have substituted concepts that can be relatively complex and not always clear. Their primary preoccupations are with such subjects as perception, problem solving through insight, decision making, information processing, and under-

Gestalt is a German word that means *whole* or *configuration* (K).

standing. In all of these processes, *awareness* (or cognition) plays a central role. Despite this focus on awareness, it is not at all unusual for cognitive psychologists to base some of their theorizing on observations of the behavior of lower animals. In this connection, Bertrand Russell has made the interesting observation that American and German rats must be basically different. He is quoted as saying,

> . . . Animals studied by Americans rush about frantically, with an incredible display of hustle and pep, and at last achieve the desired result by chance. Animals observed by Germans sit still and think, and at last evolve the solution out of their inner consciousness (in Commons & Fagin, 1954, p. 28).

He was obviously referring to the fact that American psychology was then largely dominated by the trial-and-error behaviorism of E. L. Thorndike, whereas the German school was more oriented toward insightful problem solving in a Gestaltist tradition. That rats do indeed sometimes behave as their investigators expect them to, *because* they are expected to act in that manner, has been demonstrated by Rosenthal and Fode (1963). Sixty ordinary laboratory rats were divided among twelve graduate students in an experimental psychology class. Students in this class had previously learned that some strains of rats are labeled *maze-bright* while others are termed *maze-dull*, according to their genetic background. They also knew that maze-bright rats were so called because they did, in fact, tend to learn mazes more easily than their dull cousins. For the experiment in question, half the students were told that their rats were bright, and the other half were informed that theirs were dull. All students were asked to train their rats to run a simple maze. Each rat was allowed ten trials every day for 5 days. Results of the study indicated that the rats whose handlers expected them to be bright significantly outperformed the "dull" group. In addition, they were perceived as being "brighter, more pleasant, and more likeable." A similar experiment with rats (Rosenthal & Lawson, 1964), performed over a longer period of time and involving much more complex learning, yielded highly comparable results. This finding should not be taken to mean that all rat studies invariably lead to the desired results. They do so with probably no greater frequency than do studies involving humans.

The remaining portion of this chapter consists of a description of Gestalt psychology in general terms and a discussion of Lewin's variation of a Gestalt approach. His position can be interpreted as representing a transition between a cognitivism that is largely perception oriented and the contemporary cognitive approaches of such theorists as Bruner and Ausubel.

Gestalt Psychology

Humans had their first world *war* beginning in the year 1914. A war is a method for destroying people—a highly irrational method since it is quite nonselective.

At the time that this war broke out, a young German found himself marooned on an island off the coast of Africa, unable to return to his home because of the war. His name was Wolfgang Kohler; he was a psychologist. The name of the island was Tenerife; it was inhabited by numerous apes. During the 4 years that Kohler spent on Tenerife he studied apes, and the apes studied him. Kohler reported his studies in a book entitled *The Mentality of the Apes* (1927). It is uncertain what the apes did with their observations (heh, heh!).*

Two types of studies employed by Kohler have been of particular interest, both involving the problem-solving behavior of an ape in a cage and leading to identical observations. The difference between the two lies in the nature of the problems to be solved—"stick" problems in the first study, "box" problems in the second. The problems require the ape to reach a bunch of bananas that is either hanging beyond reach over his head or is outside the cage, also beyond reach. In the first situation, the ape must move a box underneath the bananas or must pile boxes one on top of the other in order to reach his reward. In the second, it is necessary for him to reach outside the cage with a long stick, or, in some cases, to assemble two sticks in order to reach far enough.

According to Kohler, the most outstanding characteristic of the problem-solving behavior of the ape is that he employs *insight* rather than trial and error in order to solve problems. Indeed, even when he does attempt a variety of approaches, they do not ordinarily lead to the solution of the problem. That solution often comes when the ape is sitting or lying down, perhaps contemplating the problem, but not actively involved in trying to solve it. When the behavior of the ape seems to involve trial and error and when successive attempts appear to lead to a correct solution, Kohler assumes that each trial comprises a small insight.

Kohler's studies of apes led him to the conclusion that not only were apes capable of solving the banana problem, but their approach

*Heh, heh! (GRL)

to problems was essentially the same as man's in that they used *insight*. Insight has since become the cornerstone of Gestalt psychology. It is ordinarily defined as *the sudden perception of relationships among elements of a problem situation*. Three terms in this definition are particularly crucial, since they serve as key words in Gestalt psychology — insight, perception, and problem solving. The basic question asked by Gestaltists is how do people solve problems; the simplified answer is that they solve problems through insight that involves perception of relationships. Not surprisingly, one way of summarizing Gestalt psychology is to describe it in terms of laws of perception. These laws were developed and elaborated largely by the three men who are considered to be the founders of the Gestalt movement: Wertheimer (1959), Koffka (1922, 1925, 1935), and Kohler (1927, 1959). Of these three, Koffka and Kohler were the two most responsible for popularizing the movement through their writings; however, Wertheimer was the acknowledged leader. His book appeared posthumously (1945), and is concerned less with a discussion of Gestalt theory in general than with the application of the theory to education. It is interesting that the movement found much less support among psychologists, who were largely educated in a behaviorist tradition, than among educators, who claimed to have known all along that man solves problems through insight rather than through trial and error.

Laws of Perception

The first and most basic argument advanced by Gestaltists against procedures that emphasize the *analysis* of behavior is that behavior cannot be understood in terms of its parts. The classical cliché that has become the trademark of the Gestalt approach is "The whole is greater than the sum of its parts" — a statement that, as interpreted by Gestaltists, is demonstrably true. Gestalt psychology does not deny that the whole is comprised of parts, nor does it deny that the parts can be discovered through analysis. But it does contradict the notion that the whole can be understood through analysis. An example commonly cited to support this contention is the *phi phenomenon*, labeled by Wertheimer, which is simply the observation that two or more lights flashing alternately or in sequence are not perceived simply as flashing lights but rather as *moving* lights. This phenomenon of apparent motion explains how people perceive neon signs or motion pictures.

Additional evidence that the perception of wholes (*of gestalts*) is different from the perception of parts is provided by numerous daily events. When listening to music, the overall perception is not of isolated notes but rather of bars or passages. If this were not so, the order of notes and the intervals of time during which they are held, as well as the spaces of time between them, would not be so important. In addition, it is readily obvious that any physical object derives its identity not only from the parts it comprises but more from the manner in which these parts are combined. An object as simple as an apple is no longer simply an apple after it has been attacked by a blender; nor is a car still a car after it has been completely dismantled.

The first concern of the Gestaltist was, then, to discover the laws governing the perception of wholes. These laws were described by Koffka (1935) and summarized more systematically by Hilgard and Bower (1966). It should be pointed out that the laws are primarily perceptual and are discussed here as such. At the same time, it should be kept in mind that Gestalt psychologists see no discontinuity between perception and thinking and that they therefore consider these laws to be applicable to both.

There is one overriding principle — *Praegnanz* (meaning "good form"), which states that there is a tendency for whatever is perceived to take the best form possible. The exact nature of that form for all perceptual experience is governed by four additional principles discussed below.

Principle of Closure. Closure is the act of completing a pattern, or gestalt. In terms of visual perception, closure usually involves incomplete figures of various forms (see Figure 1), which humans tend

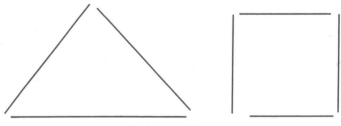

Figure 1. *Closure*

to perceive as complete forms. The same phenomenon is readily apparent in perception of a melody with missing notes or of incomplete words like p*ych*l*gy or K*ng*r. Although the term *closure* was originally employed only with perceptual problems, it has come to be used by non-Gestalt psychologists in a variety of situations, retaining much of its original meaning but also acquiring some broader significance. For example, it is not uncommon to speak of achieving closure when referring to solving a problem, understanding a concept, or simply completing a task.

Principle of Continuity. Perceptual phenomena tend to be perceived as continuous. For example, a line that is started as a curved line (see Figure 2) tends to be perceived as continuing in a curving fashion.

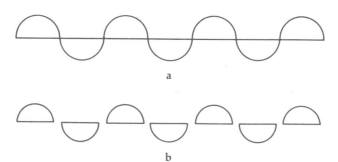

a

b

Figure 2. *Continuity.* The lines in (a) tend to be perceived as a straight line running through a curved one, not as a set of semicircles as in (b).

Principle of Similarity. This principle holds that objects that are similar tend to be perceived as related. For example, a person who hears two melodies at the same time recognizes each as a separate melody rather than hearing both as one. In Figure 3, there appear to be four rows of identical letters rather than ten columns of different letters.

```
a   a   a   a   a   a   a   a   a   a
g   g   g   g   g   g   g   g   g   g
c   c   c   c   c   c   c   c   c   c
x   x   x   x   x   x   x   x   x   x
```

Figure 3. *Similarity*

Principle of Proximity. Objects or perceptual elements tend to be grouped in terms of their proximity. Figure 4(a), for example, shows four sets of curved lines, whereas Figure 4(b) is perceived as three faces.

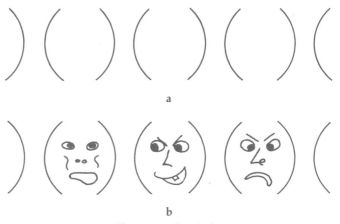

Figure 4. *Proximity*

These four principles, along with several others, were developed by Wertheimer and later applied by Koffka to thinking as well as to perception. The applications are not always clear, and are sometimes less than convincing. It is argued, for example, that the Kohler ape achieved insight perhaps because of the proximity of the stick and bananas, or of the box and the bananas. The objection can be raised that obviously there are numerous other objects (such as the bars of the cage) that are closer to the goal object than either boxes or sticks. These should form a gestalt with the bananas sooner than the solution objects. In addition, the contention (Koffka, 1925) that the banana problem is solved through closure (the tendency to perceive incomplete wholes as being complete) is, according to Hill (1963), simply to use the same name for a law about perception on the one hand and for a law about learning on the other. In other words, the fact that it is possible to conceive of a problem as involving some sort of structure with one or more elements missing is not evidence that discovering these elements involves closure. Indeed, it is relatively difficult to conceive of closure in a literal sense as involving a conceptual problem, particularly since it is defined as a natural tendency to perceive incompletes as wholes.

Learning and Memory

Since the Gestaltists were not concerned with such molecular aspects of learning and behavior as stimuli and responses, their explanations of learning and memory are considerably more global and nonspecific than those of the behaviorists. In general, the Gestalt view considers learning to result in the formation of memory traces. The exact nature of these traces is left unspecified, but a number of their characteristics are detailed. The most important characteristic is that learned material, like any perceptual information, tends to achieve the best structure possible (*Praegnanz*) in terms of the laws of perceptual organization just discussed. Hence, what is remembered is not always what was learned or perceived, but is often a better *gestalt* than the original. Wulf (1922) describes three organizational tendencies of memory, which he labels *leveling, sharpening,* and *normalizing.*

(1) *Leveling* is defined as the tendency toward symmetry or toward a toning down of the peculiarities of a perceptual pattern. Figure 5 presents a hypothetical illustration of leveling. It is assumed by Gestaltists (Koffka, for example) that the process of leveling is applicable to less perceptual cognitive content as well.

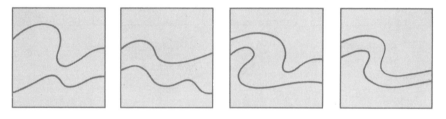

Stimulus Object   Successive Reproductions

Figure 5.   *Leveling*

(2) *Sharpening* is the act of emphasizing the distinctiveness of a pattern. It appears to be one of the characteristics of human memory that the qualities that most clearly give an object identity tend to be exaggerated in the reproduction of that object. Figure 6 is an illustration of this phenomenon.

(3) *Normalizing* occurs when the reproduced object is modified in terms of preexisting memory traces. This modification usually tends toward making the remembered object more like what it appears to be—that is, to *normalize* it. A hypothetical illustration of normalizing is presented in Figure 7.

How much simpler it would be if humans, like Korons, remembered objects as they are and not as "good" gestalts should be.

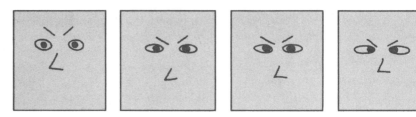

Stimulus Object   Successive Reproductions

Figure 6. *Sharpening*

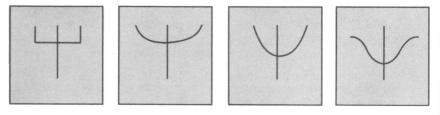

Stimulus Object   Successive Reproductions   Ψ

Figure 7. *Normalizing*

Kurt Lewin (1890–1947)

One of the men who worked with Wertheimer at the inception of the Gestalt movement, but who represents a significant departure from the Gestaltists' traditional emphasis on perception, learning, and memory was Kurt Lewin (1935, 1936, 1947). His major concerns were personality, motivation, and social psychology, but he still retained much of the orientation of his colleagues.

The concept of field plays a central role in Lewin's system, a concept that has a Gestaltic origin. Initially it was taken to mean the environment as perceived by an organism. That is, for the Gestaltists, a *field* consists of the object or objects that are being perceived (*figure*) and the background or environment that surrounds them (*ground*). Ordinarily the relationship between figure and ground is an unambiguous one—the figure is perceived, and the ground is simply its surroundings. On occasion, however, figure and ground alternate so that one moment's perception is exchanged for a different perception the next. The interesting point is that humans seem to be unable to perceive both figure and ground at the same time. The drawing in Figure 8, for example, is perceived either as a vase or as two human faces in confrontation. Unlike Korons, humans are unable to perceive it as being both at once.

Figure 8.   *Figure-Ground Alternation*

The term *field* has a slightly different connotation in Lewin's system. Instead of indicating simply the perceptual environment, it also includes cognitive meaning. A field is defined by Lewin as not only, or even primarily, the figure-ground components of the physical environment, but also the beliefs, feelings, goals, and alternatives of an individual. In other words, Lewin deals with a cognitive *and* a perceptual field—hence, the label *cognitive-field psychology*, which is often applied to his system.

Life Space

Instead of referring simply to an individual's field, Lewin employs the term *life space* to mean the world as it relates to a particular individual. Hence, a life space is a composite of all that is immediately relevant for the behavior of a specific individual. It includes not only motives, goals, means to goals and impediments to these means, but also the individual himself. The physical environment, even though it may not be of immediate relevance for behavior, is also included in life space. A diagrammatic representation of a life space is presented in Figure 9. At the center of the space is the person; he is surrounded

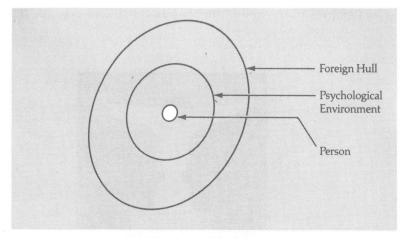

Figure 9. *Life Space*

by his psychological environment, which includes all factors that are of direct relevance for his immediate behavior. In addition, his life space includes the more remote physical environment, labeled *foreign hull* by Lewin.

Lewin's primary goal was to arrive at some representation of a behaving individual that would permit the prediction of that individual's behavior. That representation is essentially his concept of life space.

Characteristics of Life Space

Life space is a central, and relatively complex, variable in Lewin's system. It can be described in terms of a number of characteristics.

A life space is relativistic in that it is defined in terms of the environment as it is perceived by the individual and not necessarily as it actually exists. If a human persists in believing that Korons are dangerous, then dangerous Korons form a part of his life space. A woman who believes that household dust becomes lethal after prolonged exposure has lethal household dust in her life space. In order to understand her behavior in certain situations, it is necessary to know that this woman's life space contains a large corner devoted to poisonous dust.

Second, life space can be diagrammed in terms of areas representing the goals or aspirations of the individual at any given moment. In order to make such diagrams meaningful, Lewin employed a concept of *topological* space as opposed to ordinary geometry. The chief characteristic of topological representations is that the areas subsumed by them are irrelevant; only the relative positions of spaces are meaningful. Figure 10, for example, depicts the hypothetical life space of an

Figure 10. *A Student's Life Space*

imaginary student. The space contains the person, who is presently a student, and the four alternatives that he sees as being available to him. His ultimate goal is to make money. In Lewinian terminology, the goal, money, has high positive *valence* (indicated by several plus signs in the figure). The term *valence* indicates the attractiveness of various areas in the life space. Among the four alternatives open to this student are stealing money, going into his father's chicken-sexing business, drifting down the California coast, or teaching school. The representation of his life space indicates that drifting down the Pacific coast is the most attractive of these alternatives (3 plus signs). However, the likelihood of making a great deal of money while living in the lap of idealistic poverty on a beach somewhere is somewhat remote, as represented by the thickness of the line that separates the "money" and "drifting" regions. In Lewinian terminology these lines are referred to as *barriers*.

This student's life space also shows that teaching is more attractive (has higher valence) than going into business but that the barrier between making a great deal of money and teaching is even greater than that between drifting and making money. The easiest way of making money is obviously by stealing. This activity, however, has negative valence, as indicated by the minus sign in that region of the life space.

Since Lewin's system is intended to provide some basis for making predictions about an individual's behavior, the concept of a life space that comprises goals, ways of achieving goals, valences of alternatives, and the barriers impeding the attainment of goals should be of some value — at least theoretically. Obviously a great deal of information is required about an individual and his present life space before meaningful predictions can be made.

A third characteristic of life space is that it constantly varies as the person's goals change or as the alternatives he sees change. A diagram of a life space is only a two-dimensional representation. It is possible to conceive of the space itself as being three dimensional, in which case any number of slices can be cut. While each will be highly similar in that the "person" and his major goals will be the same, there might also be pronounced differences in the alternatives to these goals.

Vectors and Conflicts

In attempting to diagram the motivated behavior of individuals, Lewin not only employed the concept of a topological representation of life space but also borrowed the concept of *vectors* from physics. A vector is an arrow that is used to indicate the direction and strength of various forces. Accordingly, in Lewin's system, vectors are employed to show the directions toward which behavior tends as well as the strength of the force that is exerted. Figure 11 shows several vectors, one of which indicates a tendency to engage in navel contemplation, the other representing a weaker tendency to work. The arrow indicates the direction of force, while the length of the vector represents its strength.

Figure 11

Consideration of vectors as indicators of motivational forces leads simply and conveniently to a depiction of the three possible behavior conflicts that can beset man. The first, referred to as an *approach-approach conflict*, occurs when the individual is drawn toward two incompatible goals at the same time. Consider, for example, the case of the man who is offered a promotion from chicken counter to chicken sexer, and who, on the same day, is invited by his brother to join him as assistant manager of a 14-bird turkey ranch. Both positions are very attractive; indeed, they are equally attractive. That aspiring young executive has an approach-approach conflict.

Numerous, less facetious, examples of this type of conflict may be seen in everyday life. The reader is invited to think of some.

Approach-Approach Conflict

Consider, on the other hand, the case of the obese human housewife who likes chocolate sundaes garnished with "just a dash" of whipped cream. Her problem is of another type. She is simultaneously drawn toward sundaes (with a dash of whipped cream) and pulled in the opposite direction by her desire to regain her schoolgirl figure. Hers is an *approach-avoidance conflict.*

The third conflict situation, the *avoidance-avoidance conflict,* is clearly illustrated by the suffering human who has a toothache but passionately fears dentists. If he avoids the dentist, he must retain the toothache; yet, if he is to avoid the toothache, he must suffer the dentist. His is the classical damned-if-you-do, damned-if-you-don't double bind of the avoidance-avoidance conflict.

Lewin's System in Summary

The bulk of Lewin's theorizing is contained in his book *Principles of Topological Psychology*. A great deal of this work is more relevant to personality theory and social psychology than to learning theory and is therefore not reviewed here. His concepts of life space and its vectors, valences, and barriers can be a useful way of describing behavior *a posteriori*. However, it is of relatively limited value for predicting behavior, largely because few guidelines are provided for arriving at an accurate description of vectors and valences prior to a behavior taking place. Since life space is defined in terms of how the acting organism views *his* immediate environment, and since he is the only one who can view it in exactly that manner, he is also the only one who can come close to describing it accurately. However, since life space also includes some factors that are unknown to the individual but that nevertheless exert a powerful influence on his behavior, he is also limited in his effort to describe his own life space. Consider, for example, the human who honestly believes that he likes delivering public addresses. His description of his own life space would probably place a high valence on speaking in public. It is not uncommon, however, to find people of this type who always seem to have some excuse for not accepting invitations to display their rhetorical skills. Since life space is determined by how a person acts rather than by how he will act, an individual's personal description of his life space is not necessarily valid.

How incredibly simpler it would be for humans if they simply behaved rationally as do Korons.*

Lewin's Influence on Contemporary Psychology

The most widespread effect of Lewin's work on contemporary psychological theory and practice is probably to be found in the phenomena variously labeled T groups, encounter groups, sensitivity training, or human relations laboratories. Essentially these are training and/or therapeutic sessions involving groups of people who, through various communication exercises, perceptual activities, role-playing games, and other interpersonal activities, attempt to achieve a greater awareness of themselves and of each other. Although Lewin was not

*And how incredibly duller, my dear Kongor (GRL).

directly responsible for the inception of the training (T-group) movement, a large number of his ideas lend themselves particularly well to a
theoretical foundation for it. For example, the Lewinian notion that the
educational process consists of "unfreezing, restructuring, and refreez-
ing" one's field is ostensibly illustrated in a T-group session where
individuals are encouraged to break down interpersonal barriers (un-
freeze) in order to develop new concepts of self (restructure). Similarly, the barriers that are assumed to exist between people are often
described in terms of "psychological distance" between cognitive
fields (Lewin, 1951).

Even more fundamental to the sensitivity movement is the basic
notion that each individual reacts to his own world in a unique manner
and that in order to understand him it is necessary to begin from that
unique point of view. This notion, frequently labeled *phenomenology*,
is not only the essence of Lewin's theory but is also the basis of the
current emphasis on client-centered therapy (Rogers, 1958), as well as
on T groups and related movements.

A second, related manifestation of the influence of Lewin's theory
is the humanistic movement in psychology—a movement that is characterized by its concern with the individuality of man and with the
development of his potential through his own efforts. The phrase *self-
actualization* is ordinarily employed to describe this self-fulfillment.
Like the advocates of T groups, humanistic psychologists are typically
phenomenological. It is in this phenomenological orientation that both
are particularly indebted to the earlier theorizing of Kurt Lewin.

Life Spaces, Schools, and Teachers

Educators could use Lewinian theory as a basis for attempting
specific changes in the classroom. They could endeavor to change the
life spaces of individual students—perhaps by increasing the attractiveness of success in school or decreasing the attractiveness of socially
unacceptable behaviors. Lewin's theory could also yield ways to help
students avoid the conflicts he describes or to cope with them once
they occur.

However, the most important effect his theory might have would
be a general change in teacher-student interaction as a result of the
teacher's coming to realize that a student reacts to his world as *he* himself perceives it and that he perceives it in a way that is completely
unique to him. Such a realization might well lead to the type of student-
centered schools that are currently being advocated by a number of
psychologists (for example, Rogers, 1951, 1969).

Summary of Chapter 9

This chapter has presented an introduction to cognitive approaches to learning. The Gestalt system was described as a forerunner of contemporary cognitive psychology. In addition, the cognitive-field psychology of Kurt Lewin was described briefly. The following chapters examine some contemporary cognitive positions.

1. *Gestalt psychology* arose as a reaction against the mentalistic introspectionism of its forerunners. Unlike behaviorism, however, it did not abandon the study of the mind and of consciousness.
2. Gestalt psychology can be viewed as an introduction to *cognitivism*. Cognitive approaches to learning are characterized by a preoccupation with such topics as understanding, information processing, decision making, and problem solving.
3. The primary beliefs of the Gestaltists can be summarized in two statements: the whole is greater than the sum of its parts; people solve problems through insight. The first gives voice to the belief that the analysis of a subject (or object) into its parts is not likely to lead to knowledge of that subject. The second is a rejection of the role of trial and error in solving problems.
4. Wertheimer, Kohler, and Koffka were the founders of the Gestalt school. As a system, it has been identified largely in relation to its studies of perception and its formulation of such laws of perceptual organization as *closure, similarity, continuity,* and *proximity*. The application of these laws to learning has not received wide acceptance.
5. Gestalt studies of memory have led to the observation that structural changes in information over time involve the processes of leveling (making symmetrical), *sharpening* (heightening distinctiveness), and *normalizing* (rendering more like the object should appear).
6. *Cognitive-field psychology* is characterized by a concern with the individual as he is affected by his immediate environment (field). Kurt Lewin's system is a good example of this approach.
7. Lewin describes the behaving individual in terms of a *life space* (field) that comprises the person, his goals, the available paths to these goals, and the attractiveness of the goals, as well as the barriers that impede his progress toward them. Life space is defined in terms of the individual's *own perception* of his environment.
8. The notion of conflicts as involving incompatible approach and avoidance tendencies is represented by Lewin in terms of *vectors* that indicate both the direction and strength of a tendency to behave.
9. The value of Lewin's system is restricted by the amount of information that it is necessary to obtain about an individual before meaningful predictions about his behavior can be made. It is nevertheless of considerable value in understanding and explaining behavior, particularly *a posteriori*, and has particular relevance for teaching.
10. The influence of Lewin's work on contemporary psychological theory and practice is manifested in the T-group movement as well as in humanistic psychology.

10

Cognitivism: Bruner and Ausubel

Among the most intriguing experiments run by Blip psychologists many years ago are those that were intended to investigate the learning processes of the lower animal forms of Koros. At that time the most frequently employed animal subject was the *chunta*, a small, blue, four-legged creature that thrived in captivity and reproduced at a prolific rate. The chunta was particularly adept at learning to perform such simple tasks as pulling levers or parting curtains in order to obtain food.

An early experiment that later became something of a classic bears a remarkable resemblance to a study conducted on Earth by Tolman and Honzik (1930). The Earth study has been interpreted as evidence that there *is* "higher" mental activity, even in *rats*, that cannot easily be explained in behavioristic terms. The Koros study has similarly been taken as a manifestation of Blip-like functioning, even in as phylogenetically unfortunate a creature as the chunta. Both studies can be viewed as one explanation for the development of more "cognitive" positions in psychology.

The Tolman and Honzik (1930) experiment was a pioneering form of the *blocked-path* study. It involved releasing a rat in a maze with several alternative routes to the goal and allowing him to run in this maze until he had learned it. The next step in the procedure was to introduce barriers in some of the paths and observe the rat's reaction. An approximate representation of the original Tolman and Honzik maze is given in Figure 1. The paths are so arranged that they vary in length from the shortest, most direct route (1) to the longest (3). The rat who becomes completely familiar with the maze can be expected to develop preferences for paths 1, 2, and 3, in that order. This expectation was confirmed by the observation that hungry rats almost invariably

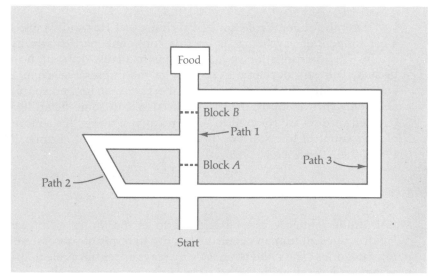

Figure 1

selected Path 1, thereby indicating a preference for it. When Path 1 was blocked at *A*, however, the rat almost invariably selected Path 2 (approximately 93% of the time). This reaction followed from S-R explanations of behavior—the next observation did not. When Path 1 is blocked at *B*, S-R theorists might still predict that the rat would select Path 2, since the entrance to it is not blocked, and it is second in preference. Obviously, however, the block on Path 1 at *B* also serves as a barrier for Path 2, thus leaving Path 3 as the only alternative that still leads to the goal. The *cognitive* argument is that if the rat selects Path 3 rather than Path 2, it is because he has developed some sort of cognitive map of the maze. This knowledge of the structure of the maze allows him to arrive at an insightful solution for his problem. Amazingly, 14 out of the 15 rats involved in the original experiment selected Path 3. This type of experimentation is often cited by such theorists as the Gestaltists or Bruner in support of their nonbehavioristic orientation.

This chapter presents a discussion of two contemporary cognitive theories—Jerome Bruner's and David Ausubel's. The first theory is treated in some detail, the second in less detail since much of what it contains is implicit in Bruner's theory.

Jerome Bruner (1915–   )

Jerome Bruner, Professor of Psychology at Harvard, is one of the most influential psychologists on this continent, particularly in education. The interpretation of his theory is relatively difficult, however, because it is still developing. In view of the impressive scope, detail, and complexity of Bruner's writings, and given the limited space available, only the "learning theory" is discussed in some detail here. Interested readers are referred to Bruner's own writings for a more complete account of his position (Bruner et al., 1956, 1966; Bruner, 1957a, 1957b, 1961, 1963, 1966, 1968).

The Theory: An Overview

Bruner's theory can be referred to as the *theory of categorizing.* He describes all human cognitive activity in terms of processes involving categories. Thus, the term *category* plays as central a role in Bruner's system as *habit* does in Guthrie's or Hull's or as *cell assembly* or *central neural correlate* does in Hebb's or Osgood's. To perceive is to categorize; to conceptualize is to categorize; to learn is to form categories; to make decisions is to categorize. The central question is, obviously, what is a category? The answer to this question can become a discussion of Bruner's entire learning theory.

Categories

If a man sees a head with long blond hair and an attractive face smiling at him over a sea of foam in a pink bathtub, does he simply see a head with long blond hair and a smiling face over a sea of foam in a pink bathtub? (The question is surely of more than passing academic interest.) Literally, yes, that is all he *sees,* but he probably goes much beyond the simple information given to him by his senses. He imagines that this must be a girl; that she probably has two arms, two legs, and two elbows; that her skin is white (if her face *is* white — it could be red); that she has toenails, and so on. Yet he cannot immediately perceive all of these qualities. Indeed, he is going beyond the information given: first, he is making the decision that this *is* a girl; second, he is inferring about this girl on the basis of what is known about *all* girls. According to Bruner, this man is making these inferences through using a category — the category *girl*. The category *girl* is a *concept,* in the sense that any representation of *related things* is a concept; it is also a percept, in the sense that a *physical thing* when apprehended through the senses is a percept.

The Category "Girl"

Categories as Rules

Another way of looking at *category* is to define it as though it were a rule for *classifying things as being equal*—a very logical definition since concepts and percepts—which are achieved through categorizing—are collections of *things* that are in some way equivalent. To state it quite simply, the concept *girl* is a category; a category is a rule; the category *girl* is the rule that allows an individual to recognize an object as a girl. In fact, this category is a collection of rules, among which may be the following.*

To be a girl, a thing must be:
1. human
2. female
3. more than 2 years old,
4. less than 29 years old,
5. attractive and so on.

Categories, as rules, obviously say something about the characteristics that objects must possess before they can be classified in a given way. Characteristics of objects are referred to as *attributes* by Bruner, which he defines as "...some discriminable feature of an object or event which is susceptible of distinguishable variation from event to event" (1966, p. 26). Attributes are therefore properties of objects that are not possessed by all objects. They are further distinguished by whether or not they play a role in the act of categorizing. Those attributes which define an object are called *criterial*. Those that do not are *irrelevant*. Femaleness is probably a criterial attribute for the category *girl*; color of hair is irrelevant.

Categorizing is defined by Bruner as follows:

> To categorize is to render discriminably different things equivalent, to group the objects and events and people around us into classes, and to respond to them in terms of their class membership rather than in terms of their uniqueness (1956, p. 1).

Categories are rules that specify four things about the objects being reacted to; they are described below in terms of the category *car*. (1) First, a category is defined in terms of certain specific characteristics that are referred to as *criterial attributes*. For the category *car* such attributes would include the presence of a motor, running

---

*This illustration, as must be evident, was given to me by Lefrancois. I personally am no more interested in this category than in any other (K).

gear, and control devices. (2) A category not only specifies the attributes that are criterial but also indicates *the manner in which they are to be combined.* If, for example, all parts of a car were disassembled and placed in plastic garbage bags, it is unlikely that anyone would treat the result as though it were equivalent to a car. The rule for *car* says that the parts must be assembled in a prescribed fashion. (3) A category *assigns weight to various properties.* A car might continue to be classed as a car even if it had no bumpers and no windows—perhaps even if it had no wheels. But if it had no motor and no body, it might be categorized as something else, for these properties are more or less necessary for membership in the category. (4) A category sets *acceptance limits on attributes.* Attributes are susceptible to variation from event to event. Such attributes as color, for example, can vary tremendously. A rule for a category such as *car* that specifies that a car has four wheels might set the limits of variation at zero. Thus, anything with three wheels or less, or five wheels or more, would not be a car.

Kinds of Categories

Bruner describes two kinds of categories, each being defined in terms of the rules just described, which are assumed to be sufficient to include all of an individual's percepts and concepts. They are called the *identity* and the *equivalence* categories.

Identity Categories. An identity category is employed where stimuli are classed as forms of the same thing. For example, different phases of the moon are all interpreted as the moon—which they are. Another example is a child at different stages of his growth; he is simply different forms of the same person.

Equivalence Categories. Equivalence categories are probably much more frequently used than identity categories. Whenever objects, events, or people are reacted to as though they were the same thing, although they really are not, equivalence categories are being employed. There are three kinds of equivalence categories, depending on the nature of the response involved.

1. *Affective categories* are established whenever an individual's emotional reaction renders events equivalent. For example, a song, Bacardi White rum, and a poem might all evoke pleasure and therefore belong to the same category.

2. *Functional categories* are defined in terms of the common func-

tion of two or more objects. Pens and pencils are both used for writing and can be categorized in the functional category *objects with which to write*.

3. *Formal categories* are defined by convention, by law, or by science. For example, there is a formal category *pen* whose criterial attributes are specified by a dictionary.

Any object can belong to any of these three categories or to an identity category. For example, an apple is the same apple when green and when ripe (identity category); it is something to eat (functional category); and it is a fruit (formal category).

Cognitivism has been described as being concerned with information processing and decision making. Jerome Bruner's description of information processing is relatively simple and useful, although it leaves a number of questions unanswered. Human beings interact with their environment in terms of categories or classification systems that allow them to treat different events or objects as though they were equivalent. Incoming information is therefore organized in terms of preexisting categories or causes the formation of new ones. In either case, the end product of the processing will be a decision about the identity of the stimulus input, as well as a number of implicit inferences about the object or event associated with the input. It is Bruner's contention that *all* of man's interaction with the world must involve classifying input in relation to categories that already exist—in his own words, completely novel experiences are ". . . doomed to be a gem serenely locked in the silence of private experience." In short, he can probably not perceive *totally* new stimulus input or, if he can, he cannot communicate it.

Decision Making

Not only is all information processed through an act of categorization, but all decisions also involve classifying. Decision making, as discussed by Bruner, involves placing events in categories. There are a number of ways of interpreting this process. First, to identify an object is to make a decision about whether or not it belongs in a given category. Second, once an object is placed in a category and therefore identified, there is inherent in the category a decision about how the object should be reacted to. For example, the almost unconscious recognition that a traffic light is red is, in Bruner's terms, the result of interpreting the input in question as though it were an example of events belonging to the category *red light*. Implicit in this act of categorizing is the decision not to walk across the street.

The nature of the decision-making process is really not explained at all clearly in Bruner's system. Nor is it ever quite clear how decision making differs from simple information processing, or whether the processing of input from the environment (perception) is different from the organization of information in the mind (conceptualization). Bruner states, in fact, that he sees no reason to believe that the processes underlying perception are any different from those involved in conceptualization (1966, p. 9). He treats thinking (Bruner, 1957a) and perception (Bruner, 1957b) in different writings, however. It should be remembered, nevertheless, that the following discussion of perception also applies to the more "central" processes.

Perception

The processes underlying perceptual activity have already been touched on in the previous section in the form of a more general discussion of the act of categorizing. Perception really does not involve anything more complicated than identification. The perceptual process itself, in a general sense, is the act of translating sensory data into awareness, knowledge, feeling, or whatever. Where the process ceases to be perceptual and becomes conceptual is a moot question.

Bruner describes two features of perception: it is "categorical" and it is "varyingly veridical." *Categorical* means that categorization is involved in perception, which is clear from the previous discussion. *Varyingly veridical* means that what an individual thinks he perceives somehow predicts, with varying accuracy, what the actual object is really like. To perceive is to categorize; to place an object in a category is to make predictions about properties that it *must* have but are not now perceptible. Take a very simple example. A white circular object, ¼ inch in diameter and 3 inches long, is held up in front of a class. One of the students who is awake is asked what the white object is. "Chalk, sir," she says. She is a bright psychology student. Implicit in her perception of this object is her knowledge that if the instructor were to hold it with one end pressed lightly on a chalkboard, and if he were to move it on the chalkboard, it would leave particles of itself behind. This is a property of the object which she cannot now perceive but which she can predict because her category for chalk, in which she has placed this object, includes the attribute "capability of leaving particles of itself behind on a chalkboard when pressed to it lightly and moved across it." She is a precise, bright psychology student. Her prediction will likely, but not necessarily, be correct. It is varyingly veridical.

Veridicality of perception will depend on a number of factors, which Bruner describes as follows:

> Adequate perceptual representation involves the learning of appropriate categories, the learning of cues useful in placing objects appropriately in such systems of categories, and learning of what objects are likely to occur in the environment (1957b, p. 229).

Bruner describes four sequential steps involved in categorizing. The first is *primitive categorization*. At this point, the stimulus event is no more than an "object" or a sound. The object is isolated and attended to in this stage. The second step is labeled *cue search* and involves looking for the presence or absence of those attributes that are likely to be useful in identifying the object. This search leads to an initial categorization after which additional *confirming* cues may be sought. This third stage is labeled *confirmation check*. The fourth stage, *confirmation completion*, is marked by a termination of cue searching. Additional cues, especially if they are not congruent with initial identification, are not likely to be reacted to. This sequence is marked by initial openness, then selectivity, and finally closedness to sensory input.

Perceptual Readiness. The accuracy with which stimulus events will be categorized is as much a function of perceptual readiness as it is of simply having the appropriate category. *Perceptual readiness* refers to the accessibility of a category, where accessibility is defined in terms of the stimulus input that is required for identification to occur. The more accessible the category, the less input is required, the wider the range of input that will be accepted, and the more likely that less accessible, but perhaps better-fitting, categories will be masked.

Obviously, then, the accessibility of an appropriate category plays a central role in the accurateness (veridicality) of perception. Two factors are assumed to determine category accessibility: the expectancies of the individual and his search requirements. These factors are determined largely by the individual's needs and by his ongoing activities. Lefrancois relates an illustration.

Several years ago, he and an undergraduate student undertook to demonstrate the effects of expectancies and search requirements on perception. The demonstration, which was conceived while they were on a moose-hunting expedition, involved setting up a target by the side of an isolated logging trail. The target was made to look remotely like a moose. It consisted of a piece of black tar paper draped over some small bushes. They predicted, on the basis of what Bruner had written about category accessibility, that due to expectancies and search requirements, the category *moose* would be extremely accessible for any hunters who happened to come down the road.

Four unwitting moose hunters who came roaring down the trail in a 4-wheel drive vehicle became the subjects. They no sooner came within sight of the "target" than the driver slammed on his brakes, and the four hunters came piling out pell-mell. At least twenty rounds were fired within 5 seconds. The intention had been to bring the bullet-riddled tarpaper into class the following week in order to demonstrate category accessibility, but not a single bullet found its mark.

Category Accessibility

Relating this event to Bruner's definition of category accessibility, the following corroborative statements can be made: (1) very little stimulus input was required to evoke categorization, for the driver stopped immediately; (2) a wide range of input was accepted, since a stimulus pattern only very remotely resembling that which would be appropriate for the moose category was identified as being a moose; and (3) some much better-fitting categories were masked. Obviously, the category *tar paper on a bush* is a better-fitting one; it was masked, however, by the moose category.

Neurological Bases

Bruner proposes four general types of mechanisms that mediate perceptual readiness. These are based largely on Hebb's concept of the cell assembly and phase sequence and as such are his closest contact with a neurological basis for his theory. He does not, however, attempt to describe anatomically and functionally a neurophysiological system that would complement his theory, but, rather, limits his discussion to what he considers must be the formal properties of such a system. Among these properties he lists four functions that need to be served in order to be consistent with his theory of categorizing. They will not be discussed in detail here since they are essentially a recapitulation of Hebb's notions. The first such mechanism is referred to as *grouping* or *integration*. It is assumed that the function of forming groupings or integrations that would correspond to categories would probably have to be undertaken by neurological organizations similar to Hebb's cell assemblies. They would reflect redundancies in the environment as do categories. A second mechanism involved in perception is an ordering one, labeled *access ordering*. This notion is highly similar to Osgood's description of associative hierarchies or Hull's concept of habit family hierarchies. Third, there is a need for some sort of neural mechanism whereby the organism will be able to tell whether or not input matches a category. Bruner does not attempt to describe how such a system might operate, but he labels it a *match-mismatch* process. The fourth function is served by a *gating process*. In order to be able to react selectively to only some of the millions of stimuli that continually bombard an organism, it is necessary that an attention process serve to gate out irrelevant stimulation. Again the anatomy of such a system is not discussed by Bruner.

Korons have no gating systems. We react to all sensory stimulation.*

Coding Systems

A concept central to Bruner's explanation of thought processes is coding systems. It is probably evident that the notion of category is

---

*I have some doubts about the truth of this assertion. Kongor himself often seemed quite unable to listen to more than two or three conversations at one time (GRL).

not sufficient to explain anything more than the simple recognition of sensory input. Going beyond the immediate sense data involves more than simply making inferences on the basis of the category into which the input has been classified. More important, it involves making inferences on the basis of related categories. For example, the inference that a new pearlike object (called a Korug) is edible is made not simply because the Korug is pearlike and pears are edible, but also because the Korug is orangelike, and oranges are edible. (As a point of information, a Korug is a blue fruit resulting from crossing a pear tree with an orange tree and painting the graft blue). In fact, the Korug is identified and predictions are made about it on the basis of a wide variety of related categories. These related categories are referred to as a *coding system* (see Figure 2).

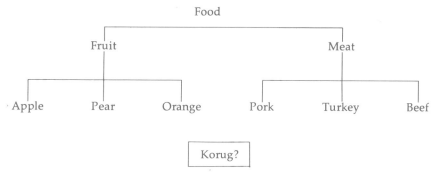

Figure 2. *A Coding System*

One of the most important characteristics of coding systems is that they are hierarchical arrangements of related categories, such that the topmost category in the system is more generic (general) than all the categories below it. In other words, as one moves up from the specific instances that define related categories, each subsequent concept (or category) is freer of specifics. According to Bruner, the non-specificity of coding systems is central in determining their role in retention and in transfer. Essentially, Bruner's contention is that in order to remember a specific it is usually sufficient to recall the coding system of which it is a member. The details of the specific instance can then be recreated. The transfer value of coding systems is implicit in the notion that a generic code is really a way of relating relatively dissimilar objects and making inferences about them. There is obviously a significant amount of transfer involved in the decision that appropriate behavior toward a Korug involves eating it.

Appropriate Behavior toward a Korug

Bruner describes four conditions that are assumed to affect the acquisition of generic codes — set, need state, mastery of specifics, and diversity of training.

Set.   Set refers to an individual's predisposition to react in a given way. It is generally recognized that predispositions can directly affect *perception* (Hebb), responding (Osgood), and learning (Bruner). Specifically, Bruner contends that through instructions or previous learning a student can be made to proceed as though new subject matter were related to other learning and were organizable in terms of an underlying structure. Obviously a *set* (attitude) of this nature is more conducive to the acquisition of generic codes than one premised on the assumption that the new learning is unstructured and unrelated to previous learning.

Need State.   Bruner's ideas on motivation are virtually identical to Hebb's. His reference to need state can therefore be interpreted as a reference to arousal level, where arousal is defined as a single drive related to the generalized need of individuals to maintain arousal at a moderate level. In the same way that learning or behavior is assumed to be maximally effective under conditions of moderate arousal, so the acquisition of generic codes is believed to be facilitated by arousal that is neither too high nor too low. In support of this inference, Bruner

(1957a) cites an experiment in maze-alternation transfer performed with two groups of rats. The rats in one group had not been fed for 36 hours and were therefore presumably under conditions of high drive; the rats in the other group had been fed recently and could therefore be expected to be at lower levels of drive. In both cases, rats had previously learned to run a simple alternating maze (that is, one where the correct turns alternate, right-left-right-left, and so on). A test of the transferability of learning took the form of placing the rats in the opposite maze (left-right instead of right-left). In this situation, those rats who had been fed most recently outperformed their hungrier counterparts. It is not immediately clear, however, that this experiment can be generalized to human behavior. Even from a Koron's point of view, it appears that there may be some differences between a hungry rat and a highly aroused human. In addition, the transfer of maze learning does not seem to be directly analogous to generic learning in man. Nevertheless, Bruner's notions about the effect of arousal level on learning are consistent with those of Berlyne, Hebb, and Osgood.

Mastery of Specifics. It can probably be accepted as self-evident that the formation of generic codes will be influenced by the extent to which the learner has mastered the information specific to the instances that are to be coded. For example, a Korug would not easily be organized into a coding system along with other fruit unless at least *some* of the specific attributes of fruit (their edibility, the fact that they grow, and so on) were well known. It would follow that knowing *more* about its specifics would enhance the codability of an event or object.

Diversity of Training. This fourth factor that is assumed to affect the acquisition of generic codes is closely related to *mastery of specifics*. Bruner's contention is that the wider the range of situations in which something is experienced, the more easily it will be related to other events. This contention can also be accepted as axiomatic, particularly because categories and codes are established on the basis of similarities and differences among events. Obviously, diversity of training may serve to highlight what is common among events as well as to point out what is unique to each.

Concept Attainment

Bruner has done some experimental work in the formation of concepts, a topic that has attracted considerable attention. Some of this original work is discussed in the remainder of this chapter.

Bruner makes a distinction between the *formation* of concepts and their *attainment.* To *form* a concept is to arrive at the notion that some objects belong together while others do not. To *attain* a concept, on the other hand, is to discover the attributes that may be useful in distinguishing between members of a class and nonmembers of the same class. For example, when a human learns that there are edible mushrooms but that there are also inedible mushrooms, he may be said to have *formed* the concept of edible vs. nonedible mushrooms. This concept formation does not mean, however, that he can now go out into a field and bring back only those mushrooms that are clearly edible. Indeed, some humans have been known to poison themselves in order to illustrate the difference between concept attainment and concept formation. When a man has learned precisely what the differences between edible and inedible mushrooms are, he is said to have *attained* the concept. It is Bruner's opinion that the process of forming concepts is active until around the age of fifteen, after which there is a prevalence of concept attainment.

Types of Concepts.   There are three types of concepts that can be distinguished by the relationship between the critical attributes that define them. *Conjunctive* concepts are defined by the joint presence of two or more attribute values. For example, a pen is an object that can be held in the hand *and* that can be used to write. *Both* of these conditions *must* be met if the object is to be a pen — therefore, the concept of *pen* is conjunctive.

A *disjunctive* concept, on the other hand, is defined *either* by the joint presence of two or more attributes *or* by the presence of any one of the relevant attributes. For example, a psychotic human may have delusions of grandeur and an intense fear of persecution as well as a mania for stealing, or he may simply have the delusions, or the phobia, or the mania. This is a disjunctive concept.

The third variety of concept is referred to as *relational.* It is defined by a specified relationship between attribute values. A rectangle, for example, not only has four sides, but two sides must also be equal in length and longer than the other two, which must also be equal in length. *Rectangle* is a relational concept.

Strategies for Concept Attainment

Bruner's work on concept attainment is premised on several assumptions, one of which is that humans tend to form concepts in order to simplify their environment and know how to react to it. Indeed, the formation of concepts is tantamount to the establishment of categories. A second assumption is that in order to reduce cognitive strain as well as to ensure that concepts are attained quickly and accurately, humans adopt certain *strategies*. These strategies take the form of regularities or patterns in the sequence of decisions that are made in determining whether or not objects belong to given classes.

In order to investigate these strategies, Bruner et al. (1956) developed a series of cards, each of which could be used as an example of either a conjunctive, disjunctive, or relational concept. The 81 cards developed for this purpose comprised all the possible variations of four attributes, each with three values (see Table 1).

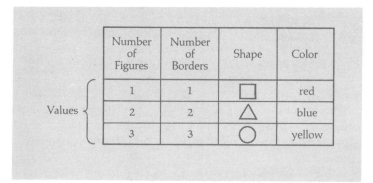

	Number of Figures	Number of Borders	Shape	Color
Values {	1	1	□	red
	2	2	△	blue
	3	3	○	yellow

Table 1. *Attributes*

In the experiments, subjects were told what a concept was and were given illustrations of disjunctive or conjunctive concepts depending on the specific study. A card with two borders and three red circles may, for example, be an example of several conjunctive concepts. One conjunctive concept is *red circles;* thus, all other cards also having red circles are examples of the same concept. If the concept *red circles* were disjunctive, any card that had either red figures on it or circles of any color would illustrate the same concept, since disjunction indicates an *either/or* element. Conjunction, on the other hand, is defined in terms of *and* rather than *either/or*.

The experimental procedure was to have the subject try to discover (to attain) the concept the experimenter had in mind. In order to make the problem soluble for a human, the experimenter told the subject how many values were included in the concept (usually two) and whether the concept was conjunctive or disjunctive.

One group of strategies for the attainment of conjunctive concepts is discussed here as illustration. They are referred to as *selection* strategies since the subject is first presented with all 81 cards, shown one example of the concept, and then allowed to *select* the card he wants tested next. After each test, the experimenter tells the subject that the card selected is or isn't an example of the concept. The object of the "game" is twofold: to arrive at the correct concept and to do it in the least number of trials possible. Four decision sequences have been identified as selection strategies for the attainment of conjunctive concepts.

Simultaneous Scanning. This strategy involves generating all possible tenable hypotheses on the basis of the first example (positive instance) of the concept and using each successive selection to eliminate all untenable hypotheses. For example, if the experimenter presents the subject with a card with two borders and three red circles on it, it would give rise to 15 tenable hypotheses (these are all two-valued conjunctive concepts) such as two borders and three figures, three circles, three red figures, red circles, two borders and red figures, two borders and circles, and so on. Unfortunately, the human mind is not ordinarily sufficient to consider so many hypotheses simultaneously. The strategy is theoretically possible but virtually nonexistent in practice.

Successive Scanning. This second strategy imposes much less cognitive strain on human subjects since it is essentially a "trial-and-error" approach. It involves making a hypothesis ("Oh, oh . . . maybe the concept is red circles.") and choosing a card to test the hypothesis directly. If the original guess is not confirmed ("Darn it, I was wrong!"), a second hypothesis is made ("Maybe it's red squares."). The concept may sometimes be arrived at very quickly, *by chance*, with this procedure — it may also *never* be attained.

Conservative Focusing. For several reasons this strategy is the most logical one for humans to employ. It imposes relatively little strain on memory or on inferential capacity, and it also assures that the concept will be attained. A subject employing this strategy begins by accepting the first positive instance as the complete hypothesis. For example, the concept is red circles (*RO*) and the first card has two borders and three red circles (*2B3RO*). The subject has as his hypothesis *2B3RO*. He then selects a second card, which varies from the original in only one value — for example, two borders and two red circles. The experimenter confirms that this card is still an example of the concept. It follows, then, that the number of figures is irrelevant. The remaining hypothesis is *2BRO*. The next selection changes one more value — the color. The card chosen has two borders and three green circles. Since the instance is now negative, color *was* relevant. The subject now knows that red is part of the concept. If his next choice eliminates number of borders or confirms shape (which it will if only one value is changed), he will have attained the concept.

Focus Gambling. A slight variation of *conservative focusing* involves varying more than one value at a time — in other words, *gambling*. If two values are changed and the card remains positive, progress is accelerated. If, however, the instance becomes negative, the subject learns little, since either or both of the changed values could be criterial.

Other series of experiments, whose results are not reviewed here, have dealt with the attainment of disjunctive concepts and with the attainment of concepts through *reception* strategies — that is, when the experimenter presents the subject with each successive card rather than allowing him to select the next one himself.

Strategies in Real Life

The results of Bruner's work on concept attainment are difficult to generalize to nonexperimental situations, for humans are not often presented with systematic examples from which to select their experiences. Nor is there usually an authority immediately available to say that "yes," this is an example of true love, and "no," that is not an example of true love. (And indeed, discovering what true love is appears to be a concept-attainment task of considerable importance for humans.) A second difficulty is that Bruner employed adult subjects in his experiments; but simpler versions of the problems presented to children have not always led to the identification of the same strategies (Olson, 1963). A third problem is that even adult subjects often employed no identifiable strategies. Difficult approaches (such as successive scanning) were never employed by any subject, and therefore remain "ideal" strategies (the terminology employed by Bruner). Last, the area of investigation has largely been abandoned by Bruner. His recent work focuses more on the development of children than on the attainment of concepts by adults.

Despite the preceding cautions, some of this work may be related to various aspects of human behavior. For example, the acquisition of inductive and deductive reasoning processes in children may involve the learning of strategies similar to those investigated by Bruner — particularly since the teaching process in schools frequently involves the presentation of related examples together with information about their class memberships. Although teachers and curriculum materials are seldom as systematic and rigorous as experimental procedures, they can occasionally be patterned after these procedures.

Summary of Bruner's Learning Theory

Bruner's theory of learning essentially maintains that people interpret the world largely in terms of the similarities and differences that are detected among objects and events. Similar objects are reacted to as though they were equal; this similarity is recognized through the placement of stimulus input into *categories*.

Categories can be compared to the phase sequences of Hebb's theory. They are essentially classifications of objects in terms of properties that are redundant for that type of object. Hence, they are based on associations developed largely through frequency or redundancy. For example, if the first people to arrive from Mars all have warts, eventually *wart* will become a criterial attribute for the category *Martian*. In Hebbian terms, the cell assemblies activated by warts will become associated with others activated by Martians.

In Bruner's system, the major organizational variable is called a *coding* system — a hierarchical arrangement of related categories, with each level of the hierarchy becoming more general, less defined by specifics, and more inclusive. The final, or most general, category in a coding system is defined in such a way as to include all of the more specific examples that lead to its formation. The act of categorizing is assumed to be involved in information processing (at both perceptual and conceptual levels) and decision making.

David P. Ausubel has advanced a position similar to Bruner's. The educational implications of these positions, however, particularly as described by Ausubel, are very dissimilar.

David P. Ausubel (1918–   )

Ausubel's orientation is explicitly cognitive, and his main concern is *meaningful verbal learning* (1963) — the type of learning he considers predominant in the classroom. He spends considerable time attempting to show that neobehavioristic views, particularly their notions of meaning, are inadequate (Ausubel & Anderson, 1965) and that his own views are both more adequate and more useful (Ausubel, 1968). The questions he attempts to answer are of particular relevance for education since they deal primarily with how children learn, organize, and remember. His research deals with classrooms rather than with laboratories.

Meaning

Ausubel's theory, which deals with the nature of meaning, can be labeled a *theory of meaningful verbal learning* or, alternately, a *theory of subsumption*. For him, the external world acquires meaning as it is converted into the "content of consciousness." That is, meaning is a phenomenon of consciousness, not of behavior. In order to clarify this last statement, Ausubel refers to Osgood's view of meaning, which he finds highly implausible. According to Osgood a thing means whatever fractional anticipatory representational responses it elicits (r_m-s_m processes). Words ". . . represent things because they produce in human organisms some replica of the actual behavior toward these things as a mediation process" (Osgood, 1957, p. 7). Osgood points out that the mediation elicited by a significate (a thing, for example) is not the same as that elicited by a sign (a word, for example). Hence the word does not really *mean* the same thing as the object it represents. Ausubel disagrees most with this aspect of Osgood's theory. Ausubel's view of meaning as involving consciousness rather than behavior is based on the notion that a signifier has meaning when its effect on the organism is *equivalent* to the effect of the object it signifies. In other words, when there is ". . . some form of representational equivalence between language (or symbols) and mental content" (Ausubel, 1963, p. 35), then there is meaning.

Learning

It should be kept in mind that Ausubel's theory is intended to deal only with verbal learning, although he does accept that there are other varieties (for example, motor, stimulus-response, contiguity). He accepts, also, that there are cognitive types of learning other than verbal. He describes these types as concept formation and problem solving. In an attempt to further clarify the issue and to delimit his theorizing, he makes an important distinction between two processes involved in cognitive learning: reception processes and discovery processes. He assumes that the former are almost exclusively employed in meaningful verbal learning and that concept formation and problem solving are more likely to involve discovery. His theory, since it is concerned with verbal behavior, deals with reception rather than with discovery learning. Insofar as Bruner's pedagogical writings are strongly directed toward the encouragement of discovery techniques, Ausubel has disagreed with him rather strongly.

Reception and Discovery: A Definition

The distinction made by Ausubel between reception learning and discovery learning is a simple one. In reception learning the material is presented to the learner in relatively complete, *organized* form. In discovery learning, the learner is expected to discover much of the material himself and to organize it in his own way. Ausubel contends that most classroom learning is reception learning.

Cognitive Structure

The concept of cognitive structure is seldom defined very specifically by human cognitive psychologists, probably because, given the lack of knowledge, it is almost impossible to do more than either speculate about neurophysiological makeup or invent labels for the elements of cognition. Both Bruner and Ausubel can be said to have adopted this second approach. The labels advanced by Ausubel are intended to define the organization of information in the human consciousness. The central label is *subsumer,* and the term advanced to describe both learning and forgetting is *subsumption.*

A Theory of Subsumption

To subsume is to incorporate new material into one's cognitive structure. Hence, to subsume is to learn. The structure itself comprises subsumers, which appear to be relatively nebulous entities somewhat similar to categories or coding systems. They are assumed to be arranged hierarchically like coding systems. They consist of all of an individual's knowledge. The subsumption process encompasses both learning and forgetting.

Subsumption and Learning

Learning can take the form of one of two processes: *correlative* subsumption and *derivative* subsumption. In both cases, no meaningful learning will take place unless there already exists a stable cognitive structure to which the new material can be related. To put it quite simply, learning will take place if the learner has the prerequisite information for the new material to be meaningful to him. If the material is completely new to him—hence, completely unrelated to anything that he knows—the only learning that can take place is what Ausubel calls *rote* learning, as opposed to *meaningful* learning.

The processes of derivative and correlative subsumption differ in the nature of the material being learned. When the new material can be derived directly from preexisting structure, derivative subsumption is said to take place. When, on the other hand, the new material is an extension or elaboration of what is already known, correlative subsumption takes place. A further distinction between these two processes is provided by an examination of the processes of remembering and forgetting.

Memory and Forgetting

When new material is learned, it is incorporated into existing structure (subsumed). In order to remember the material, it is necessary to separate or dissociate it from that structure. When material can be remembered easily, it is said to have high dissociability. If it cannot be recalled at all, it has *zero dissociability*. Ausubel labels the process of forgetting *obliterative* subsumption and describes it simply as a loss of dissociability.

Material that is learned through a process of derivative subsumption can be derived directly from existing structure and is therefore highly similar to that structure. It will, for this reason, be extremely difficult to dissociate from structure (to remember); hence, derivative subsumption leads to rapid forgetting. Material that is learned through correlative subsumption is an elaboration of existing structure and can therefore be dissociated from it relatively easily, since it is not very similar to it. Obliterative subsumption will therefore occur more slowly.

If it were possible to reduce Ausubel's views on learning to three statements, they might take the following form:

1. To learn is to incorporate material into one's "mind."
2. This learning will happen if there is already something in that mind. Otherwise, the learning will not be meaningful.
3. People remember more distinctly and for longer periods of time material that is somewhat different from what is already known. If it is too similar, it is forgotten very quickly.

Summary and Evaluation of Bruner and Ausubel

It is inevitable that psychology should lose something in the course of shifting from a preoccupation with measurable and objective indexes of behavior to those topics considered the province of cognitivism. Precision, rigor, and quantification have been lost. A stimulus can be observed; it can be measured. A response can also be observed and quantified. But what about a subsumer, or a category? That there is such a thing as sensation is self-evident. Is there such a thing as categorization or subsumption? What does obliterative subsumption look like?

The central question may be: Are these questions relevant? Despite the objections of the more hard-nosed behaviorists, perhaps behavior should not be reduced to stimuli and responses. It may well be that there is a great deal of pragmatic value in labeling and describing hypothetical properties of human functioning.

Since no easy answer can be provided for these questions, it remains impossible to evaluate cognitivism, as represented by Bruner and Ausubel, relative to behaviorism. In any case, to find in favor of either approach would be highly premature. The fruits of each will serve as evidence of their value.

Educational Implications of Bruner and Ausubel

Many of the educational implications of these two positions have been made explicit by their proponents (Bruner, 1961, 1966; Ausubel, 1968; Ausubel & Robinson, 1969). They have been summarized and discussed by Lefrancois (1972), and are therefore explained only very briefly here.

The two theories lead to apparently contradictory recommendations for instructional procedures. Bruner's emphasis on the formation of coding systems, together with his belief that the systems facilitate transfer, enhance retention, and increase problem-solving ability and motivation, leads him to advocate discovery-oriented techniques in schools. This position is not surprising since the formation of coding systems involves the *discovery* of relationships among categories.

In contrast to Bruner's eloquent plea for discovery approaches, Ausubel is a strong proponent of the more didactic techniques implied by reception learning. Among his arguments for this position is his belief that discovery is often uneconomical, inefficient, and ineffective and that most school learning is verbal learning and, therefore, reception learning. Ausubel has attacked Bruner's position in relatively detailed, if somewhat biased, chapters of several of his books (for example, Ausubel, 1968, chs. 14–16; Ausubel & Robinson, 1969, ch. 16).

Interestingly, the research on the relative merits of discovery and reception learning is somewhat equivocal. Evidence suggests that expository (reception) approaches are most likely to encourage rapid learning and retention (Craig, 1956; Haslerud & Meyers, 1958; Wittrock, 1963), but that discovery learning facilitates transfer (Guthrie, 1967).

Obviously, the kind of approach to use is not an either/or issue; there is a need for both approaches. Bruner's contention is that discovery is too often neglected rather than that it should be used exclusively. Interpreted in this way, his position has important implications.

Summary of Chapter 10

This chapter has presented a description of two theories representative of cognitive orientations: Jerome Bruner's and David Ausubel's. Each theory was discussed primarily in relation to the learning of concepts. In addition, an examination of Bruner's theory as it relates to perception and decision making was included.

1. *Cognitivism* is concerned primarily with explaining those higher mental processes not easily explained using an S-R paradigm. Cognitive psychologists have primarily been interested in such topics as perception, information processing, decision making, and knowing.
2. Jerome Bruner has advanced a cognitive theory that is a *theory of categorizing*. He uses this term to describe both perceptual and conceptual activity.
3. To categorize is to place stimulus input into classes on the basis of similarities among input. A *category* can be thought of as a rule for classifying things as being equal. As a rule, it specifies the attributes (qualities) that objects must possess before they can be incorporated into a given category.
4. Categorizing can involve identifying objects as forms of the same thing (an *identity category*) or treating different objects as though they were equivalent (*equivalence categories*).
5. Equivalence categories are distinguishable by the response involved in categorizing objects. An *affective category* is determined by the similarity of emotional responses to different events; a *functional category* derives from uses to which objects are put; and a *formal category* is established by law, science, or convention.
6. *Information processing* and *decision making* both involve categorization. An object is identified when it is placed in a category—a process that has implicit in it the possibility of "going beyond the information given." It involves making predictions about events or objects on the basis of their category membership.
7. Accurate perception not only is a function of having appropriate categories and knowing what attributes are criterial for membership in these cate-

gories, but it also depends on the *accessibility* of the appropriate category. Another term for category accessibility is *perceptual readiness*.

8. *Category accessibility* is a function of expectations and needs. The more accessible a category, the less input required for perception, the wider the range of input that will be accepted, and the more likely that other categories (perhaps better fitting) will be less available.

9. Bruner borrows extensively from Hebb in describing in broad terms the *neurological mechanisms* that would be consistent with his theory. He labels these gating processes, access ordering, match-mismatch processes, and grouping and integration.

10. *Coding systems* are arrangements of related categories in hierarchical order. Higher-level categories are said to be more *generic* in that they subsume more examples and are freer of specifics (less defined by small details).

11. Ausubel's *theory of meaningful verbal learning* is based on the notion that processes of subsumption are central to cognitive functioning and the learning of meaningful material.

12. According to Ausubel, *meaning* implies some sort of equivalence between sign and significate that goes beyond the mediating responses described by Osgood.

13. It is Ausubel's contention that the learning of meaningful verbal material is most often, and most efficiently, accomplished through a didactic, receptive approach. In this regard he is in strong disagreement with Bruner, who advocates discovery techniques in schools.

14. There are two types of subsumption involved in learning: *derivative* subsumption for very familiar material and *correlative* subsumption for material that is partly new. Forgetting is labeled *obliterative* subsumption; remembering is called *dissociating*.

15. The inferior mechanical brain of a Koron diobol employs something like categories and coding systems — only more complex. To describe Koron intellectual functioning in the same terms would be like trying to describe a computer by reference to an abacus.

11

Cognitivism: Piaget

Breasts are functional! On Earth, that is. I doubt that ours would serve the same purpose. Yet, considering that the human race is probably related to us in a remote phylogenetic sense, it is not unlikely that at some point in our evolution *we actually used our breasts!* Of course, I realize that this statement is not documented in our history, but there is that long epoch not covered in our historical archives. Nonetheless, the idea of using a breast for nondecorative purposes is almost sufficient to boggle even the Koron brain.

The really amazing thing about human breasts is that only the female* of the species is endowed with working models. They appear to be used to nourish human infants—the practice is, not inappropriately, labeled "breastfeeding." The male, who has no functional breasts, has accepted the role of advising the female on whether, how, and when

---

*Like Blips, humans come in two general types, each with different physical characteristics and each with distinct social duties. On the one hand, there is the female (girl, woman, lady, mother, wife); on the other hand, the male (man, boy, husband, father, lord, master, king) (K).

she should breast-feed her children. He has also undertaken to explain the significance of breastfeeding in the development of children. This last duty has fallen to the great Swiss psychologist, Jean Piaget. The role of advisor has been assumed by numerous philosophers, religious people, doctors, and laymen throughout history.

How very curious this all seems to my Koron mind. Even Blips do not use their breasts. But then the Blips have not produced a psychologist comparable to Jean Piaget.

Piaget

Jean Piaget was born in Neuchatel, Switzerland, in 1896. He did not begin his formal work until some time later, although there are indications that he was a precocious child. At the age of 10 he published his first "scholarly" paper.* The paper was a one-page note on a partly albino sparrow he had found. This early writing was an intimation of the wealth of published material he was to produce later. His first interests were primarily in the area of natural science, particularly in biology. Accordingly, his doctorate was obtained in this area, with a dissertation on mollusks; he received his Ph.D. at the age of 22. By the time he was 30, he had already published some two dozen papers, most of them dealing with mollusks and related topics.

After receiving his doctorate, Piaget spent a year wandering through Europe, uncertain about what he would do and where he would do it. During this year he worked in a psychoanalytic clinic (Bleuler's clinic), in a psychological laboratory (that of Wreschner and Lipps) and eventually found his way into Binet's laboratory, then under the direction of Simon. One of Piaget's duties while in the Binet laboratory was to administer Burt's reasoning tests to young children in order to standardize the items. This period probably marks the beginning of his abiding interest in the thought processes of children. It was at about that time also that he was presented with his first child. This event enabled him to make the detailed observations of breast-feeding (more specifically, of sucking behavior) that are incorporated in the origins of his theory. He has since then published close to thirty books and over two hundred articles. The bulk of his work is to be found in *Archives de Psychologie* (of which he is co-editor), in French and untranslated. Increasingly, however, his writings are being translated and summarized in response to the tremendous interest in his work which has taken hold in North America since the early 1960s.

*This is very young for humans (K).

Piaget is currently Professor at the Sorbonne, director of the *Institut des Sciences de l'Education* (successor to the *Institut Jean-Jacques Rousseau*) and director of the *Bureau Internationale de l'Education* (an affiliate of UNESCO).

Characterization of the Theory

To say that Piaget is a cognitive psychologist, while not inaccurate, is somewhat misleading. His system is cognitive primarily in the sense that it deals with the same sorts of topics that are of interest to other cognitively oriented psychologists — perception, concept formation, intellectual structure, and so on. But these topics are only a few of the many interests of Jean Piaget. Indeed, as Chaplin and Krawiec (1960) put it, "Jean Piaget is a 'school' unto himself" (p. 295). His writings deal with almost all facets of human conceptual functioning: language (1926); reality (1929); causality (1930); morality (1932); time (1946); intelligence (1950); and play, dreams, and imitation (1951), to name but a few. Throughout the development of this unified theoretical position, Piaget's closest associate and constant collaborator has been Barbel Inhelder. She continues to coauthor many of the articles and books that have not yet ceased to pour out of their center in Geneva.

Theoretical Orientation

Consistent with his early training in biology, Piaget asks questions about human development that are borrowed directly from the concerns of the zoologist. Biologists are chiefly concerned with two questions: In what phylogenetic order can the species be classified? and Which properties of organisms allow them to survive? The basic elements of Piaget's theory can be summarized as answers to these two questions as applied to human ontogeny rather than to phylogeny.* The questions can be formulated as follows (Lefrancois, 1972):

1. What are the characteristics of children which enable them to adapt to their environment?
2. What is the simplest, most accurate, and most useful way of classifying or ordering child development?

Ontogeny refers to the development of one individual from birth (or conception) to death; phylogeny refers to the evolution of a species through various forms — for example, in simplistic terms, from monkey to man (K).

Piaget's answers for these two questions will be discussed following the presentation of a 38-frame linear program. (The program is taken from Lefrançois, 1972, and reproduced with permission.) It is intended to enhance the human reader's comprehension of the material that follows—material that might otherwise be somewhat incomprehensible to the unsophisticated reader, given the strangeness of Piaget's terminology. The objective of the program is to clarify some of this jargon. After working through it, the human reader should be able to define and give examples of the following:

1. adaptation
2. functioning
3. assimilation
4. accommodation
5. invariants
6. structure
7. schemas
8. stages
9. content

Piaget's Theory

(The following program is from Lefrancois, 1972, and is reproduced by permission.)

Directions:

Fold a sheet of paper or use a strip of cardboard to cover the answers which are given in the right hand margin. With these answers covered, read frame 1 and write your answer in the blank provided. Move the paper down so as to check your answer before proceeding to frame 2.

1. Jean Piaget has developed a theory which deals with human adaptation. It is a developmental theory of human _____.

2. As a child learns to cope with his environment   *adaptation*
   and to deal effectively with it, he can be said
   to be _____ to it.

3. Adaptation therefore involves interacting with   *adapting*
   the environment. The process of adaptation
   is one of organism-environment _____.

4. One of the central features of Piaget's develop-   *interaction*
mental theory is that it attempts to explain
_____ through interaction.

5. Interaction takes place through the interplay   *adaptation*
of two complementary processes: one involves
reacting to the environment in terms of a previously learned response. This process is called
assimilation. Assimilation involves a <u>pre</u>_____
learned response.

6. Whenever a child uses an object for some   *previously*
activity which he has already learned, he is
said to be *assimilating* that object to his previous
learning. For example, when a child sucks a
nipple he is _____ the nipple to the
activity of sucking.

7. A child is given a paper doll. He looks at it   *assimilating*
curiously, and then puts it in his mouth and
eats it. He has _____ the doll to the activity
of eating.

8. Assimilation is one of the two processes which   *assimilated*
are involved in interacting with the environ-
ment. It is part of the process of _____.

9. Adaptation involves two processes. The first   *adapting or*
is assimilation. The second is called accommo-   *adaptation*
dation. It occurs whenever a change in behavior
results from interacting with the environment.
Accommodation involves a _____ in
behavior.

10. When the child cannot assimilate a new object   *change or*
to activities which are already part of his   *modification*
repertoire, he must _____ to them.

11. Johnny West was presented with a very long   *accommodate*
nipple on the occasion of his first birthday.
Prior to that time he had been sucking a short
"bulb" nipple. This long nipple matched his
nose. He had to elongate his mouth considerably more than usual in order to suck this new
nipple. Johnny West had to _____ to
the new nipple.

12. If Johnny West had been given his old, short nipple, he could more easily have _____ it to the activity of sucking.

    accommodate

13. Adaptation is defined in terms of the interaction between a person and his environment. This interaction takes the form of two complementary processes: _____ and _____.

    assimilated

14. Assimilation and accommodation are ways of functioning in relation to the world. They do not change as a person develops. Adults still interact with the environment in terms of activities they have already learned (assimilation) and they change their behavior in the face of environmental demands (accommodation). This does not mean that adults eat paper dolls, however. What it does mean is that a person's ways of functioning do not _____ from childhood to adulthood.

    assimilation and accommodation

15. Activities which do not change are *invariants*. Assimilation and accommodation can be referred to as _____.

    change

16. The twin invariants of adaptation are assimilation and _____.

    invariants (Did you see the prompt?)

17. These are also called *functional* invariants since they are activities related to human function-

    accommodation

ing. Adaptation involves _____. Functioning involves assimilation and accommodation.

18. When a Frenchman is given a bowl of pea soup and a spoon, he probably _____ the spoon and soup to the activity of eating.

    functioning (Too easy?)

19. When the same noble Frenchman is given a pair of chopsticks, it is probably necessary for him to _____ the activity of eating to these novel instruments.

    assimilates

20. A short review before continuing: adaptation involves the interaction of the functional invariants, assimilation and accommodation. These are called invariants because as ways of interacting with the environment they do not change from childhood to adulthood. Accommodation involves modifying some activity of the organism in the face of environmental demands. Assimilation is the use of some aspect of the environment for an activity which is already part of the organism's repertoire. These terms are employed in the developmental theory of _____.

    accommodate

21. Why is it that people behave in certain ways in the face of environmental demands? Part of the answer is that the activities with which they respond are part of their repertoire. Another way of putting this is to say that the activities which a person has learned comprise intellectual *structure*. Structure is a term which refers to the "mental" component of behavior. For every act there is a corresponding mental _____.

    Jean Piaget (I hope you got this one correct!)

22. If Johnny West sucks nipples, it is because he has some sort of structure which corresponds to the activity of sucking. From the fact that people behave we can infer that _____ exists.

    structure

23. When an object is being assimilated to some activity, it is really being assimilated to struc-

    structure

ture. Structure is the mental counterpart of an
_____.

24. If aspects of the environment can be assimi-   *activity*
lated to structure, then those aspects of the
environment to which a person accommodates
must cause a change in _____.

25. Assimilation can be defined as the use of exist-   *structure*
ing structure. _____ involves changes
in structure.

26. If a child can stick out his tongue, it is partly   *accommodation*
because he has some _____ which corre-
sponds to tongue-sticking-out behavior.

27. What sort of intellectual structure is a child   *structure*
born with? He is obviously born with the abil-
ity to perform some very simple acts such as
sucking, looking, and so on. These are called
re____.

28. The primitive intellectual structure of a child   *reflexes*
is defined in terms of _____.

29. Changes in reflexive behavior involve changes   *reflexes*
in _____.

30. Such changes involve the process of _____.   *structure*

31. The exercising of a reflex without changing it   *accommodation*
significantly involves the process of _____.

32. All activity involves both assimilation and   *assimilation*
accommodation. This is because new behaviors
are always based on old learning, and because
even the use of a very familiar activity can be
interpreted as involving some change in structure. That change might simply involve a higher
probability that the same response will occur
again. All activity involves both _____ and
_____.

33. The name given to the intellectual structure of   *assimilation*
a young child is schema. A schema can there-   *accommodation*
fore correspond to a reflex. The intellectual
component of reflexive behavior is called ____.

34. Schemas are related not only to reflex but also to any other early behavior. A schema is usually named in terms of a behavior. For example, there is a sucking schema, a looking schema, a reaching schema and so on. Schemas are units of intellectual _____ .

schema

35. It is obvious that structure, since it corresponds to behavior, must have something to do with assimilation and accommodation. In fact, objects in the environment are assimilated to structure. This simply means that a person reacts toward them in terms of activities he already knows. Accommodation, on the other hand, will involve a change in _____ .

structure

36. One last term—*content*. Content is simply behavior! Why not call it behavior! Paraphrasing Dr. Seuss: Are they not like one another? I don't know, Go ask your mother. In any case, behavior is called _____ .

structure

37. Again, behavior is called _____ .

content

38. Now you have it:
    adaptation
    assimilation
    accommodation
    functioning
    invariants
    structure
    schema
    content
    If you don't know what these words mean, either the program is bad, you were not paying attention, or . . . .

Human Adaptation

The preceding program describes human adaptation as consisting of the interaction of assimilation and accommodation. It could be added that the form that adaptive activity takes may be one of three alternatives: play, imitation, or intelligent adaptation. Through a discussion of these alternatives, some significant aspects of Piaget's theory can be summarized.

Play

Play is described by Piaget as involving a preponderance of assimilation. When a child plays, he continually assimilates objects to predetermined activities without regard for those attributes that fit less well. For example, when a child sits astride a chair and says "giddyup," he is not paying particular attention to those attributes of the chair that do not resemble a horse—and no one would deny that he is playing. To say or imply that this activity is less than maximally intelligent is not to deny its importance in the course of development. Indeed, Piaget does quite the opposite, emphasizing repeatedly that the young child engages in activities (such as playing "horse") simply for the sake of exercising the act. The effect is to stabilize the schema, to render it more available, and consequently to enhance further learning.

In the course of his development, a child progresses through a series of stages in the playing of games. Piaget's extensive investigation of the development of the rules by which children play as well as of the relationship between these rules and morality are reported in *The Moral Judgment of the Child* (1932). His observations in this area can serve as an introduction to Piaget's research.

First, Piaget describes game rules as comprising two aspects. There is the child's actual behavior; there are also his verbalized notions of rules. The two are not always in agreement. Both aspects are described in terms of four stages.

Stage 1 (1 to 3 years).   At the earliest stage, the child has no notion that rules exist and plays according to none.

Stage 2 (3 to 5 years).   During Stage 2 the child believes that rules are eternal and unchangeable, but he changes them constantly as he is playing.

Stage 3 (to 11 or 12 years).   In the third stage, there occurs a reversal of Stage 2 behavior. The child now admits that rules are manmade and changeable, but in practice he never alters them. His play behavior is extremely rigid, although he verbally recognizes flexibility as possible.

Stage 4 (after 11 or 12 years). With the increased maturity of Stage 4, the child arrives at a complete understanding of rules. Both in behavior and thought, he accepts these rules as completely modifiable.

Imitation

The second alternative in adaptation is imitation. Whereas play involves a preponderance of assimilation, imitation is primarily accommodation. This follows from the fact that when imitating, a child constantly modifies his behavior in accordance with the demands imposed on him by his desire to *be* something else. Again, the fact that imitation is not *intelligent adaptation* does not lessen its role in development. It is Piaget's contention that through the imitation of activity, a child internalizes his environment. Quite simply, this is intended to mean that it is through representing actions mentally that cognitive structure becomes elaborated and linked with language.

Intelligence

Piaget's concept of intelligence differs markedly from the traditional approach that is concerned with its measurement. Instead of describing it as a relatively fixed, if somewhat nebulous, quality or quantity, he describes it as a *mobile* nebulous quality. Intelligence exists *in action*. Intelligence is the property of activity that is reflected in maximally adaptive behavior; it can therefore be understood in terms of the entire process of adapting.

To review briefly, adaptation is the process of interacting with the environment by assimilating aspects of it to cognitive structure on the one hand and by modifying or accommodating structure to it on the other. Both activities, as complementary processes, occur in response to environmental demands (not necessarily *physical* environment). Also, both are guided by cognitive structure and result in changes in that structure. Obviously, however, this entire process can only be inferred from behavior (called *content* by Piaget). The substance of Piaget's concept of intelligence is summarized in Figure 1. The diagram simply depicts the relationships among the variables that comprise *intelligence-in-action*.

While this view of intelligence may be useful to a theoretical understanding of the concept, it is not of any immediate usefulness for quantifying it. Indeed, any attempt to measure *intelligence-in-action*

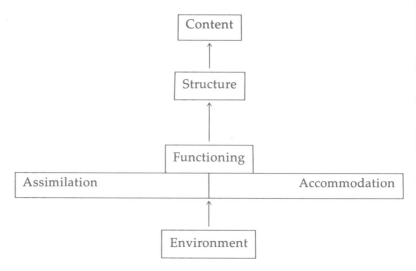

Figure 1. *Intelligence-in-action* is viewed as the interaction of an individual with his environment through the "functioning" processes. This interaction results in cognitive structures, which in turn account for the content of behavior.

would be no less presumptuous than attempts to capture souls in real space-time. But there is one aspect of this model that lends itself well to the development of tests of intelligence—the part defined by the term *structure*.

Piaget's description of structure is essentially a description of the characteristics of children at different ages—a necessary approach since the theory deals primarily with child development, and development is defined in terms of changes in structure. Obviously any detailed description of how children at a given age typically behave can serve as a guide for determining whether a specific child is below, above, or at the average.

Piaget's description of changing structure is organized around the concept of stages. His contention is that development progresses through a series of *qualitatively* different stages, each characterized by the development of new abilities—or, more precisely, each comprising a more advanced level of adaptation. This aspect of Piaget's work is currently receiving the greatest amount of attention, particularly in relation to education. Numerous interpretations of his theory have recently appeared (see, for example, Flavell, 1963; Wallace, 1965; Baldwin, 1967; Furth, 1969; Ginsberg & Opper, 1969; Phillips, 1969; Athey

& Rubadeau, 1970). Piaget's stages of development are discussed later in this chapter.

Organizing Principles in Piaget's Theory

Piaget's observations about child development are organized around a number of unifying principles, several of which have been touched upon earlier in this chapter. The most important principle is that the interaction of humans with their environment — interaction that is essential for cognitive development — *tends toward adaptation*. As was seen earlier, one way of explaining adaptation is to define it as a balance between assimilation and accommodation. Another approach to this same concept is implicit in Piaget's notion of *equilibrium* — a notion that is somewhat nebulous and complex and has been described as "excess baggage" by Bruner (1966). Nevertheless, it serves as a motivational concept of considerable importance in the system. Equilibrium, at the simplest level, denotes a balance between assimilation and accommodation. At a more complex level, it connotes an ability to "compensate for external disturbances" (Flavell, 1963) — for example, an ability to solve problems. At a still more complex level, equilibrium implies cognitive structure that is characterized by rules of logic permitting all possible transformations and combinations of data. This last definition may become clearer as the reader approaches the end of the chapter (then again it may not).

A second unifying principle is that different stages comprise qualitatively different intellectual structures. A very young human is not assumed to be simply a miniature working model of an adult but is instead considered to be discernibly different. Accordingly, a great deal of Piaget's work is devoted to the task of delineating the differences between adults and children as well as between children of different ages.

A third concept that gives structure to Piaget's work is implicit in his belief that cognitive development involves the growth of knowledge, where knowledge includes not only information but also the rules for organizing and transforming information. In Piaget's terminology, development can be viewed as the *genesis of epistemology*.* Indeed, the phrase *genetic epistemology* is frequently employed to describe his work.

---

*Epistemology is the division of classical philosophy that deals with questions about the nature of knowledge and the means by which it is acquired (K).

A fourth unifying principle focuses on the role of logic in thought. Another way of looking at development *à la* Piaget is to describe it in terms of the acquisition of progressively more advanced systems for dealing with information. The specific analogy made by Piaget in this connection is to systems of logic. At early stages of development, thought is illogical, but as the child progresses, his thinking becomes increasingly more capable of dealing with the environment in a logical manner.

The last principle is perhaps less of an orientation than a technique. It is concerned with the means employed by Piaget in gathering the data that form the basis of his theorizing. His approach is quite distinct from that of most contemporary investigators, who rely heavily on controlled experimentation with human subjects and who frequently make reference to studies involving rodents. The method developed by Piaget in his early work is referred to as the *méthode clinique*. It is a kind of semistructured interview technique in which subjects are asked certain questions, with their answers often determining what the next question will be. One of the advantages of this approach lies in the considerable flexibility it permits. Piaget's argument is that when the investigator does not know what all the answers might be, he is hardly in a position to decide *a priori* how the questions should be phrased, or, indeed, what questions should be asked. One alleged disadvantage of this flexible approach is that the data-gathering process may be difficult to replicate. Interestingly, more standardized approaches have tended to corroborate most of Piaget's findings. It is unlikely, however, that structured methods could have uncovered the findings in the first place.

The "father-experimenter" role adopted by Piaget in working with young children has led to observations that are often surprising — and to be surprised in psychology is a rare and pleasing thing, because every time a human psychologist is surprised, he knows that Grandma was wrong.

Speaking of Grandma

Speaking of Grandma, it is absolutely amazing how often the grave academic discussions of well-educated human behavioral scientists are pale reflections of the wisdom of their grandmothers — *pale* reflections because, stripped of all jargon, the scientific truths are often expressed more strongly and with greater conviction by grandmothers than by scientists. A clever psychologist will, for example, conclude "There is some evidence to indicate that there may be a tendency for human males with long nasal apparatus to serve as progenitors for offspring with similarly well-developed proboscis"—that is, he will conclude this *after* expending a $50,000 research grant. For years grandmothers have been saying "He got it from his dad, you can bet . . . his mother was never like that." That is inexpensive, hoary wisdom.

How pleasant it is for a scientist to contradict his grandmother occasionally. Hurrah for Piaget!*

Korons do not need or have grandmothers—Blips do.

The Stage Theory

Piaget describes four major stages through which children progress in their development (or more precisely, he describes children at each of four different stages):

1. Sensorimotor	0 to 2 years
2. Preoperational	2 to 7 years
Preconceptual	2 to 4 years
Intuitive	4 to 7 years
3. Concrete Operations	7 to 11 or 12 years
4. Formal Operations	11 or 12 to 14 or 15 years

Each stage can be described in terms of the major identifying characteristics of children at that developmental stage and in terms of the learning that occurs prior to transition to the next stage.

Sensorimotor Stage: Birth to 2 Years

The single most striking characteristic of child behavior in the first two years of life results in part from the absence of language and internal representation. The child's world, since he cannot represent it mentally, is a world of the *here and now* in a very literal sense. Objects exist only when the child actually perceives them; when they are beyond his perceptual field, they cease to exist. This fact can be verified indirectly by presenting a very young human with an attractive object and then removing it after he has become engrossed in it. In the earliest

---

*Another example of Kongor's weak humor (GRL).

stages of development, he will not even miss it. In Piaget's terminology, he has not yet developed the notion of the permanence and identity of objects (often called the *object concept*).

A second characteristic of the sensorimotor child is implicit in the label employed for the stage, for this is a period of sensorimotor intelligence. Not only do objects exist for the child only when he is reacting to them, but his adaptation to the world is in terms of *overt* assimilatory and accommodatory acts. In other words, his functioning in relation to the world is sensorimotor in that it involves the senses and overt behavior.

A third feature of the first stage is that the child perfects and elaborates the small repertoire of schemata with which he is born. It will be recalled that a newborn infant is capable of such simple reflexive acts as sucking, reaching, grasping, looking, and so on. A large part of his early efforts are dedicated to the exercising of these simple acts. Indeed, development through the first stage is described by Piaget as comprising six substages, each distinguishable by the nature of its reflexive activity. For example, the first substage, lasting until the end of the first month, involves the simple exercise of relatively unmodified reflexive behavior. The second substage (1 to 4 months) is marked by acquired adaptations that are called *primary circular reactions*. These activities are centered on the child's body (hence *primary*) and are circular in that the behavior elicits its own repetition. Human infants occasionally suck their thumbs. Since it is likely that the activity of sucking produces sensations that lead to a repetition of the sucking that produced the feeling that led to the first repetition that had led to another sensation . . . At any rate, thumb sucking in a human child is one example of a primary circular reaction. Later substages witness the coordination of separate activities, the evolution of language, and so on. A more detailed account of these substages is provided by Flavell (1963) and by Baldwin (1967).

The last characteristic of the sensorimotor child is egocentricity. The term is used in a descriptive rather than a derogatory sense. An egocentric child is incapable of adopting the point of view of others. The young human is egocentric in a literal sense. It can be demonstrated that he is incapable, for example, of describing what a physical object looks like from a vantage point different from his own (see Piaget, 1961). His world is the world as *he* reacts to it.

Achievements by Age 2. A Piagetian stage is not necessarily defined in terms of the characteristics a child acquires prior to transition into the succeeding stage, but more often in terms of the characteristics that prevail throughout most of the stage. Obviously, the sensorimotor stage is so labeled because throughout most of the stage the child reacts to his world in a sensorimotor fashion. Each stage, however, is a preparation for the next. The achievements of each are therefore of critical importance in explaining the transition to the succeeding stage.

While it is true that a sensorimotor child reacts primarily in activity, this fact is linked with his lack of language facility. Toward the end of the period he will have begun to acquire language. Hence, one of the achievements of the first two years of life is the development of the ability to symbolize and to communicate—a significant attainment, since language accelerates thinking and makes possible the transition to a more cognitive interpretation of the world.

A second achievement of this stage is the development of the *object concept*, which is tantamount to discovering that objects have a permanence and identity independent of the perceiver's perception. In other words, the world continues to exist even when it is not being seen, felt, heard, smelled, or tasted—or does it? Humans don't really know. In fact, they have had some prolonged philosophical debates about the question but have never quite resolved it. Piaget's work at least points out that it is a childish question (Heh, heh!).*

At any rate, adult humans behave as though their world is permanent and stable; very young children don't, but by age 2 they have changed their minds.

Two other related achievements mark the culmination of sensorimotor learning. First, the child learns to coordinate separate activities. Although this ability may not appear to be of any great significance, particularly since humans tend to take it for granted that numerous activities can be coordinated, it is no small or unimportant event for the child. In the absence of cooperation between such simple activities as looking and reaching, humans could not obtain the objects they look at and desire. Indeed, for such an uncomplicated behavior as picking up a pen, not only must vision direct the arm, but the hand must also be pressed into service. Perhaps even other parts of the body may need to be brought into play.

The other achievement is the recognition of cause and effect relationships. Obviously, a child is not born knowing that if he reaches toward an object he can grasp it and bring it closer to himself—he must learn. And it is precisely this kind of learning that allows him to develop intentionality, for until the child knows what the effects of his activities will be, he cannot clearly *intend* these effects.

*Heh, heh! (GRL)

Preoperational Thinking: 2 to 7 Years

The next stage in the evolution of a child is a marked improvement over the first in terms of the child's increased understanding of his world—but relative to an adult, it exhibits serious shortcomings. The stage is ordinarily divided into two substages. The characteristics and achievements of each are discussed below.

Preconceptual Thinking: 2 to 4 Years. This stage is characterized primarily by the child's inability to understand all of the properties of classes. Having acquired the ability to represent objects internally (mentally) and to identify them on the basis of their membership in classes, he proceeds to react to all similar objects as though they were identical. Thus for some time all men are "daddy"; all women, "mommy"; animals are all "doggie," and the world is simple. If a child sees a teddy bear like his at a friend's place, he knows that it is *his* teddy bear—and the tricycle at the store is also clearly *his*. The child understands something about classes since he can identify objects, but his understanding is incomplete since he cannot yet distinguish between apparently identical members of the same class—hence the term *preconceptual*. This mode of thinking occasionally has its advantages for parents. Santa Claus continues to be the one and only individual of his type, even though he may be seen in ten places on one day.*

Another feature of the child's thinking during this stage is that it is *transductive* as opposed to *inductive* or *deductive*. The last two types of reasoning are "logical"; inductive thinking proceeds from specifics to a generalization whereas deductive reasoning begins with the generalization and terminates with specifics. Transductive reasoning, on the other hand, involves making inferences from one specific to another. For example, the child who reasoned "My dog has hair; that thing there has hair, although it's only a little pink tuft; therefore that thing is a dog" is the same child who called me "doggie." She was the youngest of the Lefrancois children. It is somewhat embarrassing (and not a little demeaning) for a mature Koron to be called "doggie" by an immature human. This child was engaging in transductive reasoning.

Santa Claus is an imaginary and obese person invented by humans for some unknown reason—and for some other unknown reason, human children are duped by adults into believing that this gross person, Santa Claus, is capable of stuffing himself and a bag of toys through the chimney in order to bring them toys on Christmas Eve (December 24, Earth calendar) (K).

The Period of Intuitive Thought: 4 to 7 Years. By the time a child reaches the age of 4 he has achieved a more complete understanding of concepts and has largely ceased to reason transductively. His thinking has become somewhat more logical, although it is governed more by *perception* than by logic. In fact, the role played by perception in the intuitive-stage child's thinking is probably the most striking characteristic of this period. It is a role that is particularly evident in the now famous conservation tasks. A conservation problem is typically one in which the child is presented with two identical objects; one object is then deformed, rearranged, or otherwise changed in appearance, but not in quantity. The subject is then asked a question about one of the quantitative attributes of the objects. If he thinks they have changed, he is assumed not to have acquired conservation. A more detailed discussion of conservation is presented in the section on concrete operations. One example is given here, however. The task concerns the conservation of liquid quantity. The subject is shown two identical beakers filled to the same level with water (as in Figure 2a). The experimenter then pours the contents of one of the beakers into a tall thin

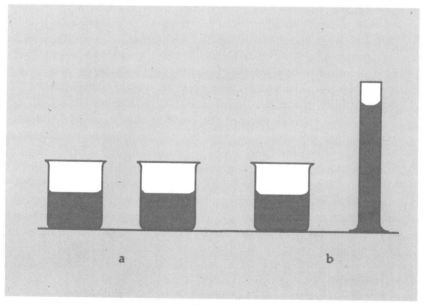

Figure 2

tube (as in Figure 2b). The subject, who at first admitted that the amounts in each were equal, is now asked whether there is as much, more, or less water in the new container. At the intuitive stage, he will almost invariably say that there is more *since it is much higher in the tube.* In other words, he is attending to the misleading perceptual features of the stimuli.

A second characteristic of a human child somewhere between the ages of 4 and 7 is that his reasoning is very egocentric. In the same way that a sensorimotor child finds himself unable to adopt the *physical* point of view of another person, so the intuitive child has difficulty accepting the *mental* point of view of others. This orientation is clearly illustrated by an experiment involving a boy and a girl doll side by side on a piece of wire. The experimenter holds one end of the wire in each hand, hides the dolls behind a small screen that has been placed between him and the child, and asks the child to predict which doll will come out first if they are moved out on the left. The child's answer is noted, the dolls are returned to their original position, and the question is repeated. Again the dolls are coming out on the left; obviously the same doll is coming out first. The procedure is repeated a number of times. A reasonably intelligent human child will at first generally answer correctly. After a while, however, he will change his mind and predict that the *other* doll will come out. If asked why he thinks so, he is very unlikely to admit that he distrusts psychological investigators since he has probably not learned to distrust them yet. Instead he may say something like "It's not fair. It's her turn to come out next." It is this solution of a simple logical problem by reference to how things *should* be from the child's *own point of view* that illustrates the role of egocentricity in intuitive thinking.

A final characteristic of the child at this stage is that he has not yet attained the ability to classify. Although he can deal with single classes, he cannot reason about subclasses nested within larger groupings. A 4-year-old child who is shown a handful of seven candies, two of which are chocolates and five of which are gums, immediately recognizes that they are all candies, and, if asked, will probably say so. If the experimenter says, however, "Tell me, young 4-year-old human child, are there more gums than candies, or less, or the same number?" he will almost invariably say that there are more gums than candies! Try it! Find a 4- or 5-year-old human child, buy some candies, and try it! Grandma is wrong again! Yeah!

This experiment is interpreted to be indicative of the fact that when a class is broken down into subclasses and the child is asked to reason about the subclass (gum) and the larger class (candy) he cannot do so, since the original subdivision destroyed the parent class as far as the child is concerned.

The preconceptual and intuitive stages are parts of a larger class, the preoperational stage. It is of some importance to realize that the label *preoperational* is descriptive of the two stages in a literal sense. Prior to age 7, the human child does not reason with operations. As the labels for the next two stages clearly indicate, after the age of 7 (or thereabouts), the average child achieves operational thinking. The term *operation* is therefore central in Piaget's system.

An operation can be defined as an internalized activity that is subject to certain rules of logic, the most important of which is reversibility. Indeed, it is not inaccurate to say that an operation is a *reversible* thought, since an internalized act can be interpreted as *thought*. A thought is reversible when it can be unthought. This is a somewhat inelegant and crude definition of a usually sophisticated and nebulous concept, but it is not incorrect (although it may still be nebulous). In order not to confound the issue further, the definitions given are not elaborated at this point. Some examples of operations and of operational thinking are instead provided in the sections dealing with the last two of Piaget's stages.

A Break

I again find myself borrowing from Lefrancois (1972). While writing a difficult chapter on Piaget, he suddenly realized that the human reader had almost reached the end of his capability—he himself was nearly asleep. At that point he inserted the section that is reproduced here (from Lefrancois, 1972; reproduced with permission).

A Break

Stop! It would probably be wise for the reader who is not already familiar with Piaget to stop at this point. If you have available an electroencephalograph machine, a cardiograph, a thermometer, and a pupillometer, as well as any other graph or meter, these should be connected and read at once. Alpha waves, together with decelerated heartrate, normal temperature and reduced pupil size are symptoms of imminent *jargon shock.* This condition in an advanced stage can be highly detrimental to concentration and learning. Several hours of sleep usually brings about a significant amelioration of the condition.

If you don't have any of this sophisticated electronic gadgetry readily available, you can substitute a hand mirror. Hold the mirror up to your face and look at your eyes. If they are closed you are probably in the terminal stage of "jargon shock."

Jargon Shock

Concrete Operations: 7 to 11 or 12 Years

The major features of the period of *concrete* operations can be arrived at most easily by distinguishing it from its preceding and following stages. This section is organized in accordance with this observation, beginning first with a discussion of the distinctions between preoperational and concrete thought and concluding with an analysis of the differences between *formal* and *concrete* thought.

Concrete Operations and Preoperational Thought. The major difference between these two periods, as is intimated in the previous section, is that a child does not acquire the ability to utilize operations until he reaches the age of 7 or 8. More specifically, he then manifests three new abilities: the ability to deal with classes, with seriation, and with number. In addition, largely as a result of the appearance of the logical properties of thinking that define *operations*, the child now begins to acquire the various conservations, which are discussed below.

(1) *Classes*. The child's ability to classify is assumed to result from activities that he has previously engaged in with real objects. As

a result of combining objects, dissociating them, and arranging them into groups, he has come to learn about class membership and is now able to reason about nested classes. The candy problem would, for example, present so slight a problem for the concrete-operations child that he might well laugh in derision if the question were put to him.

(2) *Seriating.* Also as a result of experiences with real objects, a child acquires the ability to order them in series and to set up correspondences between more than one series. Piaget has investigated the understanding of seriation by presenting children with various objects that can easily be ranked in one dimension—for example, dolls and canes as in Figure 3. Prior to concrete operations the child ranks objects by comparing two of them at once, but seldom makes the necessary inference that if *A* is greater than *B* and *B* greater than *C*, then *A* must also be greater than *C*. The preoperational child is not embarrassed about putting *C* before *B* if he has just been comparing *A* and *C*. The concrete-operations child seldom makes an error with the problem, even when it involves setting up *two* series in one-to-one correspondence as in Figure 3.

Figure 3. *Correspondence between Two Ordered Series.* A concrete operations child who is presented with a random arrangement of dolls and canes of varying length can arrange them as illustrated when requested to place them in order so that the dolls and canes match.

(3) *Number*. The ability to deal with numbers is a logical result of classifying and seriating, since a complete understanding of number requires some comprehension of its cardinal properties as well as knowledge of its ordinal meaning. Cardinal properties are simply the *class* properties of number. The number 4 is an abstraction that signifies a collection of a group of specified magnitude—hence, a *class* of related objects. Ordination refers to the rank characteristics of a number. The ordinal properties of the number 4 are specifically that it precedes 5 but follows 3—hence, ordinal properties refer to seriation.

The Conservations. The Piagetian type of learning which has probably attracted the greatest amount of attention on the North American continent has to do with the acquisition of concepts of *conservation*. Conservation can be defined as "the realization that quantity or amount remains invariant when nothing has been added to or taken away from a collection of objects despite changes in form or spatial arrangement" (Lefrancois, 1966, p. 4). In the experiment involving water that has been poured into a tall, thin tube, the child has not acquired conservation until he answers that the amounts are indeed unchanged.

There are numerous types of conservation, each relating to a specific quantitative attribute of an object, and each acquired in a highly similar order by most children. For example, conservation of substance is typically achieved by the age of 7 or 8, whereas conservation of area is not learned until 9 or 10, and conservation of volume does not appear before the age of 11 or 12. Some attributes seem to be more difficult to apprehend than others. For example, *volume* is more remote to a child's direct experience than *substance* (see Piaget, 1957). While this distinction might explain the order of acquisition for the different conservations, it sheds little light on why the conservations do not appear until concrete operations. Piaget, however, has provided an answer for this question. The fact that a child says "more" when an object *appears* larger, longer, or fatter is obviously partly due to the fact that he *perceives* it as appearing to have more. Hence, *perception* dictates the nature of his answer. It is not perception *per se*, however, but rather lack of appropriate operational thought structures that makes it impossible for the child to answer correctly in the first place. Quite simply, if a child is presented with the conservation of liquid problem discussed earlier, and he answers correctly, he may be reasoning in one of three ways; each of these different reasons is illustrative of a new *logical* property that now governs his thinking. The child might be thinking, "If the water were poured out of the tall tube and back into its original container, it would still have as much water as before so it mustn't have changed." This thought would be illustrative of what Piaget calls *reversibility*—a property that was alluded to previously. Not only is the action capable of being unthought (or undone mentally) but there are also some necessary, logical consequences. The most important consequence is obviously that the process of transforming does not alter quantity.

The child might also reason that nothing has been added to or taken away from either container and that there must then still be the same amount in each. This is an example of the rule of *identity*, a rule that states that for every operation (action) there is another operation that leaves it unchanged. Obviously, adding or taking away nothing produces no change.

A third alternative might be this: "The tube is taller but it is also thinner, so it balances out." Piaget and Inhelder (1941) refer to this reasoning as *combinativity (or compensation)*, which is a property defined in terms of the logical consequences of combining more than one operation or, in this case, more than one dimension.

A further clarification of these notions can be provided by direct reference to some specific examples of conservation problems. The reader is invited to replicate them with young humans, wherever he finds them. It might be amusing to perform them in front of Grandma, *after* having explained the procedure to her and *after* she has predicted what the child's response will be. Employ a 4- or 5-year-old in order to ensure that your Grandma will be wrong. (The following five experiments are reprinted from Lefrancois, 1972, with permission. Note: the ages indicated in parentheses should not be considered to be more than very imprecise approximations.)

1. *Conservation of Number* (6–7).   Two rows of counters are placed in one-to-one correspondence between the experimenter (*E*) and the subject (*S*):

One of the rows is then elongated or contracted:

S is asked which row has more or whether they still have the same number.

2. *Conservation of Length* (6–7). *E* places two sticks before the subject. The ends are well aligned:

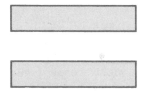

S is asked if they are the same length. One stick is then moved to the right:

The question is repeated.

3. *Conservation of Substance* (7–8). Two plasticene balls are presented to *S*. He is asked if they have the same amount of plasticene in them. If *S* says no, he is asked to make them equal. (It is not at all uncommon for a young child to simply *squeeze* a ball in order to make it have less.) One ball is then deformed:

S is asked again whether they have the same amounts.

4. *Conservation of Area* (9 or 10).   S is given a large piece of cardboard, identical to one that E has. Both represent playgrounds. Small wooden blocks represent buildings. S is asked to put a building on his playground every time E does so. After nine buildings have been scattered throughout both playgrounds, E moves his together in a corner.

S   E

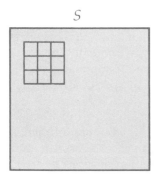
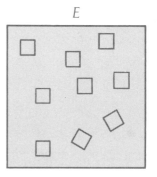

S is asked whether there is as much space (area) in his playground as in E's.

5. *Conservation of Liquid Quantity* (6 or 7).   S is presented with two identical containers filled to the same level with water.

One of the containers is then poured into a tall thin tube, while the other is poured into a flat dish.

S is asked whether the amount of water in each remains equal.

<u>*Can Conservation Be Taught?*</u>   Just as Grandma has almost succeeded in overcoming her exasperation and is about to issue a pearl of ancient wisdom that will serve to explain and denigrate the results of science, turn to her, dear Reader, and issue this challenge: "Grandma, I challenge you! I challenge you! I say, Grandma, I challenge you!" (It is often necessary to repeat things several times with human grandmothers.) There is certainly no point in explaining the challenge until your grandmother has understood you well enough to repress her pearl of wisdom, at least momentarily, and to say "What?" At that point, you might continue by saying, "I'll bet you, Grandma dear, that *you* cannot teach little Norbert to answer correctly when I squish this plasticene into a pie."

Grandma will probably fail, as did many human investigators—notably Smedslund (1961a, b, c, d, & e) in his earlier experiments. True, a number of psychologists have recently been successful in accelerating the appearance of concepts of conservation in *some* children (never

A Human Grandmother

all), but only after extensive, systematic, and theoretically based training (for example, Lefrancois, 1968; Towler, 1967; Cote, 1968; Travis, 1969). None of these psychologists has clearly shown that such acceleration studies have a generally beneficial effect on other aspects of child functioning. Indeed, it is Laurendeau and Pinard's (1962) contention that contrived experiences of the kind ordinarily employed in acceleration studies are not likely to be of sufficient moment to significantly alter the course of development.

Grandma will fail!

How amusing it would be if Korons had grandmothers.

Concrete Operations and Formal Thought. Concrete thinking differs in several ways from the type of thinking that characterizes the period of formal operations. The thought structures of concrete operations are applied directly to real objects or to objects that are capable of evocation. In other words, the child does not yet deal with that which is merely hypothetical unless it can be tied directly to concrete reality. Also, he is incapable of dealing with *combinatorial analysis*, which Piaget describes as the systematic generation of all possible combinations. It is sometimes said, for example, that the logic of concrete operations is the logic of classes but not the logic of class products (Peel, 1960). This distinction can be defined by reference to Table 1,

Table 1

A 2 × 2 Classification

	Red	Blue
Circle	Red circle (RC)	Blue circle (BC)
Square	Red square (RS)	Blue square (BS)

(a)

All Possible Combinations of the Products of A

NOTHING	RC	BC	RS
BS	RC BC	RC RS	RC BS
BC RS	BC BS	RS BS	RC BC RS
RC BC BS	RC RS BS	BC RS BS	RC BC RS BS

(b)

which shows a four-way classification system (a), as well as a recombination of the products of these four original combinations (b). The first ordering can be executed by a concrete-operations child, but not the second, as is illustrated in the next section.

A third limitation of concrete operations is that the child's understanding of such rules of logic as identity and reversibility is not completely general — in other words, he acts according to these rules in only some situations. For example, he solves a conservation of number problem much before he can answer a conservation of area question — yet the same process of logical reasoning can be applied to both.

Formal Operations: 11 or 12 to 14 or 15 Years

The last stage in the evolution of human thought begins around the age of 11 or 12. It is marked by the appearance in behavior of propositional thinking — that is, thinking that is not restricted to the consideration of the concrete or the potentially real but that deals in the realm of the hypothetical (a proposition is any statement that can be true or false). The child can now reason from the real to the merely possible or from the possible to the actual. He can compare hypothetical states of affairs to actual states, or vice versa, and, as a result, he can become profoundly upset at the seeming irresponsibility of a generation of adult humans that has brought itself to the edge of untold disasters.

Two experiments can illustrate the differences between formal thinking and earlier stages. The first (Piaget, 1961) is a simple test of verbal reasoning of the type: $A > B$; $A < C$; which of A, B, or C is greatest? (For example, John is thinner than Bill; John is fatter than Sam; who is the fattest of the three?) Human children under the age of 11 or 12 have a great deal of difficulty with such problems unless they pertain directly to objects they can see. The reason is that the solution of the problem requires propositional thinking — that is, it requires reasoning about hypothetical statements.

A second experiment (Piaget, 1961) involves having the subjects combine colored disks in all possible ways (by twos, threes, and so on). The formal-operations child will do so completely and systematically, whereas a younger child will ordinarily produce some, but seldom *all*, combinations since his approach is haphazard rather than systematic.

Logic and Piaget's Theory

Piaget's extensive use of models of logic as analogies to thought has not met with as wide acceptance as his more descriptive work. The lack of acceptance may stem from the difficulty level of symbolic logic, particularly as it is interpreted by Piaget. A second reason is, ostensibly, that the logic really does not serve to increase clarity or to further knowledge. It is, in a sense, an extremely clever and complex academic exercise. For these reasons, logic is mentioned only tangentially throughout this chapter. (The interested reader is referred to Piaget (1957) or to Peel (1960) for a more detailed account.)

Piaget's Theory: An Overview

Piaget's position is primarily a theory of development. However, largely because of its emphasis on genetic epistemology, it is also a theory of learning. Obviously, since the subject matter of genetic epistemology is the genesis of knowledge, and since learning is concerned largely with knowledge, it is inevitable that Piaget's theory should serve as a theory of learning.

As a theory of learning it can be simplified and reduced to the following set of statements:

1. The acquisition of knowledge is a gradual developmental process made possible through the interaction of a child with his environment.
2. The sophistication of a child's representation of the world is a function of his stage of development. That stage is defined by the thought structures he then possesses.
3. Maturation, the environment, equilibration, and socialization are the forces that shape learning.

So What?

Throughout this chapter little effort has been made to make obvious the relevance of Piaget's theory—for two reasons. First, the chapter is already relatively long and relatively substantive; second, the astute reader will have realized that any theory that describes children and their development in as much detail as Piaget's must be relevant at least to the study of children—and children are subjects who may be studied for a wide variety of reasons, one of which is that a great many people are interested in teaching them.

The impact of Piaget's theory on school curricula, on instructional procedures, and on measurement practices appears to be profound and significant. Numerous authors have attempted to delineate specific educational recommendations based on the work of Piaget (for example, Hunt, 1961; Furth, 1970; Athey & Rubadeau, 1970; Ginsberg & Opper, 1969; Phillips, 1969). Others have attempted to develop intelligence scales based on Piaget's descriptions of structure (Goldschmid & Bentler, 1968). Unfortunately, it is impossible to do more than summarize the implications of a theory such as Piaget's in a section as short as this one. These implications point to the importance of understanding the present level of a child's development, the consequent limits of his cognitive abilities, the usefulness of presenting material at an optimal level of difficulty for him, and the value of encouraging the child to become involved (active) in his own learning. Further elaboration of these general implications is provided by Lefrancois (1972).

Evaluation of Piaget's Position

There is little doubt that Jean Piaget's stature in contemporary cognitive psychology is unequaled. Not surprisingly, he has attracted a number of critics as well as a host of devoted followers. A rather standard criticism has to do with the paucity of subjects in his earlier work—often his samples included only one subject, his own child. It is true, however, that this criticism is irrelevant unless further work done under more rigorous conditions fails to replicate his findings.

Others have criticized his work on the grounds that it is extremely difficult to understand. This criticism is justified, but its difficulty is not necessarily a weakness of the system (it may be a weakness of the reader). A third criticism centers around his use of logic and whether or not it is really necessary. There are, indeed, indications that the theory would not be substantially different without the extensive use of the concepts and symbolism of logic. Again, however, this criticism does not point out an inaccuracy in the theory. A last criticism is leveled at Piaget's use of such nebulous and imprecise terms as schema, operations, equilibrium, and so on—terms which are sometimes made even more confusing in the translation from French to English.

On the other hand, it is widely recognized that Piaget's contributions can hardly be ignored (the programs of most recent psychology and education conventions attest to this). Various authors have praised his role in clarifying the relationship between experience and the development of intelligence (for example, Hunt, 1961). Others (Marx & Hillix, 1963) see his interdisciplinary approach as particularly worthwhile. Isaacs (1961) believes that the introduction of Piaget's inquiry technique is a valuable contribution. Lefrancois (1967) draws attention to the comprehensiveness and detail of Piaget's observations. In short, the work of Jean Piaget, which appears to be far from finished, is exercising a profound influence on current psychological thought throughout the world.

Summary of Chapter 11

This chapter has presented a review of the work of Jean Piaget. Content in the many specific areas investigated by Piaget (such as time, space, geometry, and so on) was not detailed, but instead the general developmental theory and the characteristics of children at various stages were discussed.

1. *Jean Piaget*, the noted Swiss psychologist, is by training a biologist and by avocation a philosopher, mathematician, logician, and writer. By occupation he is a psychologist.
2. Piaget's theory can be viewed as an attempt to answer two biology-related questions: What are the characteristics of children that enable them to adapt to their environment? and What is the simplest, most accurate, and most useful way of classifying or ordering child development?
3. Early human *adaptation* can take the form of one of three types of activity or, more often, of a combination of these: play, imitation, and intelligent adaptation. Each is defined in terms of the balance that exists between the functional invariants, assimilation, and accommodation. *Play* involves a preponderance of assimilation; *imitation*, a primacy of accommodation; and *intelligent adaptation*, an optimal balance of each.
4. Piaget's concept of *intelligence* varies from the more traditional model that typically represents intelligence as a somewhat fixed and measurable quality. Rather he describes it in terms of activity in relation to the environment.
5. Piaget's experimental approach is referred to as the *méthode clinique*. It involves a flexible interview approach in which the subject's answers influence subsequent questioning.
6. Human grandmothers are not always right!
7. The *sensorimotor stage* is characterized by a "here-and-now" understanding of the world, extreme egocentricity, absence of language, and the elaboration of schemata.
8. Among the important achievements of the first two years of life are the development of the object concept, the discovery of causal relationships, the acquisition of language, and the appearance of intention.
9. During the *preconceptual stage* the child expands his ability to verbalize. His thinking is fraught with errors of logic. In particular, he reasons *transductively*, and he understands concepts incompletely.

10. At the age of 4 (or thereabouts) the human child begins to solve many problems correctly on the basis of his *intuition*. His thinking continues to be egocentric and perception dominated, however, and he always disappoints his grandmother on conservation tasks.

11. The transition from preoperational to operational thought is marked by the appearance of the ability to conserve. In addition, the child can now deal with classes, series, and number. His thinking is tied to the concrete, however.

12. *Formal operations* are defined by the appearance of propositional thinking. The child's thought processes are freed from the immediate and real and are potentially as logical as they will ever be.

4

Cybernetics

12

Feedback, Machines, and Men

Unlike Korons, humans have not yet achieved any degree of weather and climate control. As a result, living on Earth exposes one to all sorts of strange experiences. For example, it *rained* last night. Rain is the word used to describe water falling from the sky in the form of little drops. We sat in front of the glass doors, the good doctor, his wife, the two children, and I, looking at the rain. A million things were happening all at the same time. The surfaces of the little pools that had formed where the water collected in tiny hollows were being dimpled ceaselessly by falling drops; water bounced on the concrete walks and spattered into countless droplets; curled bundles of water rolled reluctantly from the soaked leaves of maple trees, assaulting the sopping blades of grass they hit. Occasionally, great sheets of water propelled by a stubborn wind were hurled about, drenching all that they touched. And throughout this downpour, huge, magnificent exchanges of electricity, called lightning, leaped about the sky. These sheets and flashes of light were followed shortly by a reverberation of thunderous sounds. I had never witnessed such a spectacle, and I was so impressed by it that at the height of the storm I went out and stood shivering in the center of the yard with water streaming all over me. What a marvellous sensation!

I fear now that I am in for another bout with that dangerous illness, the cold.

I have been living with humans for almost 9 months; yet it is the first time that I have done something that is not clearly rational. I hasten to assure you, however, that it is certainly not clearly *irrational* either.* I don't believe that I have broken the first of the Eleven Great Laws.

I have been reflecting for some time on the seeming irrationality of human behavior, and inevitably I end up comparing it in some detail with the behavior of Korons. It has been amusing to study the models advanced by man in explanation of his own behavior, particularly since very few of these models take into consideration the problem of rationality (predictability) or irrationality. One class of these models — cybernetics — is especially intriguing since it shows much more promise as a description of Koron behavior than as an explanation of human activity.

The term *cybernetics* was coined by Norbert Wiener (1948) to signify the application of *feedback theory* to the study of human learning. The term is derived from the Greek and means "steersman" or "helmsman" — hence *control*. The application of the principles of cybernetics to human behavior can take the form of abstract models that incorporate *feedback theory* or of analogies to physical models that also make use of feedback. This chapter discusses one example of each. First, a direct analogy between human problem solving and the functioning of a digital computer is provided through a discussion of some of the work of Newell, Shaw, and Simon. Then a more abstract model in the form of the work of Miller, Galanter, and Pribram is presented.

Can Machines Think?

Humans have for some time been concerned with the problem of whether or not machines can think (see, for example, Anderson, 1964; Ashby, 1961; Moray, 1963). It appears to be a question of some relevance, particularly for cybernetics, since this science can take the form of attempts to simulate human behavior with machines. Since the possession of a *mind* or the ability to *think* is considered by humans

*Heh, heh! (GRL)

to be particularly *human*, the ability or inability of a machine to do likewise can be of critical importance.

The classical answer for this question is provided by the late A. M. Turing (1950). Turing rephrased the question and asked, "Can machines imitate?" In an amusing discussion of "The Imitation Game," he then proceeded to outline a situation that would determine whether or not machines can imitate the behavior of people. The *a priori* conclusion is that if the machine succeeds in imitating, it *ipso facto* demonstrates that it can think.*

The problem involves two people, a man (*A*) and a woman (*B*), who are placed alone in a room. An interrogator (*C*) in another room must discover whether *A* is a man (*X*) or a woman (*Y*). In Turing's words, at the end of the game he must say "*X* is *A* and *Y* is *B*" or "*X* is *B* and *Y* is *A*". In order to discover who *A* and *B* are, *C* is allowed to ask them questions. *A* and *B* type out their responses. The object of the game for *A* is to impede the interrogator. He may, for example, answer questions as though he were a woman — or he may tell the truth. *B*, on the other hand, attempts to help the interrogator. Obviously, if she attempts to do so by telling the truth — "I'm *B*, I'm the woman! Believe me!" — *A* can do exactly the same thing — "Don't believe *B*, I'm *A*, I'm the woman!"

The next question asked by Turing is the crucial one: "What will happen when a machine takes the part of *A* in this game?" His eventual answer is that it will soon be possible to construct a machine that will stump the interrogator at least 70% of the time. By implication, then, the answer to the original question, "Can machines think?" is in the affirmative.

As a sequel to the often-quoted Turing article, Gunderson (1964) presents the "toe-stepping game," also in an attempt to answer the question "Can machines think?" In the "toe-stepping game" two people, a man (*A*) and a woman (*B*) are placed together in a room. At the bottom of one wall in this room there is a small aperture through which a third person, the interrogator (*C*), has placed his foot. The object of the game for *C* is to discover which of *A* or *B* is a man (*X*) and which is a woman (*Y*). As in the *Imitation Game*, he will be asked to phrase his answer in the form, "*X* is *A* and *Y* is *B*," or "*X* is *B* and *Y* is *A*." In order to discover who *A* and *B* are, he is allowed to insert his foot in the opening in the wall, and to have either *A* or *B* step on it.

---

*The unemotional Kongor became progressively more attached to Latin expressions so that he eventually went about saying such things as "Ergo," "Et cetera" almost continually. We finally had to reprimand him for the sake of the children (GRL).

The object of the game for *A* is to confuse *C*, whereas *B* attempts to help him. Again the question asked is "What would happen if a machine were substituted for *A*?" This machine would simply need to be a "rock box"—that is, a box filled with rocks of various shapes, sizes, and weights. These could be dropped on *C*'s foot and retrieved before rolling on the floor.

Gunderson's answer for this last question is analogous to Turing's earlier conclusion—namely, that in 50 years it will be possible to develop a rock box that will confuse the interrogator at least 70% of the time.

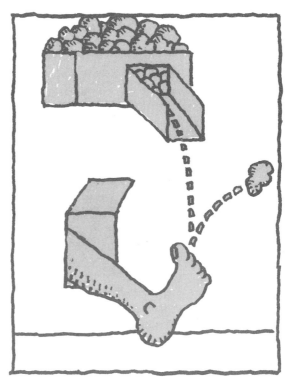

A Rock-Box Machine

The point of Gunderson's parody of the Turing article is that illustrating that a machine can imitate aspects of human behavior is not equivalent to demonstrating that it can think. Obviously, few people would maintain that the rock box could think. But, as is pointed out by Gunderson, the rock box does not *need* to think—it accomplishes its objective better than a human without thinking. He concludes (Gunderson, 1964): "In the end the steam drill outlasted John Henry as a digger of railway tunnels, but that didn't prove the machine had muscles; it proved that muscles were not needed for digging railway tunnels" (p. 71).

Despite the intuitive appeal of Gunderson's argument, it remains true that the simulation of human cognitive processes differs from the imitation of more physical activities. The relationship of machines to men is discussed in the remainder of this chapter.

Feedback and Behavior

Human behavior can be considered to involve three separate components: *input, processing,* and *output.* The early behaviorists were concerned only with input and output—not with making the "black box," in which processing ostensibly occurs, any less mysterious. Later behaviorists attempted to open the box and to label its contents, which were seldom observed unless they were reduced to neurological units but were instead inferred on the basis of input and output. Nor were input and output the most fashionable expressions until just recently; formerly, the terms *stimulus* and *response* did quite well in indicating what psychologists were talking about. More recently, particularly since the early part of the fifth decade of this century, psychologists have again become concerned with the black box. One of the forms that this interest has taken is reflected in contemporary cognitive positions; a second form is that of cybernetics or feedback theory.

The central assumption of feedback theory is that the organism or machine is self-regulated. The term *machine* can accurately be employed here even though we are still considering human behavior, for it is largely correct that cybernetics deals with the machine like aspects of human functioning. A self-regulated machine, when activated, continues to function until conditions in the environment dictate that it should cease or modify its functioning. The important point is that the machine *must itself sense those external conditions that regulate its performance.* A system that can be activated and then shuts itself off automatically after a period of time is not *self-regulated* but is simply *regulated.* It is obvious that if man is to be compared to a machine system, that system will have to be self-regulating.

One of the most frequently cited examples of a simple self-regulated system is a household furnace and thermostat. The input that affects the system's performance via the thermostat is the surrounding temperature. The system's output affects the temperature, thereby modifying the input to which it responds. Hence, its sensors are affected by the results of its own activities. Two types of feedback are involved in this system, as in any other feedback system. (Feedback is defined as the information that the system obtains about the effects of its own activities.) One type of information—*negative* feedback—indicates that the activity of the system should be discontinued because of modified environmental conditions. When the system receives information indicating that functioning should continue, it is receiving *positive* feedback. Referring to the illustration of the household furnace, the input that initiates the firing of the furnace is a temperature reading below what is indicated as desirable on the thermostat. As long as the furnace continues to function, it is receiving positive feedback. More accurately, as long as it *is* receiving positive feedback, it will continue to function. But when the actual temperature reaches the desired level, the system receives negative feedback and ceases to function.

Processing

Input (and *output* insofar as it affects input) can be discussed in terms of feedback, and the effect of feedback on a self-regulated system presupposes some sort of processing device. In the case of the heating system, the processing device is the thermostat. As a processing device of the simplest kind, it merely evaluates input according to predetermined criteria and acts on the basis of whether or not a match occurs.

The processing unit in the human being is not so simple or obvious (which is one of the reasons psychologists continue to speculate about human learning and behavior). Nevertheless, it can be accepted as axiomatic that there is a processing system or, more likely, a series or arrangement of such systems. The possibility that the nature of these systems can be clarified by drawing analogies between known machine systems and man justifies cybernetics.

Mention should be made here of one of the central problems of cybernetics (also of philosophy, and, indeed, of man). The problem is how to determine the extent to which human behavior is predictably affected by feedback and the extent to which output remains erratic. This question is central in that it hinges on the necessity of employing relatively straightforward, *deterministic* models of behavior in the one case, and *stochastic* models in the other. In a deterministic model, the action (operation), which is selected from among a number of alternatives, can be predicted on the basis of the information and processes contained in the system. In a stochastic model, on the other hand, the probability of the selection of an alternative can be computed within some error range, but there always remains a degree of probability that another alternative will be selected instead. Because of the minimal influence of random variables in most machine systems (such as computers), stochastic models are less frequent than deterministic ones.

The problems of arriving at a model that is basically an accurate reflection of human behavior have been discussed by Carl Hovland (1960). To choose between stochastic versus deterministic systems is one such problem. Another problem is how to deal with the complexity of the processes that cyberneticians attempt to simulate. At best a machine can be made to duplicate the behavior of one *specific* individual in one very *clearly defined situation.* Hovland believes that the next step of simulating the behavior of individuals who vary from the prescribed pattern may prove to be extremely difficult. A second source of difficulty stems from the fact that simulation has typically been accomplished where terminal performance can be defined *a priori* in terms of a set sequence of procedures. Hovland's contention is that human perception and thinking often involve parallel processes that cannot easily be broken down into the steps required for simulation.

Computers and Problem Solving

Carl Hovland's (1958, 1960) work has dealt largely with attempts to simulate human information processing and problem solving with digital computers. A number of other investigators, notably Newell, Shaw, and Simon (1957, 1958; Newell & Simon, 1956) have been concerned with essentially the same problem.

It is important to note that direct comparisons between human functioning and a computer are seldom made but that the computer is used as nothing more than an analogy. The fact that man behaves *as though* he were in some ways like a machine cannot be taken as evidence that he possesses the same mechanisms and organization as does the machine. The analogy simply serves to clarify, and perhaps to simplify, the nature of human activity. At one level, there are the numerous analogues to the nervous system that are evident in digital computers. In discussing these analogies, Miller, Galanter, and Pribram (1960) summarize some of them as follows:

. . . the open-or-shut relay was analogous to the all-or-none neuron, the electrical pulses in the computer were analogous to the neural impulses, the mercury delay lines were analogous to the reverberating circuits in the nervous system, the memory circuits of the computer were analogous to the association areas of the brain, and so on and on (p. 49).

At another level, the computer simply serves as an analogy to the processes that humans employ. This type of analogy forms the basis for the remainder of this chapter.

A Theory of Human Problem Solving

Newell, Shaw, and Simon have advanced a proposal for a theory of human problem solving that serves as a classical example of one cybernetic approach. Their theory is designed to be simulated on a computer and is intended to illustrate the solving of problems through "information processes." Central to the theory is the notion that the explanation of human behavior is inherent in a description of the "program" of information processes that lead to behavior. In this sense, they do not use a computer model as an analogy to human behavior, but simply as a means to describe behavior in terms of a program. *The program is the analogy.*

The development of the theory has taken the form of a complex program for discovering proofs for theorems in symbolic logic. Specifically, the program is based on *Principia Mathematica* (Whitehead & Russell, 1925). It is called the *Logic Theorist* and has come to be referred to as LT in the literature. Its authors point out that it was not constructed in order to arrive at a model of human behavior but that it was written simply to develop a program that would prove theorems. Analogies to human problem solving were made later.

The LT program consisted essentially of storing the axioms of *Principia Mathematica* in the computer together with all of the processes necessary for discovering proofs. The first 52 theorems of the text were then presented to LT. It succeeded in proving 38 of the theorems, almost half of them in less than one minute. Longer proofs took more time. Variations of this initial experiment involved presenting the theorems in isolation so that previous proofs could not be employed in the solution of later problems. As a result, the LT often had to give up before finding a solution.

That the behavior of the Logic Theorist is like that of a human is supported by several observations. Newell, Shaw, and Simon (1958) indicate that LT did, in fact, solve problems — as human subjects sometimes do.* They also found that the probability of finding a correct solution appeared to be very much a function of the order in which information is presented. This same fact is assumed to hold for humans as well. Other similarities between the Logic Theorist and human problem solving are subsumed under four headings:

Set. In the same manner that human learning and problem solving are affected by set (see, for example, the chapters on Hebb or Bruner), so the LT responds to instructions. These instructions are ordinarily technical, indicating the order in which various operations are to be performed.

Insight. The authors define insight in solving a problem as the process of grasping its "structure" rather than as a process of trial and error. Their contention is that the Logic Theorist's behavior is not simply blind trial but that alternatives are attempted in reasonable order and that discarding a possible solution determines the next process. In other words, the proof is not arrived at through the "brute force" of a high-speed computer trying innumerable approaches until the right one is found, but instead the process is based on the *logical* elimination and selection of alternatives. According to the authors, the controversy between the insight and trial-and-error groups can be accounted for by confusion about the meanings of the terms. In their words, the controversy "rests on ambiguity and confusion." A problem solver may appear to be engaging in trial-and-error behavior, but to the extent that his actions are governed by rules, he is demonstrating insight.

Concepts. Concepts are involved in the behavior of the LT in that all theorems or axioms having something significant in common can be considered to be concepts.

Hierarchies of Processes. The authors reason that in the same way that the LT makes use of sequences of operations by generating problems and subproblems and keeping a record of them, so a human organizes his approach to problems in a somewhat hierarchical fashion.

In summary of the theory, it can be said that Newell, Shaw, and Simon have attempted to simulate human problem-solving behavior by programming a computer so that it would, in the course of solving

*Heh, heh! (GRL)

problems, acquire information necessary for the solution of other problems. The description of human problem-solving behavior that they have presented is implicit in the program itself. It is not immediately obvious that the model provides new information about human behavior. It appears to be somewhat more likely that the general approach may instead lead to a clarification of existing information. At least two problems remain unsolved. The first problem of what type of model to employ (deterministic or stochastic) has already been discussed. The second problem stems from the simple observation that computer memories are vastly superior to human memories. Computers do not forget. In addition, their application of rules and procedures is much more logical, although more rigid as well. At best, one can say that the LT simulates the problem-solving behavior of an extremely intelligent human being (who is probably nonexistent). The Logic Theorist does simulate the behavior of very young Korons. Even some of Bruner's strategies, which are relatively simple by comparison, were never employed by human subjects but remain only logical possibilities.

A second model illustrative of a cybernetic approach is provided by what is referred to as the TOTE theory of Miller, Galanter, and Pribram (1960), discussed in the following section.

TOTE

Last night I observed a man picking his teeth. He was a round, bulbous, obese human with huge jowls that waggled unpredictably as he talked or munched on his food. His great red beard was faintly streaked with the milk and meat of other meals; otherwise he gave the appearance of always taking great care with his person, as his small, well-manicured nails attested. After his meal last night, breathing heavily, he reached into his pocket and extracted from it his greatest luxury — a gold toothpick in a small case. Judging from the many dents and scars which it bore, it had likely been owned by his father — and perhaps by *his* father before that. He grasped the toothpick delicately with the thumb and forefinger of his right hand and opened his mouth, revealing a row of superb, gold-capped uppers; his lowers remained concealed behind the heavy fringe of beard. With his mouth open he ran his tongue gently over the teeth, uncovering in the process a formidable piece of turkey that had become firmly lodged next to his left eyetooth. Unerringly he guided the toothpick toward the offending meat and flicked at it quickly and decisively. Again he ran his tongue over the teeth, and again it encountered the stubborn turkey. Once more he aimed the golden toothpick, and again he merely weakened its precarious hold between the teeth. He confirmed this fact yet another time with his tongue, proceeding immediately to launch another attack on the tender *viande*—and this time he was successful. Breathing sonorously, he replaced the toothpick in its case and returned it to his pocket. "Now that," I thought, "is a marvellous example of a TOTE sequence."

A TOTE Sequence

The TOTE unit is the basic concept in the account of human behavior presented by Miller, Galanter, and Pribram (1960). It is also the basic unit in any feedback system, containing as it does all of the elements of such a system. The letters stand for the phrase *TEST—OPERATE—TEST—EXIT*. The phrase summarizes the sequence of functioning in a self-regulated machine. First, behavior is initiated by a test designed to reveal whether environmental conditions match the test standard(s). For example, using the earlier illustration of a heating system, the initial test might reveal that the temperature is below the indicator setting. The next step is the *operation*, which is the activity designed to modify environmental conditions to the point that feedback will become negative. The furnace ignites. The operation is followed by another test. For example, the thermostat again senses whether the temperature is up to the indicated level after the furnace has been fired. The *exit* phase is simply the termination of an operation after negative feedback. Obviously, there may be a long series of tests, each followed by operations, before feedback becomes negative. In other words, behavior is of the TOTE variety only at the very simplest level. More often it is of the TOTOTO . . . TOTE type. For example, it is possible to conceive of the thermostat in a heating system as *continually* testing temperature. The model can then be thought of as comprising an infinite number of overlapping tests and operations.

The behavior of the fat man picking his teeth is only one of many possible examples of TOTE units in human behavior. The operation involved using the toothpick, the test was accomplished by means of a sensitive tongue, and exit occurred only after three test-operate sequences had taken place. A diagrammatic representation of a TOTE unit is given in Figure 1.

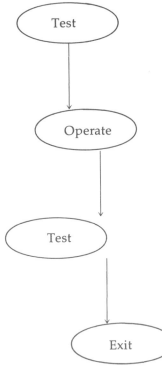

Figure 1. *The TOTE Unit*

For Miller et al., the TOTE unit is expressly an admission that human behavior is governed by feedback. At the same time, it provides a framework within which to advance some notions about the nature of operations and of tests. Two concepts form the essential basis of these notions — *plans* and *images*.

Plans

The authors begin with the assumption that behavior does not consist of sequences of conditioned responses. Nor do they believe that the reflex is the basic unit of behavior. On the contrary, their contention is that the reflex as an unlearned response arc is a much overrated, formerly useful concept that may well be more mythical than real. In place of the reflex, they have substituted the feedback loop. They have linked behavior, one fundamental component of this loop, with the term *operation;* the term operation is in turn linked to the concept of *plans*. At the simplest level, a plan is a blueprint for activity. It is a plan of attack or a strategy in much the same sense that a computer program is a strategy. More precisely, a plan is "any hierarchical process in the organism that can control the order in which a sequence of operations is to be performed" (Miller et al., 1960, p. 16). At the highest level, plans for human behavior are *molar*. That is, they govern large segments of behavior without specifying *a priori* what each specific operation will be in the sequence of activity. At the same time, however, they also include sequences at a more *molecular* level. It is in this sense that plans are *hierarchical*. The molar units of behavior can be viewed as comprising *strategy*, whereas the molecular aspects correspond to *tactics*. The decision to write a report, for example, is one example of a plan. It specifies in a general sense that my activity in the future will include writing a report. This is the molar aspect of the plan. As the operations go into effect, however, more precise tactics emerge. The decisions to write the report in chapters, to use a blue ball-point pen with blue ink in it, to write on blue paper, and to have it typed by a secretary dressed in blue are all molecular aspects of the same plan.

In short, a plan is a pattern for behaving — a pattern that is hierarchical in the sense that it is comprised of behaviors of greater or lesser specificity. A plan is executed when it serves as a guide for behavior.

According to the authors, plans need not involve *overt* behavior, since there are plans for gathering information or storing it, for solving problems, for making decisions, and for transforming information, as well as for engaging in overt behavior.

Image

The second concept that plays a central role in the theoretical position advanced by Miller, Galanter, and Pribram (1960) is *image,* which the authors define as "all the accumulated organized knowledge that the organism has about itself and its world" (p. 17). This concept is not essentially different from Kurt Lewin's notion of life space (see Chapter 9).

When drawing an analogy between computer functioning and human behavior, the image can be seen as analogous to a fully programmed computer. It corresponds to the store of knowledge that the computer has, together with the operations possible for it. In the same sense, the image contains all information that an individual possesses, together with all the alternatives for activity. Quite simply, images contain plans.

The Role of Images and Plans in Behavior

The account of human behavior presented by Miller et al. (1960) has less to do with the relationship of images to plans than might appear to be the case from reading parts of their book. In actuality, the TOTE model they present is a description of a plan-in-action-*sans*-image. It is the plan that contains both the organization of behavioral sequences *and* the test standards.* The role of the image is relatively minor, except for its involvement in decisions about plans or their modifications.

The contributions of this model to an explanation of behavior can best be summarized by reference to Figure 2, which illustrates behavior as consisting of TOTE units where there is a possibility at each test-point for exit if the feedback is negative, for repetition of the same operation, or for the execution of a new operation.

Evaluation of Plans and the Structure of Behavior

Although the model described by Miller et al. is a relatively clear and interesting example of cybernetics, its value in adding to human knowledge about learning or behavior has not been immediately ap-

---

*Images also contain tests, which serve as sources of information for forming plans (K).

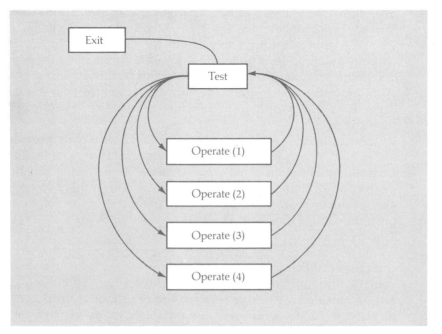

Figure 2. *Feedback Loop*

parent, partly because of ambiguity in the model.

1. The relationship between images and plans is not at all clear. Images contain plans, since the totality of an individual's knowledge must include the awareness that he can act on that knowledge. At the same time, however, plans are based on knowledge and can be modified on the basis of knowledge. In addition, the provisions for *testing* that are an integral part of plans are also based on knowledge or on values — both of which are assumed to be part of the image. Probably the clearest distinction between the two is provided by the declaration that plans govern behavior directly, whereas images do so mediately through plans.

2. Some further confusion is caused by the authors' description of values as being a part of the image while intentions "refer to the uncompleted parts of a plan whose execution has already begun" (p. 61). The artificial separation of values and intentions presents a problem for understanding the relationship between the two. Are plans

determined by values? All or in part? Are plans intentions only after they are begun or before as well? Are intentions then caused by values?

3. A third difficulty arises from the use of the plural of image without a definition of image that is sufficient to allow the reader to determine how images might be differentiated. Since images contain all of an individual's information, are they separable on the basis of differences among units of information? If so, how are they different from concepts?

4. A fourth problem stems from the explanation provided by Miller et al. (1960) for the origin of plans. Plans are assumed to result from the modification of old plans, from habits learned largely through instruction or imitation, and from instincts. The authors do not, however, name or describe a single human instinct, but simply make a few favorable comments about the work of such ethologists as Lorenz and Tinbergen, whose work has been with animals.

5. Last, it remains somewhat uncertain whether the model accomplishes the purpose explicitly adopted for it by the authors — namely, bridging the gap between cognition and action. True, a plan can be considered a bridge between image (cognition) and a sequence of activity. This is, however, an extremely global representation of human behavior. According to the authors, to say that a person behaves is to say that he has a plan. Conversely, of course, to say that he is executing a plan is to say that he behaves. Indeed, Miller *et al.* contend that an individual will be as close to planlessness as is possible (short of death) only when he is asleep. But to say that an individual has plans is of no more value than to say that he behaves — unless this particular way of looking at behavior leads to new hypotheses and eventually to new discoveries.

Despite the fact that a number of problems remain, there is hope that humans will eventually arrive at some of the Eleven Great Laws. At least one of them can be achieved through cybernetics.

Summary of Chapter 12

This chapter has presented an introduction to cybernetics, the application of machine models to human behavior. Feedback systems were discussed and their application to human cognitive processes was illustrated by direct reference to the work of Newell, Shaw, and Simon on the one hand, and Miller, Galanter, and Pribram on the other.

1. The term *cybernetics* refers to the application of feedback theory to the study of human learning. Aspects of cybernetics include attempts to explain behavior through the functioning of self-regulated machines or to devise such machines in order to simulate behavior.

2. The question of whether or not machines can think cannot easily be answered. Nor is it clear that they *need* to be able to do so in order to simulate human activity.
3. Behavior can be thought of as comprising *input, processing,* and *output.* In a self-regulated machine, input (which is modified by output) affects processing. As a machine, man's sensation of changes in the environment regulates his behavior.
4. Positive feedback maintains ongoing behavior, whereas negative feedback indicates that the operations (activities) in progress should be altered or should cease.
5. *Computers* are often used as models for human problem solving. It is possible to draw an analogy between computer components (hardware) and the human neurological system. More often, however, cybernetics draws the analogy between computer programs (software) and human functioning.
6. Newell, Shaw, and Simon have developed a program, called the *Logic Theorist* (*LT*), which is capable of *discovering* proofs for theorems in symbolic logic. Its functioning simulates some aspects of human problem-solving behavior.
7. Miller, Galanter, and Pribram have also advanced a cybernetic model. It describes behavior as comprising *TOTE* units. A TOTE unit is essentially an operational feedback loop in a self-regulated machine.
8. *Plans* (blueprints for activity) and *images* (organized totalities of knowledge) are central concepts in the position advanced by Miller et al. The terms represent relatively global conceptualizations of behavior and are therefore characterized by some lack of clarity.

5

Learning Theories:
An Integration

14

Human Socialization

Humans are not completely rational. I have made this point in earlier parts of this report but wish to reiterate it here since it is so essential to know this in order to arrive at some understanding of human behavior. Indeed, it is man's irrationality that makes Skinner's work with rats and pigeons relevant to human behavior. Consider, for example, the fact that some of Skinner's pigeons insisted on standing on one leg while pecking at a disk. Then relate this to the behavior of those humans who cross their fingers when engaged in games of chance. And this practice is only one of a large number of good-luck signals. Rabbits' feet, 4-leaf clovers, horsehoes, the appropriate stars, number 3, a rainbow, two rainbows, number 7, half a rainbow, three rainbows, pink clouds, number 9, old underwear, mascots, sun dogs, the evening star, bubbles on tea, and a found penny are also signs of imminent good fortune. Dropping cutlery means that company is coming; salt over the left shoulder wards off evil spirits; touching wood prevents the occurrence of dire calamities; mentioning catastrophes that haven't yet occurred hastens their arrival; upright ladders should be walked around; black cats shouldn't cross in front of humans;

Human Superstition

potatoes should be sown when the moon is full; and whoever catches the bride's bouquet will be next to marry.

Humans are *superstitious!*

Like Blips.

Unlike Korons.

Most apartment buildings on Earth do not have a thirteenth floor. They go from twelve to fourteen.

This is Chapter 14—the first of two chapters to be presented as partial integrations of the preceding twelve chapters.* It deals with

---

*It is ironic that Kongor accepted my facetious suggestion that there be no Chapter 13; he later insisted that it be omitted, although he vehemently denied that he was superstitious (GRL).

the application of general learning theory to the topic of human socialization. Chapter 15 presents a second type of integration—an attempt to include a variety of *different* explanations of learning in one theory. It consists in part of short summaries of each of the major theoretical positions, followed by a comparison of various positions. The comparison stems largely from the notion that jargon hides many similarities among theoretical positions.

Social Learning: A Definition

It might appear from reading the preceding chapters that most human learning involves acquiring information and learning how to deal effectively with the environment. The emphasis throughout has been primarily on environment-learner interaction. Actually, however, since humans, like Blips, are born relatively free of knowledge or behavioral predispositions, it is important for them to learn how to relate one to the other as well as how to relate to the environment. The learning of behaviors that are socially acceptable (as well as learning which ones aren't) defines *social learning*. In effect, social learning theory simply attempts to describe the processes by which humans come to know what behaviors should or shouldn't be engaged in when in different social situations. The theories themselves are simply *learning* theories that have been applied to social situations. Interestingly, learning theories that have been applied directly to problems of social learning have generally been *behavioristic* rather than cognitive. In addition, the topic of social learning has not received a great deal of attention in learning textbooks, probably because it seems logical to assume that *social psychology* is the area that should deal with social learning. However, social psychology textbooks typically deal with small, large, middle-size, huge, and tiny *groups*, and with such topics as group dynamics, peer influences on learning and behavior, mob psychology, and so on. Only rarely do they deal with the learning of social behavior —commonly referred to as *socialization*—the process that is defined by Brim and Wheeler (1966) as ". . . (that) by which persons acquire the knowledge, skills, and dispositions that make them more or less able members of their society" (p. 3).

The term *social learning*, as employed in this chapter, refers specifically to the learning of behaviors that are appropriate for a culture. The discussion of social learning is based largely on the theoretical formulations of Bandura and Walters (1963) and Bandura (1969).

Socialization

A treatment of social learning can deal with two aspects of socialization — the *process* itself, which may be highly similar across a variety of cultures, and the *content* of social learning, which may be highly dissimilar across societies. Although this chapter is concerned primarily with the process, content is discussed briefly prior to a consideration of the work of Bandura and Walters. The content of social learning is the actual catalog of behaviors that includes those that are appropriate and excludes those that are inappropriate. Two characteristics of such a catalog are noteworthy.

1. Acceptable behaviors vary from culture to culture. For example, in some Oriental countries it is highly appropriate to present university professors with gifts as tokens of appreciation. The same practice is looked upon with considerably less favor in North America. In the same manner, the appropriateness of sex-related behavior varies widely among cultures. What appears to be normal behavior for North American teen-age children would be regarded as highly promiscuous among rural Ghanians as well as among many Oriental societies. The same behavior might be viewed as relatively inhibited by some primitive African or South American tribe.

2. The appropriateness of specific behaviors varies among individuals in the same society. Even in a relatively classless society, some social behaviors can be engaged in only by those who hold certain positions. As Lefrancois (1972) observed, an employer can offer a member of his staff a drink when he comes into his office. On the other hand, an employee would probably be well advised to refrain from offering the boss a drink in *his* office. At the same time, however, the same employee may offer his boss a drink when the latter visits his home. Put quite simply, for the same individual, behavior varies in appropriateness depending on the person(s) with whom he is interacting and the particular situation in which he finds himself.

From a learning-theory point of view, a description of behaviors that are appropriate in different circumstances for different people is not as important as a discussion of how humans learn such behaviors — the topic that forms the basis for the remainder of this chapter.

Alternative Explanations of Socialization

Consider the simple problem faced by all human children of learning that it is not acceptable to kick strangers in the shins. A number of different explanations for the fact that this learning does take place can be derived from learning theory.

1. *Classical Conditioning.* An explanation based on notions of classical conditioning cannot easily explain complex social learning. It is extremely difficult, in fact, to conceive of situations involving the kicking of shinbones in which contiguity could account for learning. It is less difficult to imagine that the consequences of engaging in this behavior might lead to its rapid suppression. Neither of these explanations, however, can clearly explain why the behavior does or does not occur in the first place.

2. *Cognitive Explanations.* In order to account for social learning in terms of one or more of the cognitive positions that are discussed in this report, it is necessary to extrapolate beyond the specific formulations of the theorists in question. Typically, *cognitive* theories are more concerned with the properties of cognitive structure, the determinants of perceptual activity, and the factors governing awareness or insight than with the acquisition of simple behaviors. Accordingly, such

Probability of Escape = 10%

theories are not easily applicable to problems of social learning. It is possible, however, to assume that engaging in or refraining from a behavior such as kicking shins involves reaching a decision, and decision making is a topic of some interest to contemporary cognitivists. The typical approach to the subject is to examine it in the light of information processing. In this context, it is reasonable to assume that when a child is faced with a shin, he, in a Brunerian sense, evaluates the probability of various outcomes of the choices he can make and estimates (subjectively) the payoff associated with each. More simply, he can be imagined to reason as follows: "If I kick the old codger I will feel good in my awareness but he will probably catch me (p approximately equal to .90) and beat the living _____ out of me—that has a negative valence. If I pass up this splendid opportunity, I will not be beaten by the old geezer, but I will feel unhappy because of my frustrated aggressive tendencies." Having completed this reasoning process, the child, being human, will in all likelihood kick the old gentleman and run like a frightened gazelle in order to take full advantage of his 10% probability of escaping.

3. *Operant Conditioning.* The third explanation of social learning resembles the second in that the consequences of the behavior are assumed to be important in determining whether or not a behavior will be engaged in. In addition, the position can be employed to provide some explanation for the occurrence of the behavior in the first place. Indeed the most widely accepted social learning theories are those premised on an operant-conditioning model (for example, Miller & Dollard, 1941, and Bandura & Walters, 1963). An operant-conditioning explanation of social learning says simply that reinforced responses tend to be retained, whereas those that are not reinforced (or that are punished) tend to be eliminated. The position also assumes that the initial occurrence of the response is relatively independent of environmental circumstances—it is simply *emitted*. Two problems are implicit in an operant-conditioning explanation of social learning. First, it does not account for the initial occurrence of the response. Obviously, if the behavior does not occur, it cannot be learned. Second, the model described above provides a less than adequate explanation for the suppression of undesirable behavior—an explanation that maintains, first, that nonreinforced responses will be suppressed and, second, that through generalization other related responses will also be suppressed. The first explanation is obviously not completely accurate since numerous behaviors are not engaged in even though they have never occurred. The second alternative may well account for the fact that many behav-

iors never occur at all, but it is nevertheless true that in order to account for all learning through generalization (or discrimination), the processes must be defined in an extremely broad sense.

4. *Grandmother* must be allowed to present her explanation: "He knowed better 'cause he seen his brother git slapped fer it," or "Shure he knowed how to 'cause he seen them other boys doin' it." Interestingly, it is possible to combine Grandma's explanation with that of other theorists in order to arrive at an apparently reasonable explanation for a great deal of social learning. An early attempt to do this took the form of Miller and Dollard's (1941) theory of social learning based on the role of imitation. Their theory was essentially an assertion that imitation rather than trial and error is the chief learning mode for humans. It can be reduced to the following set of statements about learning and the elements involved in the process:

1. Learning involves *cues, drives, responses,* and *rewards.*
2. A *drive* is a force that impels an organism to action. It is the motivational factor in learning.
3. Drives are attached to specific stimuli that can be external (like a sound) or internal (like hunger). Stimuli that give rise to response-producing drives are referred to as *cues.* In a literal sense, they serve as cues or signals for behavior.
4. The *response* occasioned by a drive will become learned if it leads to a reduction in drive. Since drives are the result of stimuli, reducing drives involves eliminating drive-producing stimuli.
5. The elimination of these stimuli is said to be *rewarding.* Miller and Dollard contend that learning does not take place in the absence of reward.
6. Learning involves attaching responses to specific stimuli. The initial occurrence of a response, particularly where social learning is involved, is more often the result of imitation than of trial and error.
7. Imitation is learned through the same process by which other learning occurs. Behaviors that are engaged in by a child *and are imitative of the behavior of someone else* will be learned if rewarded. Since children are often rewarded when they imitate adult behavior, it is inevitable that a large number of imitative responses will be learned in this way. Through *generalization,* a child eventually comes to imitate specifically as a means of learning.

The most obvious theoretical objection that can be raised to this explanation of learning is that it is not realistic to assume that *all* or even *most* human behavior is motivated by the desire to eliminate stimulation. It appears evident that humans engage in many activities that have the objective of seeking rather than avoiding stimulation (see Chapter 3). A more recent formulation, also based on a theory of imitation but without the limitations of a rigorous drive-reduction approach, is provided by Bandura and Walters.

5. *An Integrated Explanation.* Bandura (1969) and Bandura and Walters (1963) present a theory of social learning that integrates all of the explanations described above. It is a theory that is based on operant conditioning, that admits of classical conditioning, and that accounts for learning partly in terms of the effectiveness of imitation in determining human behavior. In addition, Bandura (1969) describes imitation as involving a cognitive element. Despite its seeming eclectic nature, the theory presents a highly unified conception of human behavior.

Bandura and Walters

The most recent description of this position is provided by Bandura (1969) in *Principles of Behavior Modification* — a book concerned primarily with the application of social learning principles to the modification of behavior. This chapter deals with the principles *per se*, as they are discussed by Bandura in this book and by Bandura and Walters in an earlier book (1963). While a brief discussion of behavior-modification techniques is also provided, the interested reader is referred to the original sources for more detailed information.

Behavior-Control Systems

The Bandura and Walters theory can be considered an integration of a variety of theoretical positions in that it admits that behavior is controlled by several "systems," each of which relates directly to a specific school of psychological thought. It is true, however, that their theory deals primarily with only one of these behavior-control systems. Nevertheless, each system is clearly implicated in social learning.

Bandura (1969) maintains that it is impossible to explain human behavior solely by reference to either internal or external stimulus events, but instead both are inevitably involved in most human behavior. Since behaviorism can be defined in terms of its preoccupation with *external* events whereas cognitivism deals with *internal* mediation of behavior, an admission that both are involved in human activity can be interpreted as an attempt to integrate behavioristic and cognitive positions.

When Bandura refers to *external* stimulus events, he means simply the physical environment that is at least partly responsible for human behavior. It is patently obvious that humans do, in fact, respond to their environments. Indeed, not to do so would be a mark of a totally nonfunctional being. Even such phylogenetically low forms of Earth life as planaria are responsive to external stimulation. *Internal* stimulation refers to the more "cognitive" events, in the form of images, memories, feelings, instructions, verbalizations, and so on, which comprise human thought processes. That these events influence behavior is clear—Grandma needs no convincing whatsoever. Interestingly, Earth psychologists sometimes do. To this end, Bandura (1969) cites an experiment performed by Miller (1951) in which a group of subjects were conditioned by means of electric shocks to react negatively to the letter *T* and positively to the number 4. After conditioning, subjects consistently gave evidence of greater autonomic reaction (arousal) for the stimulus associated with shock—in this case, *T*. Miller subsequently instructed subjects to *think* "T" and "4" alternately as a sequence of dots were presented to them. That is, the subjects were asked to think "T" for the first dot, "4" for the second, "T" for the third, "4" for the fourth, and so on. The fact that there was now greater autonomic reaction to odd-numbered dots is assumed to be indicative of the effect of internal processes on behavior.

In describing the forces that cause human behavior, Bandura notes three separate *behavior-control systems* which are assumed to interact with each other in the determination of behavior.

1. *Stimulus Control.* One class of human behaviors consists of activities that are directly under the control of stimuli. Such behaviors include the host of autonomic (reflexive) acts that people engage in when responding to certain specific stimuli. Sneezing, withdrawing from pain, flinching, the startle reaction, and so on are all examples of behavior that is controlled by *external* stimuli. In addition, a wide variety of nonreflexive behaviors come under control of stimuli through conditioning. For this reason, the first behavior-control system described by Bandura can be interpreted as including the types of learning that are of most direct concern to behavioristic psychologists.

The group of behaviors under control of stimuli also includes responses learned through reinforcement, where a specific stimulus is always present at the time of the reinforcement. This stimulus acquires control over behavior in the sense that it comes to elicit a response because of its relationship to the reinforcement. A clear illustration of this type of control is provided by the contrast between the deportment of many school children when their teacher is present and when she isn't. Through the administration of rewards for good behavior and punishment for less desirable activity, teachers become stimuli that are capable of eliciting either obedience, fear, caution, respect, love or a combination of these responses.

2. *Outcome Control.* The second *behavior-control system* described by Bandura refers to the group of behaviors that are under the control of their consequences rather than under the control of antecedents (or stimuli). Obviously, this system has been extensively investigated by B. F. Skinner. It relates specifically to those human activities that become more probable as a function of reinforcement or less probable as a function of nonreinforcement or of punishment. Control is achieved through operant conditioning in this behavior-control system (see Chapter 5).

3. *Symbolic Control.* The last behavior-control system includes the range of human activity that is influenced by "mediation" or internal processes. There are several ways in which human behavior can be affected by thought processes. Covert verbalization of rules (self-instructions) can direct behavior, as in the Miller (1951) experiment in which subjects can be assumed to have "mentally" told themselves to think "T," then "4," and so on. A second sense in which symbolic processes direct behavior relates to the way *imagining* the consequences of behavior affects ongoing activity. It appears obvious that were it not for the ability to represent long-range outcomes symbolically, a great many tasks that are neither under immediate stimulus control nor likely to be rewarded immediately would not be undertaken. The importance of symbolization for human behavior appears to be much greater than that of the other two behavior-control systems. It also appears that as one goes down the phylogenetic scale, the importance of outcome control and of direct stimulus control increases. Lower animal forms seem to react more to specific external stimulation than to behavioral outcomes. In addition, it is not at all evident that symbolization plays an important (if any) role in the direction of the behavior of lower animals.

Behavior-Control Systems and Social Learning

While stimulus-control, outcome-control, and symbolic-control systems relate to three classes of behavior that are clearly distinguishable on theoretical grounds, they are not necessarily separate in practice.

Indeed, much human activity is probably directed by a combination of these three. For example, a man who pursues a buck-toothed, cross-eyed, knock-kneed, pigeon-toed, skinny, red-headed woman may well be directed by stimuli, outcomes, and symbolization. In the first place, the pursued redhead is a woman, and because of stimulus generalization the pursuer reacts to this woman as he would to any other. His pursuing behavior is under the direct control of the stimulus *woman*, because *woman* is the stimulus that has been present at the time of many previous reinforcements. But human behavior is not this simple. The pursuer does not just respond to this signal in the blind manner expected of an unsophisticated rat, but he responds in a manner directed by its immediate outcomes. If his initial approach is met by strong resistance, he may modify it; if it is rewarded, he may intensify it; if the intensification leads to more reward, it may be reintensified; if it leads to a cessation of reinforcement, it may be de-intensified. Quite simply, the human male is capable of changing his behavior in accordance with its outcomes. But the direction of activity is not this simple either. Man does not react solely to stimuli or to the consequences of his behavior, although it is obviously necessary that he do so to some extent. Also, his actions are guided by symbolic processes. For example, the human male pursues an unattractive redhead because he can represent imaginally the consequences of being successful in his attempt to capture her. He can clearly visualize that such an ugly woman must possess hidden talents to offset her lack of obvious qualities — she must certainly be an excellent cook.

The relevance of Bandura's discussion of the control of behavior for social learning is implicit in the assumption that learning involves bringing responses under the control of stimuli, rewards, or symbolic processes. In this respect, social learning does not differ from other forms of learning, except insofar as the *content* of the learning may itself be different, since it relates to *socialization* rather than to the simple acquisition of knowledge or information.

The theory of social learning advanced by Bandura and Walters (1963) is based on all three of these behavior-control systems. Their most important contribution, however, is their explanation of social learning in terms of the effects of imitation. They contend that a great deal of the learning of social behavior is achieved by observing the behavior of others. This learning is referred to as observational learning. The theory is discussed below in terms of the answers it advances for four related questions:

1. What is the relationship between imitation and operant conditioning?

An Excellent Cook

2. How prevalent is imitative behavior?
3. What is a *model?*
4. What are the results of observational learning?

Imitation and Operant Conditioning

Skinner's model of operant conditioning describes learning as an increase in the probability of occurrence of an operant (emitted response) as a function of reinforcement. In order to relate this model to the process of learning through observation, it is necessary to assume that imitative behavior possesses the characteristics of operants and that it is subject to reinforcement. That both aspects of the assumption are valid can easily be illustrated. First, an operant is a response that is not elicited by a stimulus but is simply *emitted* by an organism. This description does not contradict the possibility that some environmental condition(s) may be partly or wholly responsible for the appearance of the response, but it does assert that the antecedent conditions are not of any direct consequence to the actual learning. Thus, it can be said that imitative behavior may result from the observation of a model, *but the learning itself* will involve the formation of some sort of relationship between the reinforcement and the behavior rather than between the model's behavior and the observer's behavior.

The second aspect of the assumption is that imitation is subject to reinforcement. That this assumption is true is readily evident from the behavior of humans. Indeed, four separate sources of reinforcement are apparent in observational learning—three involving reinforcement for the observer and one involving the behavior of the model. An imitator is often reinforced directly by the model whose behavior he is copying, particularly if the imitator is a young child. Proud human parents are prone to praising their children for behaviors that resemble those of Daddy or Mommy. Even grandmothers are occasionally heard saying, "Look at little Norbert standing there with his finger in his nose, *just like his daddy.*"*

A second source of reinforcement for the observer derives from the actual consequences of the imitated behavior. If the activity is socially acceptable and/or if it leads to the obtaining of reward, it is reinforced by its own consequences. A child who learns to say "milk" as a result of hearing his mother say "milk" forty times a day for 3 years, not only incurs the praise of that proud parent but may also receive real *milk* as a result of saying the word. Hence, the consequences of learning socially appropriate behavior through imitation are often desirable.

Third, the observer in a modeling situation often appears to be influenced by what Bandura (1969) labels *vicarious* reinforcement. This type of reinforcement derives from the assumption that if a model engages in a behavior there must be some reinforcement that leads him to do so and that this reinforcement will also result if the observer imitates the behavior. The fact that an observer will often imitate without any expectation of reward and continue to do so even after he has discovered that he is not being reinforced is interpreted as evidence that he derives secondhand or *vicarious* reinforcement from the imitation itself—a reinforcement that is linked to the model's assumed reward.

The fourth source of reinforcement for imitative behavior affects the model rather than the observer. For this reason it is not directly pertinent to observational learning, but it does serve to explain why

*Heh, heh! (GRL)

some of the model's behavior is (or isn't) maintained. It often appears that when a human is imitated, there is an increase in the probability that he will engage again in the behavior that was imitated. For example, some years ago some entertainers let their hair grow much longer than the social norm. This fashion was widely imitated, and the entertainers continued to let their hair grow. Had they not been imitated it is much less likely that they would have continued to do so. In other words, it appears that to be imitated is reinforcing for a human.

In summary, observational learning can be understood in terms of an operant-conditioning model if it is assumed that imitative behavior is operant or instrumental in nature. Although an obvious external stimulus often seems to elicit the behavior initially, this stimulus (the model) serves only to account superficially for the appearance of the behavior but not for the fact that it may or may not be learned. A second assumption that relates imitation to an operant paradigm is that reinforcement is often a consequence of imitating.

Prevalence of Imitation

Currently, some emphasis is placed on originality and creativity in many human societies. Consequently, there is a concomitant denigration of imitation since to imitate is, by definition, not to be original. Yet not only is it abundantly obvious that imitation is extremely common, but it is equally clear that organized societies would no longer be viable if their members did not imitate one another. Consider the chaos that would result if humans decided to drive on either side of the street, to park vehicles anywhere, and to interpret traffic signals in original ways. The very basis of communication among humans is imitation. In the same manner, the storage of knowledge and the transmission of culture requires imitation.

Primitive societies are sometimes cited as examples of learning through imitation. Bandura and Walters (1963) described the Cantalense people, a Guatemalan subculture. In this society a little girl is provided with miniature *working* replicas of all of the tools employed by her mother in caring for the household. As soon as she is old enough, she follows her mother about, *observing* her, and imitating her actions with miniature brooms and corn-grinding stones. Throughout the learning process there is *little or no direct tuition.* Hence, the learning is more clearly a result of imitation than is the learning of young children in more highly verbal cultures.

A second example of a primitive culture in which early learning is largely observational is provided by Lefrancois' (1972) discussion of the Canadian Ojibwa Indian. This tribe lived largely on the fruits of hunting, fishing, and trapping. Early in life a young Ojibwa boy would follow in his father's footsteps, learning how to hunt, to set traps, and to fish. At a young age he would be given his own traps and would go out by himself. In the same way, a young Ojibwa girl learned how to prepare game, clothing, cooking fires and so on, by observing her mother. As in the Cantalense culture there was little direct tuition.

The prevalence of imitative learning in highly developed technological societies is not as evident. Obviously, it is virtually impossible for parents to provide their children with miniature *working* replicas of the tools and machines that they employ in the course of their daily activities. Nor would it be particularly wise to do so, since children frequently enter occupational fields that are very different from those of their parents. Nonetheless, observational learning is highly prevalent in advanced societies. Through imitation children learn appropriate (acceptable) ways of doing things, acquire behavioral patterns that conform to those of peer groups, and so on—indeed, when imitative learning is defined as all learning that results from observing *models*, and *models* are defined according to Bandura and Walters, it becomes apparent that the most highly developed society may well be characterized by the greatest degree of observational learning.

Models

Although there is a tendency to think of models as *people* whose behavior is copied by others, a model is more appropriately defined as any representation of a pattern for behaving. Humans do serve as models for other humans—parents serve as models for children, children are models for other children, and sometimes for adults, and adults continually imitate one another. Television is also a model since it presents a variety of patterns for behaving. In the same sense, books, verbal instructions, animals, and directions are all models. They are referred to as *symbolic models*; each plays a significant role in the socialization of the contemporary human child.

Effects of Imitation

From the preceding sections it might appear that learning through imitation simply involves a model who does something and an observer who copies his behavior and is reinforced for doing so. However, the process is somewhat more complex than this. Bandura and Walters

(1963) and Bandura (1969) distinguish three separate results of observational learning, which they describe as the three *effects* of imitation.

The Modeling Effect.   When an observer learns (through imitation) something that is *new* for him, he is said to *model*. Hence, modeling involves the acquisition of *novel* responses. That such an effect does exist is corroborated by anecdotal evidence. Grandmothers eagerly describe how their grandchildren acquire undesirable habits from the neighbor's undisciplined ruffians—habits that are clearly novel since they were never engaged in previously. In further support of grandmother's position, Bandura et al. (1963) describe a series of often-replicated experiments dealing with aggression in young children. The experiments typically involve subjects who are exposed to filmed, real-life, or cartoon models of other children or of adults engaging in *novel* aggressive behavior with a large inflated plastic clown. Occasionally the model is verbally aggressive; at other times he (or she) strikes the clown with fist, foot, or mallet, or he sits on it, scratches it, or otherwise attacks it. Subjects are later exposed to the same clown and their reactions are noted. Frequently, these reactions take the form of precisely imitative aggressive responses. When the responses are clearly new for the child, he is assumed to be *modeling*.

The Inhibitory and Disinhibitory Effects.   The second effect of imitation does not involve *novel* responses but deals instead with the suppression or disinhibition of previously learned *deviant* behavior. *Deviant* behavior is defined as socially unacceptable responses (such as excessive aggression, for example). Inhibition and disinhibition usually occur as a result of seeing a model punished or rewarded for engaging in deviant behavior. For example, a group of thieves may stop stealing after a member of the group is apprehended and punished. On the other hand, the same group may have begun stealing as a result of seeing a member become wealthy through stealing. The first instance exemplifies the inhibitory effect; the second example illustrates the disinhibitory effect.

A rather striking illustration of the power of models in disinhibiting deviant behavior is provided by a series of experiments sometimes referred to as the *punishment studies* (Walters & Llewellyn, 1963; Walters, Llewellyn, & Acker, 1962). In these studies subjects were asked to volunteer for what was ostensibly an experiment in memory. The subjects were shown a short sequence from one of two films: either a violent episode from the movie *Rebel Without a Cause* or an excerpt from a film showing adolescents engaged in art work. Those exposed to the sequence with aggressive content comprised the experimental group; the second group served as controls. After the films were presented, subjects were asked to help the experimenter with another study designed to investigate the effects of punishment on problem-solving behavior. A person who posed as a subject, but who was in reality a stooge, sat at a panel working out problems and signaling his answers by pressing a switch. Whenever he answered correctly a green light would flash on a second panel; when he was incorrect, a red light would go on. The second panel also contained 15 toggle switches that were labeled 15 volts, 30 volts, 45 volts, and so on. The switches appeared to be connected to the electrodes fastened to the stooge's wrists. Instructions given to the subject (after he had been administered a mild shock in order to ensure that he realized what he was doing) were simply to administer punishment in the form of an electric shock every time an error was made. Results strongly supported the prediction that exposure to aggressive models would result in an increase in the intensity of the shocks administered. Even more striking is the fact that very few subjects refused to participate in the experiment, despite the fact that they were being asked to inflict pain on their colleagues.

The inhibitory effect cannot be so easily demonstrated experimentally, probably because systematic attempts to inhibit deviant behavior often show little evidence of success. Contemporary North American criminal law is often justified on the grounds that punishing an offender serves as a deterrent for others who might also become criminals. The person punished is therefore intended to serve as a model for the inhibition of the behavior punished. There is some indication, however, that humans are not particularly susceptible to this behavior-control technique. Grandmother has known this for some time. Indeed, she has summarized the whole ineffectiveness of criminal punishment in the brilliant and insightful phrase: "He thinks it can't happen to him." Interestingly, Grandmother still insists that criminals must be punished: "They just deserve it, that's all! The idea!"

The Eliciting Effect. A third manifestation of the influence of models on human behavior is referred to as the *eliciting effect.* It involves *eliciting* responses that are not novel and not identical to those of the model but are related to the model's responses in two ways. First, there is an obvious relationship in that the model's behavior serves as a stimulus for the appearance of the observer's response. Second, the observer's responses and the model's behavior are related in that they belong to the same class of behaviors. A rather common example of the eliciting effect is provided by the behavior of those who try to excel in one area because someone else excels in *another* area. The acquisition of accents through exposure to people who speak differently and being generous in one way because one's neighbors are generous in another are two examples of the eliciting effect. Whenever a model is responsible for the appearance of a response that is not novel, *nor precisely imitative, the eliciting* effect is manifested. A further example of this effect is provided by Lefrancois (1972):

> Another clear example of the eliciting effect is provided by the behavior of teachers, who are, as is well known, highly underpaid. Being underpaid they cannot take full advantage of the summer holidays so generously given to them by the people whose children they teach. Many teachers have to spend their summers working.
>
> Teachers are quiet, God-fearing, well behaved pillars of conservative communities — they have to be since they are the self-chosen transmitters of a quiet, God-fearing, hardworking culture. They occasionally find themselves, however, working, sometimes at hard labour, with rough, unwashed and uncouth individuals — individuals whose short-sentenced conversations are liberally sprinked with four letter words. Only extremely rarely does a teacher in such circumstance succeed in serving as an effective model of God's, the Queen's and the President's English. More often he becomes the "observer," and adopts the manner of speech of his co-workers. Evidence that this change is illustrative of the eliciting effect is found in the fact that the teacher's behavior is not ordinarily a direct imitation of the language around him but is often an embellishment of that language. The improvement is probably derived from expressions that had effectively been inhibited by a teacher-training program.

Imitation and Social Learning

Imitation ranks high among the alternative explanations for complex social learning, primarily because those explanations provided by operant- or classical-conditioning models, while useful in accounting for the acquisition of simple responses, are not clearly applicable to a great deal of complex learning. Such skills as learning to drive a car are not acquired solely through contiguity or trial and error but require the presentation of models. These models can take the form of other drivers or of verbal or written instructions. Humans would probably never learn to speak if they needed to do so through trial and error, without benefit of the models that are presented by other speaking humans. Indeed, it can truthfully be stated that people learn what is acceptable and unacceptable in matters of speech, dress, and behavior largely by observing the speech, dress, and behavior of others.

Behavior Modification

Given the effectiveness of models in determining human behavior, it follows that systematic attempts to modify deviant behavior can make use of modeling procedures. Bandura and Walters (1963) describe five techniques that can successfully be employed to this end and that are based on operant-conditioning principles as well as on the specific use of models.

Positive Reinforcement. The use of rewards for modifying behavior is a well-known and widespread practice in everyday life. It is a technique invented by some ancient grandmother. In order to toilet train a child, his parents give him a candy when he goes on the "pot"; hard work is repaid with increased wages; the diligent student is smiled at, and so on. The systematic use of rewards in therapy, however, is not as common as Grandmother might expect. The *psychoanalytic** orientation of many therapists leads them to approaches intended to uncover the causes of deviant behavior rather than to deal with their manifestation. Behavioral approaches to therapy are contrasted to the psychoanalytic techniques mainly in terms of their treatment of symptoms rather than causes. There is some argument about whether the removal of symptoms constitutes a *cure*. At the same time, there is doubt that *cures* are frequent as a result of psychoanalysis.

The Ninth Great Law could resolve this minor controversy.

Positive reinforcement is one behavioral technique. It is employed primarily where there is a behavioral deficit. In principle, the procedure involves simply arranging for the appearance of a response and following it with reinforcement. Several investigations (for example, Lovaas, 1966; Lovaas *et al.*, 1966; Risley & Wolf, 1967) have demonstrated that autism can successfully be treated in young children through the use of positive reinforcement. Autism is characterized by extreme withdrawal, undeveloped communication habits, and general nonsocialized behavior. Therapy can take the form of rewarding such children for verbal responses elicited through games (Ferster, 1961; Ferster & de-Myer, 1962).

Counterconditioning. This impressive term refers to the technique of conditioning responses that are incompatible with the undesirable

---

*Psychoanalysis is a term used to refer to the therapeutic school that follows the methods developed by Freud. These techniques are the traditional patient-on-the-couch, what-happened-in-your-childhood, what-do-you-dream approaches (K).

behavior but occur for the same stimuli. Wolpe (1958), a behavior therapist, has developed this method in a procedure he labels *systematic desensitization,* or *reciprocal inhibition.* In addition, the three techniques presented by Guthrie for the elimination of habits are all examples of counterconditioning since each involves learning responses for the original stimulus that are incompatible with the undesirable behavior (see Chapter 4).

Wolpe's *systematic desensitization* is a method used primarily in the treatment of anxieties and phobias (fears). It may be described in simplified form as involving three steps. First, the patient describes all of the situations that bring about his unwanted behavior. These situations are arranged in hierarchical order beginning with the stimulus that elicits the mildest response and culminating with the stimulus associated with the strongest reaction. The second step is to teach the patient a response that is incompatible with the one he wants to be rid of. Almost invariably, this step takes the form of training the patient in relaxation, since relaxing is incompatible with fear or anxiety. The third step is to present the subject with the mildest stimulus *while he is relaxing* and to continue presenting stimuli in hierarchical order until he begins to feel uncomfortable. At that point treatment is discontinued, and relaxation is again practiced. The object of the procedure is to eventually present the strongest stimulus without eliciting the unwanted reaction.

This procedure is evidently a sophisticated version of Guthrie's *threshold* technique or of Grandmother's "don't-throw-him-in-the-water-let-him-get-used-to-it-slowly-damn-it" approach.

Extinction. Even as Skinner's rats could be made to cease depressing a lever simply by withdrawal of rewards, so humans can often be made to stop engaging in some unwanted form of behavior by removal of their source of reinforcement. The application of this technique requires that the behavior be maintained by positive reinforcement and that this reinforcement be under the control of the experimenter or therapist. The second requirement is probably not often met since deviant behavior often leads to intrinsic satisfaction that is not under any external control. On the other hand, there are numerous attention-seeking behaviors in young children that can be extinguished simply by ceasing to pay attention to them. Ayllon and Michael (1959) describe the successful treatment of a child who cried every time he was put to bed. This treatment involved letting the child cry. In less than a week the behavior had stopped altogether.

Modeling. The fourth behavior-modification technique involves the deliberate application of modeling procedures in an attempt to eliminate deviant behaviors. These procedures can take the form of any of the three effects of imitation. For example, a child might be taught something new by being shown what to do (modeling effect); he might be discouraged from doing something by witnessing someone else being punished for the behavior (inhibitory effect); or he might be encouraged to engage in a certain class of behaviors after being exposed to a relevant model (eliciting effect). Ferguson (1968) reports an investigation in which adult subjects were effectively treated for snake phobia by being exposed to a model who, in successive stages, worked around a live snake, fed the snake, and eventually held and played with it. It has similarly been demonstrated that fear of animals in young children can be eliminated through exposure to models who show no evidence of fear (Bandura, Grusec, & Menlove, 1967).

Discrimination Learning. Discrimination learning is the formation of discriminations among stimuli such that the individual responds appropriately in similar situations requiring different responses. For example, aggressive behavior is appropriate in football; it is less appropriate in baseball. Similarly, a child is punished for striking his sister, but may be praised for attacking the local bully.

One procedure for teaching discriminations is described in the report of an experiment conducted by Freund (1960). Subjects were male homosexual patients who volunteered for treatment and were then shown slides of nude males at the same time that the effects of a previously injected emetic mixture were felt. In a later session, they were shown slides of females after being injected with testosterone (a sexual stimulant). The procedure resulted in considerable success with these volunteer patients but less success with others who had not volunteered for treatment.

Social Learning and Teaching

The relevance of the preceding discussion for teaching centers around two facts. First, it is probably correct to assume that not only does a teacher's behavior serve as a model for a great deal of student behavior, but that instructions, descriptions of behavior, and explicit and implicit expressions of values for which he is responsible also serve as symbolic models. Second, each of the five behavior-modification techniques that were described can be applied in situations involving learning as well as in those involving discipline (behavior control). The reader is invited to attempt to apply these techniques himself. (Chapter 15 of Lefrancois' book [1972] may be of value.)

Social Learning Theory in Review

The social learning theory presented by Bandura and Walters attempts to account for learning by means of an imitation theory. The theory is closely related to an operant-conditioning model with one major distinction, which is carefully pointed out by Bandura (1967, 1969). The traditional operant-conditioning paradigm is premised on the assumption that a discriminated stimulus that is present when an operant is emitted and reinforced comes to acquire the ability to elicit the response. In learning through imitation, however, the discriminated stimulus is the model, and the model does not acquire the ability to elicit the imitative response. Nor is the reinforcement necessarily an immediate, tangible consequence of imitating. Indeed, frequently the model has been presented a long time prior to the emission of an imitative response, and the reinforcement might well remain vicarious rather than real. According to Bandura, this time lapse makes an operant-conditioning paradigm somewhat insufficient for explaining observational learning. For this reason, a symbolic behavior-control system can usefully be employed in the theory.

The behavior-modification techniques that are a logical outgrowth of social learning theory are receiving a great deal of attention in contemporary psychological research, theory, and practice. The entire area is relatively new but is characterized by more experimental research than most, if not all, other therapeutic approaches.

It is interesting that humans, like Blips, are gregarious and that therefore social learning is a topic of major significance for them.

Summary of Chapter 14

This chapter has presented a definition of socialization and a discussion of various theoretical explanations of social learning. The theory advanced by Bandura and Walters was examined in some detail. A brief account of behavioral therapeutic techniques was also given.

1. Social learning can be defined as the process of learning to behave in a socially acceptable manner. The term *socialization* is used synonymously with the expression *social learning*.

2. Appropriate behavior varies across cultures and for different people within cultures. Hence, a description of the *content* of social learning would be extremely complex. The *process*, however, is probably more uniform across cultures.
3. Among the explanations for social learning phenomena that can be derived from learning theory are those based on classical conditioning, operant conditioning, cognitivism, and Grandmother's imitation position. No explanation taken alone is entirely adequate to account for much significant social learning.
4. An integration of all of these extrapolated explanations is provided by the social imitation theory of Bandura and Walters.
5. The major points in this theory are that much significant social learning results from imitation, the effects of imitation are explainable in terms of a model of operant conditioning, and symbolic processes are often involved in social learning.
6. Dollard and Miller also present a social learning theory based on the role of imitation. Theirs is essentially a drive-reduction approach. As such it suffers from the fact that not all human behavior is designed to reduce stimulation.
7. Bandura and Walters describe three *behavior-control systems* distinguishable by the differences among the responses involved. First, there are responses that are under direct stimulus control; second, there are responses that are affected by their consequences; and, third, there are responses that are directed by means of symbolic processes.
8. *Models* are not only *people* but also symbolic patterns for behavior, such as are provided by books, instructions, religions, television, and so on.
9. *Observational learning* can be manifested in terms of one or more of the three effects of imitation: The modeling effect involves novel, precisely imitative responses; the inhibitory or disinhibitory effects involve the suppression or appearance of deviant behavior, usually as a function of consequences to the model; and the eliciting effect involves non-novel, and not precisely imitative, behavior, which is nonetheless related to the model's behavior.
10. Techniques for *modifying behavior* include positive reinforcement, extinction, counterconditioning, modeling, and discrimination learning. Each technique can be clearly contrasted to psychoanalytic approaches.
11. Imitation appears to be much more prevalent in social learning than trial-and-error or insightful learning.
12. The superstitious behavior of humans is as difficult to understand as their social learning. It is certainly much less rational. Neither is of much relevance on Koros since we are not superstitious — nor very sociable. It was Lefrancois who suggested that there not be a Chapter 13.*

---

*I was merely joking. It was Kongor who *insisted* that there not be a Chapter 13 (GRL).

15

An Integration and Evaluation

One way to summarize the state of Koron knowledge about behavior is simply to recite the Eleven Great Laws. Summarizing the state of human knowledge about learning is somewhat more complex, for one major reason—namely, that in this area it is difficult to make clear distinctions among knowledge, speculation, and wishful thinking. It is known, for example, that the human brain is grayish and convoluted and that it weighs 3¼ pounds in the average adult male—as is pointed out in Chapter 2, the female brain weighs *less*. It is also known that human infants ordinarily respond to oral stimulation by sucking. On the other hand, it is merely suspected that neural transmission usually involves some chemical activity at synaptic junctures. In the same manner, there is some evidence to suggest that the memory function resides in the RNA molecule. Some other beliefs are not even speculative. Numerous statements about human qualities and human behavior are the hopeful echoes of ancient grandmothers who have, over the years, repeatedly uttered such phrases as "Man is rational," "Man is a paragon of virtue," "Oh, what a work of art is man," "Man is wise," "Man is intelligent," "Where there is a will, there is a way," and so on.

While the examples cited above are clearly factual, speculative, or wishful, a great deal of the content of psychology partakes of all three qualities in confusing proportions or, equally confusing, is not clearly either fact, fiction, or wish. For this reason, the integration of knowledge about human learning presented here takes the form of summaries and comparisons of the major theoretical positions discussed in earlier chapters. Since the Eleven Great Laws are not applicable on Earth without some major revisions, and since these principles would in any case be quite incomprehensible to the average human reader, I am unable to state clearly what is actually known about learning. However, I fully intend to sonarduct the revised laws back to you some day through my good and kind friend, Guy Lefrancois.

The first part of this chapter consists of summaries of each of the major learning theories discussed earlier. The second part deals with a comparison and evaluation of these theories. The intention is to provide a clear overview prior to the synthesis and evaluation of these positions.

Major Divisions in Learning Theory

Learning has been defined as changes in behavior that result from experience. The point has also been made that the phrases *learning theory* and *behavior theory* are employed synonymously. Among the various ways of looking at human behavior or learning, two broad orientations which give rise to the classical divisions among psychological theory can be identified. The first orientation assumes that man's behavior is, at least in some measure, influenced by the activity that goes on in his brain. Grandmother's expression for the same orientation is that man thinks, has a will, feels, and behaves because of the way he thinks, feels, and intends. Fortunately for her, she is seldom asked to define the terms she uses. The second orientation does not flatly contradict the first but merely asserts that very little scientifically valid knowledge about human behavior can be derived from an investigation of the nebulous processes of the mind. Instead, advocates of this orientation concentrate on an examination of human behavior and the observable conditions that lead to the behavior. Obviously, prebehavioristic and cognitive psychologists have the first orientation in common, whereas behaviorists are characterized by the second. It is important to bear in mind, however, that few positions are clearly *only* behavioristic or cognitive; such terms are simply convenient labels to describe distinct theoretical orientations. In addition, the labels are also indicative of somewhat different areas of interest. For example, behaviorism deals largely with investigations of stimuli and responses as well as of mediation (neobehaviorism). On the other hand, topics of interest to cognitive psychologists typically do not include stimuli and responses *per se* but deal instead with more *central* processes such as problem solving, decision making, perception, information processing, and concept formation. Table 1 (adapted from Table 1 in Chapter 4) distinguishes among the major divisions in learning theory, the theoretical positions that are representative of each, and the topics of greatest concern to the theorists in question. Each of these positions is summarized in the following section.

Table 1. *Divisions in Learning Theory*

	Symbolic Representation	Variables of Concern	Representative Theorists
Behaviorism	S-R	Stimuli Responses Reinforcement	Watson Thorndike Guthrie Skinner
Neobehaviorism	S $\overset{O}{\diagup\diagdown}$ R	Stimuli Responses Reinforcement Mediation	Hull Osgood Hebb
Cognitivism	O	Perception Organizing Information Processing Decision Making Problem Solving	Gestaltists Ausubel Bruner Piaget

Analysis

Behavioristic Positions

Watson. J. B. Watson was among the first Americans at the turn of this century to attempt to define the science of psychology in objective terms. He saw psychology as a science that dealt with the observable rather than the merely hypothetical—a definition that gave rise to American behaviorism. Watson's behaviorism was characterized by a rigorous subscription to the laws of classical conditioning that had been investigated by the Russian physiologist Pavlov. Watson assumed that individuals are born with a behavioral repertoire consisting only of a few reflexes and that these early responses become conditioned to other stimuli as a function of the simultaneous occurrence of stimulus or response events. For this reason, Hill (1963) refers to him as a *contiguity theorist in the connectionist* tradition.*

Watson is also recognized as one of the chief spokesmen for environmentalism — the belief that personality, intelligence, and all other human qualities are determined by the environment (the nurture side in the historical nature-nurture dispute). He is reported to have said that he could make whatever he wanted out of a dozen healthy infants providing he was given a free hand in their upbringing.

Guthrie. Edwin Guthrie is also referred to as a *contiguity theorist in the connectionist tradition* (Hill, 1963). Like Watson, he takes a rigidly behavioristic approach. It can be summarized quite simply in several major laws, which state essentially that whenever a response follows a stimulus, there will result a tendency for the same response to occur again the next time the stimulus is presented. Specifically, Guthrie maintained that learning was complete on the occasion of the first pairing of a stimulus with a response and that further practice would not strengthen the response. Similarly, he believed that forgetting does not occur — in other words, when a bond has been formed between a stimulus and a response, that bond will never be broken. However, it is possible to remove undesirable habits by learning new ones that are incompatible with the old ones. Guthrie suggests three ways in which this can be done: the fatigue technique, the threshold approach, and the method of incompatible stimuli. It is important to note that for both Watson and Guthrie, the consequences of the behavior are not instrumental in bringing about learning. The effects of punishment and reward are, according to Guthrie, simply to change the stimulus situation, thereby preventing the unlearning of a response.

Thorndike. E. L. Thorndike is generally credited with introducing the notion of reinforcement in contemporary learning theory through the introduction of the laws of Effect and of Exercise. The Law of Effect states that learning is a consequence of the effect of behavior.

---

*Connectionism is sometimes employed synonymously with *behaviorism.* It refers to a concern with the links (or connections) that appear to form between stimuli and responses when learning occurs (K).

Specifically, those responses that lead to a satisfying state of affairs will tend to be repeated, whereas those which lead to an unpleasant or annoying state will tend not to be repeated. The Law of Exercise says that stimulus-response events that are practiced will tend to be more strongly linked, whereas those that fall into disuse will tend to be forgotten.

For Thorndike, learning consisted of the formation of bonds between stimuli and responses as a function of their repetition and of the consequences of the responses. He labeled the process of learning a *stamping-in* process; forgetting involves *stamping out*. The system can be further detailed through a discussion of five subsidiary laws, the most important of which is the law of multiple responses. This law states in effect that humans faced with a problem situation tend to respond in a variety of ways until one of the responses emitted is reinforced. In other words, learning occurs through a process of *trial and error*. Additional laws are simply formalizations of the observation that behavior is generalizable, that man responds to the most striking features of the environment, that cultural background affects behavior, and that learning through contiguity does occur.

Skinner. B. F. Skinner stands out as one of the great system-makers in twentieth-century psychology. Interestingly, his aim has not been to develop a system or theory of behavior but simply to make careful observations of the behavior of various organisms. The learning model that has resulted from his work is *operant* conditioning, a model that can be described simply as the assertion that learning results from the reinforcement of responses that are emitted by an organism. Skinner's major preoccupation has been with discovering the relationship between reinforcement and response variables. For this reason, his work has dealt largely with the effects of different ways of presenting reinforcement (schedules of reinforcement) on the rate of learning, the response rate, and the extinction rate. Extinction refers to the cessation of a response after reinforcement has been discontinued. Among his most important findings is the fact that learning is facilitated in its initial stages by continuous reinforcement, but extinction time is increased by intermittent reinforcement. Although most of his experimentation was carried on with animals, these results are assumed to be generally applicable to human behavior as well.

One of the techniques developed by Skinner for teaching complex behaviors to animals is *shaping*, which involves reinforcing *successive approximations* to the desired behavior and is widely employed by professional animal trainers.

The applications of Skinner's work to human behavior are discussed by him in two books: *Walden Two* (1948) and *Science and Human Behavior* (1953). In addition, a direct educational application of Skinner's theory is that of programed instruction.

Neobehaviorism

Hull. Clark L. Hull's theoretical approach is labeled hypothetico-deductive. He undertook one of the most ambitious tasks ever undertaken by a psychologist—that of formalizing all knowledge about human behavior in order to make it possible to predict responses on the basis of knowledge about stimuli. The system was never quite completed but nevertheless stands as a monument to formal theory building.

Hull's investigations and consequent formulas and equations deal with three aspects of human behavior: *input* variables, which include physical stimuli as well as such factors as drive conditions, previously learned habits, and amount of reward available; *intervening* variables, which consist mainly of the effects of input variables on the organism; and *output* variables, which are the characteristics of actual behavior in terms of response latency, frequency of responding, and time to extinction. The system may be partly summarized in terms of the following equation: $_sE_R = {_sH_R} \times D \times V \times K$.

Hull described his system in 17 postulates, 133 theorems, and innumerable corollaries from which the nature of his beliefs about learning emerges. One of the central concepts in the theory is habit, which is an S-R connection, or a collection of such connections that forms a *habit family hierarchy*. This habit family hierarchy is a hypothetical ordering of related alternative behaviors by preference. The relatedness of habits results from the fact that they have common goals. According to Hull, behavior is purposive in that it is goal oriented. Reinforcement in the form of the attainment of a goal or in the form of what he labels *antedating goal responses* accounts for the formation of habits. An antedating goal reaction is any one of the many reward-related responses that an organism makes as it nears a goal. For example, as he turns the last corner in a maze, a rat may lick his chops—an antedating goal reaction.

Hull's use of the concept of intervening variables provides a link between his system and neobehaviorism. It is important to note, however, that the Hullian variables are tied directly to input and output variables. They are not intended to be simply inferred hypothetical constructs.

Spence. The Hullian tradition was further carried on by Kenneth Spence. An obvious, but superficial, distinction between Hull and Spence is that some of the symbols employed by Hull have been changed. The major formula is no longer $_sE_R = {_sH_R} \times D \times K$ . . . but is $E = H \times (D + K)$. Interestingly, however, the symbols have the same referents. One other less superficial change is evident in the Spence formula—the change from a multiplicative to an additive function. Drive (D) or reward (K) can be zero without necessarily reducing the potential for responding (E) to zero. In addition, whereas Hull had relied largely on a drive-reduction explanation of motivation, Spence substituted the notion that the antedating goal responses are themselves reinforcing in the absence of the actual reduction of drive. Also, Spence assumed that the strength of a habit is not dependent on reinforcement (as Hull had contended) but that it is related only to the frequency of S-R pairings.

In the final analysis, the two systems resemble each other much more than they differ. Indeed, it is not at all unusual to see references to the Hull-Spence system.

Hebb. D. O. Hebb has advanced a somewhat speculative, neurophysiological proposal for a neobehavioristic theory of human behavior. The mediational activity that is the basis for his explanation of higher mental processes in man is assumed to consist of activity in neurons or groups of neurons arranged in closed loops, or of activity in more complex arrangements of such loops. The closed circuit of related neural cells is labeled a *cell assembly.* Hebb assumes that it is comprised of a number of smaller neural units called *reverberatory loops.* The more complex arrangements of cell assemblies are labeled *phase sequences.* The property of these neural organizational units that is absolutely central to Hebb's theory is that transmission among neurons appears to be facilitated as a function of repeated firing among them. This phenomenon of neural activity ostensibly accounts for learning. A cell assembly corresponds to some simple sensory input—for example, the color of an object or one part of one of its dimensions. Activity in an entire arrangement of assemblies (a phase sequence) corresponds to the whole object. Through learning, cell assemblies and phase sequences eventually achieve some correspondence to the environment. That is, since different parts of an object are usually sensed in contiguity, cell assemblies related to different aspects of an object will often be simultaneously active and will therefore become related.

Hebb has been largely responsible for the development of an arousal-based theory of motivation. This theory is premised on the assumption that optimal human functioning is made possible by a moderate level of arousal and that an organism therefore behaves in such a way as to maintain that level. Other theorists have subsequently incorporated these same notions in their systems (for example, Osgood and Bruner).

Osgood. Charles Osgood presents probably the clearest example of neobehaviorism in contemporary Earth psychology. The model he describes is not intended simply as a proposal for a theory, as was Hebb's, but is meant to encompass all of human behavior — in scope if not in detail.

According to Osgood, human interaction with the environment is a two-stage, three-level process. On the one hand stimuli are sensed and interpreted (decoding); on the other, intentions are translated into behavior (encoding). Each stage consists of three levels distinguishable by the complexity of the neural organization characteristic of each. At the simplest level, impulses are simply transmitted to or from the cortex (projection); at a more complex level, the formation of relationships among neural events occurs (integration); at the highest level, the implicit fractional responses (r_m-s_m) that define *mediation* and account for meaning emerge and are themselves organized (representation).

Within this model, learning consists of changes in neural organization as a function of the repeated co-firing of neurons that relate to sensory or motor events. These neurons are labeled central neural correlates. Integrations involve dependency relationships among central neural correlates and serve to explain conditioning phenomena.

One of Osgood's major contributions takes the form of his explanation for the acquisition of meaning and is reflected in a psycholinguistic test based on his theory: the Illinois Test of Psycholinguistic Ability (ITPA).

A related contribution is in the form of a research tool designed to uncover the meanings that specific stimuli have for people, the *semantic differential*. It consists of a series of bipolar adjectival scales (such as *hot, cold*) on which the subject indicates his spontaneous reaction to a word.

Like Hebb, Osgood espouses a single-drive, arousal-based explanation for human motivation.

Cognitivism

The Gestaltists. Gestalt psychology can be interpreted as a second reaction against the mentalism of pre-twentieth-century Earth psychology. However, unlike the behavioristic reaction, it did not seek to objectify the science so much as to change its methods. Introspection was unacceptable, not because it investigated the wrong topics but because it sought to discover facts about behavior through *analysis*. The Gestalt approach is one of *synthesis;* it asserts clearly that even physical objects cannot be completely known or understood through an analysis of their parts. That *the whole is greater than the sum of its parts* became the familiar Gestalt watchword.

The chief concern of Gestalt psychology was to discover the laws governing perception. It is responsible for the elaboration of such "laws" as *closure, proximity, symmetry, continuity,* and *Praegnanz*. It is largely because of this preoccupation that Gestaltism is considered to be the forerunner of cognitivism.

Among the better known Gestalt psychologists were such men as Kohler, Koffka, and Wertheimer. Lewin's system is also an example of a Gestalt approach. These positions are unified not only in terms of their preoccupation with perception, but also through their rejection of trial-and-error explanations of human learning; their alternative explanation was that people learn through insight.

Ausubel. David P. Ausubel is clearly a cognitive psychologist. He has attempted to develop a nonbehavioristic definition for meaning and, subsequently, to develop a theory to explain meaningful learning. Specifically, he deals primarily with meaningful *verbal* learning, not because other types of learning do not exist but because most classroom learning is of this type — such is the explicit area of his interest.

Ausubel's theory is sometimes referred to as a theory of *subsumption,* which is the process through which new information is learned. Learning involves incorporating (subsuming) material into preexisting cognitive structure. The process appears somewhat complicated. It involves either derivative subsumption, which leads to rapid subsumption and rapid loss of dissociability, or correlative subsumption, which is marked by slower subsumption and longer time to zero dissociability. In other words, obliterative subsumption is a function of the type of initial learning process.

Bruner. Jerome Bruner has developed a loose-knit cognitive theory intended to explain various phenomena in perception, decision making, information processing, conceptualization, and development. Those portions of his work that deal primarily with learning comprise his earlier writings; his more recent interests are largely in the area of development.

The theory is sometimes referred to as a theory of categorizing. The term *category* is synonymous with both *percept* and *concept*. Essentially, to categorize is to treat objects as though they were in some ways equivalent. Accordingly, a category can be thought of as a rule for classifying objects in terms of their properties (attributes). Much of Bruner's early work was devoted to an investigation of the strategies employed by people in learning how to categorize stimulus events both for simple perception and for the attainment of concepts.

Bruner's approach to learning and problem solving is premised on the assumption that the value of what is learned is measurable largely in terms of how well it permits the learner to go *beyond the information given*. He argues that concepts and percepts are useful when organized into systems of related categories (coding systems) that have wide generality.

Bruner also makes use of an arousal-based explanation of motivation — an explanation that is virtually identical to Hebb's. He also borrows extensively from Hebb in describing the neurological mechanisms that humans must possess in order to behave in a manner consistent with his theory.

Piaget. Jean Piaget is not as clearly a cognitive theorist as are Bruner and Ausubel, nor is he as clearly a learning theorist. Indeed, his theory is really a system unto itself. It is not easily compared to other positions.

Piaget's major focus is development. Given the close relationship between learning and development, however, it is not inappropriate to make reference to his *learning* theory. He describes development as the evolution of a child's ability to interact with his world in an increasingly appropriate, realistic, and logical fashion. Part of his work is therefore devoted to a description of children at different stages of development, labeled the sensorimotor stage (birth to 2 years), the preoperational stage (2 to 7 years — comprising preconceptual and intuitive thinking), the period of concrete operations (7 to 11 or 12 years), and the stage of formal operations (11 or 12 to 14 or 15 years). Each stage is marked by characteristic abilities and errors in problem solving, results from activities and abilities of the preceding period, and is a preparation for the next stage.

Another part of Piaget's work is devoted to a discussion of the properties of human children that enable them to make progress in their ontogeny. In this connection, he has evolved a biologically oriented definition of intelligence as an interactive process. Essentially, it is a process involving the two ways of functioning that humans possess. One is defined as the process of exercising previously learned activities (assimilation), and the other consists of modifying behavior (accommodation). An optimal balance between these processes (equilibrium) constitutes maximally adaptive behavior (or maximally *intelligent* behavior).

In addition to studying the characteristics of development *per se*, Piaget has devoted a large portion of his writings to specific topics such as the development of children's concepts of time, space, causality, logic, geometry, and so on.

Cybernetics

A short summary of cybernetics is not given here, largely because it does not represent a new body of knowledge about human behavior, nor does it clearly represent a new approach to that study. Indeed, the attempt to use machines to replicate the behavior of man may well be limited by the amount of information that can be derived about man *from other sources.* Essentially, at this stage in its development, cybernetics is an intriguing game that may well lead to some extremely useful discoveries and/or applications of knowledge. But it is not now a learning theory.

Miller, Galanter, and Pribram have advanced a model of human behavior premised on the notion that man behaves in the manner of a well-programmed self-regulating machine. The TOTE unit that forms the basis of this model provides a simple and potentially useful approach to understanding behavior. Taken alone, however, it too does not represent a new theory or new information regarding human behavior.

Synthesis

The preceding summaries are a brief analysis of the learning positions described in this report. This section and the next constitute a synthesis of the information presented in the summaries.

Two different syntheses are provided: the first in the form of a tabular representation of the vocabulary of each theoretical position; the second in the form of a reduction of theoretical jargonism to the statements of a wise grandmother.

Table 2 is presented as something of a pedagogical device for the student of human learning theory. It may prove useful, particularly for review and examination purposes, to study the contents of the table. The terms associated with each theorist are simply those words or expressions that most clearly identify the position in question and distinguish it from other theories. Table 3 is presented for those who are

Table 2. *Key Words*

Behaviorists			
Watson	*Thorndike*	*Guthrie*	*Skinner*
behaviorism	effect	contiguity	operant
classical conditioning	exercise	one-shot	respondent
reflexes	stamping in	learning	schedules
environmentalism	stamping out	habits	extinction
contiguity	trial and error	threshold	rats
	connectionism	fatigue	shaping
		incompatible	superstition
		stimuli	programed
			instruction

Neobehaviorists			
Hull	*Spence*	*Osgood*	*Hebb*
habit strength	habit	decoding	reverberation
hypothetico-deductive	reaction	encoding	cell assembly
reaction potential	potential	projection	phase sequence
drive	r_G-s_G	integration	neurophysiology
goal reactions	drive	representation	arousal
habit families		semantic	perception
		differential	

Cognitivists			
Gestaltists	*Ausubel*	*Bruner*	*Piaget*
perception	meaningful	categorizing	equilibration
wholes	verbal	perceptual	stages
Praegnanz	learning	readiness	assimilation
closure	subsumption	attributes	accommodation
field	obliteration	coding	operations
vectors	structure	systems	logic
life space	reception	strategies	
	learning		

more visually oriented. It consists of diagrammatic or symbolic representations of aspects of each theory. It should be noted that neither Table 2 nor Table 3 pretends to be a complete representation of the theories in question. Each is based on my own notions of what would be most useful to an Earth reader. Obviously, the tables would both be quite useless for a Koron.

Jargonism

While it would be relatively simple to dismiss differences among theoretical positions as superficial and resulting only from the use

Table 3. *Diagrammatic and Symbolic Representations*

Behaviorism			
Watson	*Thorndike*	*Guthrie*	*Skinner*
$UCS \rightarrow UCR$	1) $S_1 \rightarrow R_1$ (pleasant)	$S_1 \rightarrow R_1$	$R_x + \underline{reinforcement}$
$CS \;\; \rightarrow ?$	2) $S_1 \rightarrow R_1$	$S_1 \rightarrow R_1$	$+ S_1$
——————	1) $\overline{S_2 \rightarrow R_2}$ (unpleasant)		$\downarrow$
$\overline{CS \rightarrow CR}$		$S_1 \rightarrow R_1$	$S_1 \rightarrow R_x$
	2) $S_2 \rightarrow$		

Neobehaviorism			
Hull	*Spence*	*Osgood*	*Hebb*
$_sE_R = {_sH_R} \times D \times V \times K$	$E = H \times (D + K)$		

Cognitivism			
Gestaltists	*Ausubel*	*Bruner*	*Piaget*

content

↑

structure

↑

function

of different terms for the same concepts, it would not be entirely accurate to do so. Obviously, there are some *real* differences among the theoretical positions described in Tables 2 and 3; the respective theorists would probably be among the first to make this assertion. Indeed, it appears to have been somewhat fashionable in the development of theoretical positions to begin by demonstrating how earlier theories could not account for various phenomena judged to be of some psychological significance. For some theorists, the deprecation of other theoretical positions has been a major concern.

However, despite these alleged theoretical distinctions, it is nevertheless true that there are many more similarities among theories than would appear to be the case from a superficial examination of them. Jargon hides many of these similarities, since each theorist seems to feel that it is his right to coin new terms or to use old ones in new ways. But jargon sometimes does more than simply hide the resemblance of a new theory to an old one — frequently it hides the absence of substance. For example, it is difficult to see how a subsumer and a category are different, or to see how subsumption and categorization differ. True, the respective theorists say somewhat different things about each, but if they are saying different things about the same thing (this sentence should cause a small boggle in the human brain), then it would perhaps be wise to use the same terms. A reasonable alternative would seem to be to point out how various definitions of a term are inadequate and then to modify the definition, rather than to begin by changing the label and then providing a definition.

A casual look at Table 2 reveals numerous terms that could almost be used interchangeably. In many cases, another, more familiar, but less jargonistic expression could substitute for either. For example, *integration* is really *classical conditioning* — but so is the formation of a *cell assembly*. A *cell assembly* bears a strong resemblance to a *percept* or *concept*, as does a *category*. A *phase sequence* is the neurological analogue of a *category*, or perhaps of a *schema*. To reach *zero dissociability* is to forget; to forget is to undergo *obliterative subsumption; obliterative subsumption* is defined by *zero dissociability;* to reach zero dissociability is to forget; to forget . . . (even the Koron mind boggles a wee bit). To *stamp in* is to *learn; to stamp out* is *to forget; to forget* is to undergo *obliterative subsumption* . . . whoa! To *decode* is to sense; to *encode* is to respond. *Projection* is *neural transmission* . . . .

But there are some differences. In order to obtain a clearer understanding of these, the reader is advised to study Chapters 1 to 14 of this report (omitting Chapter 13).*

Some Criticisms

If I were to evaluate the state of Earth knowledge about human learning as compared with the Eleven Great Laws, it would be neces-

*Heh, heh! (GRL)

sary to dismiss a great deal of the alleged substance of various theoretical positions. Lefrancois has advised me against making this comparison on the grounds that it might offend someone and drastically reduce his royalties (he is rather stricken with poverty—and other things).*
I have therefore agreed to present some evaluative comments in a relatively systematic way in this section, without totally dismissing any one position. These comments are not meant to be an exhaustive catalogue of all the good and bad features of each theory; indeed, since the comments are somewhat subjective in the first place, they are presented here only as suggestions. The interested reader is invited to expand the evaluation in his own subjective fashion or, alternatively, to consult his grandmother.

Behaviorism. The principal criticism of behaviorism is that through its mechanization of man, it has dehumanized him. Critics point out that man possesses awareness, that feeling is very much a part of behaving, that surely human interaction with the environment is more than simply a matter of stimuli and responses. They contend further that conditioning, in all of its varieties, is not sufficient to explain a great deal of human behavior. They also react negatively to the use of animals in studies whose results are then generalized to human behavior. Behaviorists, on the other hand, maintain that it is only by dealing with those aspects of human functioning that are clearly measurable and definable that valid and reliable conclusions can be reached. They point at the chaotic and confused nature of "mentalistic" psychology. They ask what images, feelings, and sensations are. They also wonder what the significance of these concepts is except as they affect human behavior.

Clearly, then, behaviorism stresses objectivity; in so doing, there is some loss of immediate and obvious relevance. Nevertheless, the approach has proven fruitful in terms of applicable research and theory and appears to be in little danger of being abandoned.

Some specific criticisms can also be leveled at each of the major behavioristic positions. It has been pointed out, for example, that a model of classical conditioning, such as that espoused by Watson, cannot easily account for the acquisition of novel responses. In addition, Hill (1963) raises a number of criticisms of Watson's theory, most of which focus on its incompleteness and lack of logical consistency. It is nevertheless true that Watson, more than anyone else, is responsible for the development of American behaviorism.

*Ditto (GRL).

Guthrie's theory, like Watson's, suffers from its failure to recognize that the effects of behavior are related to learning. In addition, the notion that learning always occurs and is complete in one trial appears to be somewhat unrealistic. Thorndike's work has been subject to a great deal of criticism by early Gestalt psychologists, particularly for its almost exclusive reliance on a trial-and-error explanation for human learning.

The work of B. F. Skinner has also been severely criticized, not so much because of theoretical inconsistencies or errors, but rather because he represents a behaviorism that is sometimes viewed as a potential weapon that will be used against humanity by Machiavellian psychologists. The "theory" itself is expressly not a theory but simply an organized collection of observations. To the extent that the observations are accurate, the system *per se* is relatively impervious to damaging criticism.

Despite the obvious shortcomings of the early behaviorist positions, their influence on the development of human learning theory has not been insignificant. A great deal of the emphasis on experimentation and scientific rigor that characterizes much contemporary theorizing stems from the work of such people as Guthrie and Watson; much of the emphasis on the practical applicability of theory is attributable to the work of Thorndike; and Skinner's contribution to a practical science of behavior can hardly be overestimated.

Neobehaviorism. Critics of neobehavioristic positions advance many of the same arguments that were used in connection with early behaviorism. They point to the disparity between man as he is intuitively understood by grandmothers and man as made up of stimuli, responses, and the intervening processes of neobehaviorism. They argue that surely awareness is more than implicit responses, that thought is sometimes couched in images or feelings not easily reducible to mediating processes, and that the complexity of human information processing and decision making does not easily lend itself to the mechanistic analyses of neobehaviorism. The neobehaviorists counter with the observation that they have retained the precision and objectivity of early behaviorism—an objectivity that seems essential to building a science. At the same time, they have opened the "black box" and have begun to make inferences about processes that obviously intervene between stimuli and responses. But in so doing they have based their inferences solely on observable events or neurological fact. In other words, they claim not to have gone *too* far beyond their data.

The first of the neobehaviorists, Hull, developed a very formal and elaborate, but often imprecise, system. Critics have drawn attention to his use of numbers in equations where the figures are often taken from studies involving only one or two subjects; they have noted the failure of his system to increase the accuracy of predictions about responses, and they have commented on the fact that although Hull ostensibly dealt with human behavior, his experimentation was usually limited to studies of the behavior of rats or, at best, studies of conditioned eyeblink responses in man.

Spence's system can generally be criticized on the same grounds as Hull's since it is not substantially different from it.

Osgood's theory has been attacked by Ausubel primarily on the grounds that although it is intended to account for the acquisition of meaning, it does not really do so. The r_m-s_m processes which, according to Osgood, define meaning are described by Ausubel as representing only connotative aspects of meaning. Accordingly, it is argued that the semantic differential measures only connotation and not denotation.

The proposal for a theory advanced by Donald Hebb is admittedly based on neurophysiological speculation as well as fact. It has been argued that neurologizing is not likely to lead to any new discoveries about learning but is more apt to result in logically plausible but practically useless conceptions of neural functioning. In other words, it is unlikely that neurological speculation will lead to anything more than an explanation for what is already known or suspected about behavior. Of course, the opposite argument can also be advanced. It can be countered that not all neurologizing is based on speculation, that there are sources of information about human neurology that are quite distinct from psychological experimentation, and that it is quite conceivable that knowledge about human neural activity may eventually lead to a better understanding of learning and behavior.

Cognitivism. The critics of cognitive approaches to human learning base many of their objections on the cognitivists' relatively less precise and more subjective approach to information gathering and to theorizing. The extensive use of jargon by many contemporary cognitivists and the seeming lack of agreement among different positions has also been the source of some criticism. Cognitivists counter by pointing out that they are dealing with topics that are of more relevance to human behavior than are questions relating to stimuli and responses and that the investigation of these topics sometimes requires the making of inferences from relatively limited data.

Gestalt psychology has been largely abandoned by some contemporary theorists, partly because the laws of perception do not appear to be directly applicable to learning processes. (Humanistic and group-oriented psychologists are frequently Gestaltic, however.) Both Ausubel and Bruner can be criticized on the grounds that their terminology is sometimes confusing and therefore camouflages similarities between the positions. In addition, it is likely that the use of jargon also serves to make the theories appear more complex and more substantive than they really are.

Piaget's work has been heavily criticized on several counts. His experimental methods, his lack of sampling procedures, the extremely small numbers of subjects employed in most of his studies, and the lack of statistical analysis in his early work have met with some opposition, particularly on the part of experimentally oriented American psychologists. In addition, Piaget has been criticized for overgeneralizing and overtheorizing from his data.

Summary Evaluation

The preceding section is essentially a selected listing of criticisms that can be leveled at each of the major theoretical positions in learning. The evaluation would not be complete without repeating again that each position also has some unique strengths and contributions, as is made evident in earlier chapters of this report.

Contrasting theoretical positions and attempting to discredit some explanations of learning have served as useful devices in the development of new theories. Such apparent disagreement among theorists, however, is often discouraging and frustrating for the student who is searching for *the* correct theoretical position. Perhaps, that position does not exist.

An Alternative

Historically the search in learning theory has been for *one* best way of explaining human behavior. Obviously this effort has been premised on the assumption that there *is* one best explanation. An alternative assumption that leads to a drastically different and potentially extremely useful theoretical orientation can also be advanced. One can assume that there is no one correct theory and that since there are numerous kinds of human learning, there is a need for a large number of different explanations. The resulting "theory" could well be an integration of a variety of concepts that have traditionally been associated with separate positions.

Several recent attempts at integrating knowledge about human learning are based on the assumption described above. Bandura's (1969) description of behavior-control systems is one example of this approach. Melton (1964) provides a second example in his book that describes categories of human learning. These "categories" include topics of interest to most theoretical positions. A third, more detailed and more comprehensive, integration is provided by Robert Gagné (1965, 1970). It is described briefly in the next section, with less emphasis on Gagné's own descriptions of learning than on showing how his theory relates to other theoretical positions.

Robert Gagné: An Integrated Position

Gagné describes eight types of human learning, each relating to one or more of the theories described in this report. However, before listing and defining these eight types of learning, a number of comments should be made about Gagné's general approach. First, the learning types are not completely independent from one another but are in fact hierarchical. The simplest, most basic learning is necessary before the learner can go on to more complex types of learning. A second point is that these types of learning are distinguishable largely in terms of the *conditions that permit the learning to take place;* knowledge of subordinate types of learning is only one of these conditions.

Gagné's Types of Learning

Type I: Signal Learning

Definition: Simple Pavlovian conditioning.

Example: A car horn blasts. A man jumps wildly. The same man sees another car — a quiet one. He jumps wildly again.

Important Theorists: Pavlov, Watson

Type II: Stimulus-Response Learning

Definition: The formation of a *single* connection between a stimulus and a response.

Example: A fat sow is turned clockwise as her proud owner, a psychologist, says gently, "turn." After each complete turn the smiling sow is given a piece of apple. The psychologist does this every day for two years. After 730 apples and 1459 turns (the psychologist ate half the apple once), the sow can now turn when the psychologist says "turn." That is slow stimulus-response learning.

Important Theorists: Skinner, Thorndike, Hull, Spence

Type III: Chaining — Motor Chains

Definition: The connection of a sequence of motor stimulus-response behaviors.

Example: A man is seen removing his teeth. He reaches to his mouth with his hand, opens his mouth and inserts his hand, places the thumb and forefinger on the right upper canine, and pulls. He then does the same for his lower teeth. The S-R chain may be simplified as follows:

```
S → R -------- S ——→ R ------- S ——→ R ---------- S ——————→ R
hand  open      mouth  insert    hand   position     fingers       pull
at    mouth     open   hand      inserted fingers    positioned
mouth
```

Important Theorists: Guthrie, Thorndike, Skinner

Type IV: Chaining — Verbal Associations

Definition: The connection of a sequence of verbal stimulus-response behaviors.

Example: One, two, three, four, five, . . .

Important Theorists: Osgood, Hebb, Bruner

Type V: Discrimination Learning

Definition: Learning to discriminate between highly similar stimulus input. The learning of discriminations is ". . . essentially a matter of establishing numbers of different chains" (Gagné, 1965, p. 115).

Example: The learning of a foreign language involves learning verbal chains in that language. Since these chains are already present in the mother tongue, the learner must discriminate between the two.

Important Theorists: Bruner and Ausubel as well as Hebb and Osgood.

Type VI: Concept Learning

Definition: Concept learning is the opposite of discrimination learning. It involves responding to a set of objects in terms of their similarities.

Example: A child learns that an English setter is a dog. He sees a cat and says "doggie." He has developed a "doggie" concept, albeit an incorrect one.

Important Theorists: Hebb, Osgood, Bruner, Ausubel

Type VII: Rule Learning

Definition: "A rule is an inferred capability that enables the individual to respond to a class of stimulus situations with a class of performances" (1970, p. 191).

Example: A simple rule is exemplified by the statement "psychology is fun." Understanding this rule involves understanding the concept "psychology" and the concept "fun." Many students understand neither.

Important Theorists: Bruner, Ausubel

Type VIII: Problem Solving

Definition: The application of rules in the generation of "higher-order rules." This is the inevitable outcome of applying rules to problems.

Example: Consider the elementary problem of catching a dorabotur. Four rules can be employed in the solution of this simple problem:
1. Doraboturs like snrapes.
2. Snrapes grow in holes 2 feet deep.
3. Doraboturs have tails that are always at least 3 feet long.
4. Doraboturs are harmless.
The solution can be expressed in terms of the higher-order rule: Doraboturs can be pulled out of snrape holes by their tails.

Summary of Chapter 15

This chapter has presented summaries of each of the major theoretical positions discussed in this report. The summaries were followed by a tabulation of the terms that can be employed to identify each position and by an evaluation of these theories. In addition, a brief description of the theory of Robert Gagné was given.
1. One of the problems in evaluating human learning theory is to differentiate among fact, speculation, and wishful thinking.

2. The major divisions in learning theory — behaviorism, neobehaviorism, and cognitivism — can be distinguished in terms of the variables of greatest concern to the theorists in question as well as in terms of the approach to data gathering and science building employed by each.

3. Watson, Guthrie, Thorndike, and Skinner were among the early behaviorists. Watson and Guthrie can be classed as "connectivists in the contiguity tradition," whereas Thorndike and Skinner are "connectionists in the reinforcement tradition" (Hill, 1963).

4. Hull, Osgood, Spence, and Hebb are neobehavioristically oriented. Hull and Spence have attempted the development of a formal hypothetico-deductive system; Hebb has advanced a neurophysiological model of perception and learning; and Osgood has described an explicitly neo-behavioristic two-stage model of human behavior.

5. The Gestaltists, Bruner, Ausubel, and Piaget, can be considered cognitive psychologists. Gestaltism is concerned more with perception than with learning; Bruner has described an information-processing theory; Ausubel's position attempts to explain meaningful verbal learning; and Piaget's system is largely developmental.

6. Jargon hides many similarities among learning theories. It can also serve as effective camouflage for lack of substance.

7. When evaluated in terms of how well they account for all types of human learning and behavior, each theoretical position can be subjected to criticism.

8. Recent attempts to describe various kinds of learning (for example, Bandura, Melton, and Gagné) are premised on the assumption that there is a need for a variety of explanations.

9. Gagné's eight types of learning can be related directly to the theories discussed in this report.

10. The Eleven Great Laws will make all of this meaningful for you, as you approach nearer to the rational perfection we have on Koros.

16a

Kongor's Epilogue

Where Man Now Walks

The development of a science can be compared to a man taking a walk in unfamiliar surroundings. First, he is certain about only one thing—that he desires to investigate the area. He does not yet know where to go or how to get there. But as he walks he gathers information, and sometimes he returns to reexamine something he had seen earlier. Often he pays little attention to his surroundings, heeding only what is already inside himself; at other times he reacts excitedly to his world. As he progresses, he develops prescribed ways of doing things; he also begins to limit the range of phenomena to which he will pay attention. His search becomes more controlled, less haphazard, and more manageable. It also seems to become more fruitful. (But is it really?)

Earlier chapters of this report have retraced the steps of psychology, particularly as it relates to human learning and behavior. Throughout these chapters, a picture has been drawn of men attempting to map the whole of the area they explored, often from very different perspectives but always with the hope of arriving at explanations that would be accurate for large segments of human behavior. To conclude the report at this point, however, would be to leave it more incomplete than it should be—for one major reason. That is, it is not possible, on the basis of the preceding chapters, to know precisely where man now walks or in what direction he is going. It is probably true that much of his wandering in the area of human behavior has taken the form of large circles —this fact, in itself, would make it difficult to project a continuing direction of exploration. In addition, this wandering has been guided by the hope of making significant discoveries about the whole area.

It is largely correct to say that the contemporary psychologist has not changed the direction of his steps; nor has he abandoned those areas that most concerned his predecessors. *He is simply walking in smaller circles.*

This last sentence is meant less as a derogatory statement than as a simple description of contemporary learning "theorists." In effect, the analogy is meant to highlight the primary distinction between the psychologists discussed in earlier chapters of this report and those whose work is currently gaining prominence. Whereas the psychologists of past decades were theoreticians and researchers, today's psychologists are researchers first and *sometimes* theoreticians. Two developments in learning psychology are of special note—a de-emphasis on theory *per se* and on the establishment of new theoretical positions in contrast to other existing theories, and a growing emphasis on the explanation of *small* aspects of human behavior. Accordingly, it is becoming increasingly difficult to find integrations of knowledge about human behavior in recent psychological literature. Instead, books and journals abound with detailed descriptions of specific phenomena such as memory and recall, attention, verbal learning, discrimination learning, and operant behavior. Texts on learning and related processes are often not so much summaries of information on these subjects as they are detailed compendia of related pieces of research. In summary, the current approach appears to be in the direction of a decreased preoccupation with theories and increased specificity. Indeed, the label *cognitive*, as it applies to a great deal of contemporary *learning psychology*, refers more to a collection of topics than to an integrated explanation of selected behavioral phenomena. These topics are precisely those mentioned earlier in this report—perception, problem solving, concept formation, and so on. The recent research on these topics and in such other currently exciting areas as verbal learning, attention, and applications of operant research are not detailed in this report. As the assiduous reader has probably discovered by now, the report deals primarily with *theories* of learning. In addition, a more extensive coverage of this research is provided in another report I have left with the good doctor. The present text can be considered a necessary introduction to this other report since contemporary research is typically premised on the better-known theories of learning. The following tabulation is provided as a partial summary of some learning-related areas of research that are presently receiving a great deal of attention. In addition, some representative researchers are referenced for each area.

Topic	References
1. Operant behavior	D. M. Baer et al. (1967) S. W. Bijou & D. M. Baer (1961a, 1961b) O. R. Lindsley (1960, 1963) O. I. Lovaas (1966)
2. Verbal learning	A. W. Staats (1964) A. W. Staats & C. K. Staats (1961) B. J. Underwood & R. W. Schultz (1960)
3. Discrimination learning	J. S. Brown (1965) H. F. Harlow (1959) W. Kintsch (1970)
4. Concept formation	H. Kendler (1964) V. Neisser (1967)
5. Attention	D. Zeaman & B. House (1963)

The interested reader is invited to pursue these topics further through his local library — or, alternatively, to await the appearance of my next report.

Farewell, my children.*

---

*P. S. If you enjoyed this text, buy a copy for a friend or for your grandmother. Lefrancois needs the royalties. (K)

16b

Lefrancois' Epilogue

Kongor is no longer with us. He has now been gone for almost 3 months, but the children still ask for him every day. He was our friend.

We didn't understand him very well, especially when he first arrived. I remember how proud he was when he talked about his people, the Korons, about their cold, calculated, deliberate adherence to reason — about their complete lack of emotion. If there is a God on Koros, then it must surely be the most rational and logical being possible, and if there is a devil he must be highly emotional. Indeed, Kongor was forever making comments intended to show how much better we would be if we were rational rather than emotional. And in doing so he made two fundamental errors, one of which prevented him from really understanding human behavior. The other may, by now, have cost him his life.

Kongor's first error was his failure to realize that emotion and reason are compatible — indeed, both are necessary for human and, I suspect, for Koron functioning. So deeply ingrained was Kongor's belief that one cannot be both emotional and rational at the same time that he failed to see the contradiction between this belief and several of the passages of his report. For example, in Chapter 3 he wrote:

333

> While emotion and reason are often contrasted, they are not necessarily incompatible. Indeed, it is often abundantly *reasonable* to react on the basis of emotions and quite unreasonable not to do so.

Or again, also in Chapter 3:

> The role of emotions in behavior can be summarized in Piaget's (1967) terms. He sees emotion or affect as the force that energizes behavior, whereas reason or more intellectual factors determine the course. It appears axiomatic that learning will not occur unless there is *interest* — and interest is an emotion.

It is highly ironic that a being as intelligent as Kongor obviously was could arrive at such statements on the basis of psychological literature but remain unable to relate them to our behavior. Even more ironic is the second basic error made by Kongor — his inability to admit that he himself (and probably all other Korons) was subject to emotional reactions. The emotional aspect of his personality was almost immediately clear to us, despite Kongor's anxious protests. He initially *feared* our dog; he was *lonesome* for his Blip; he *wished* that humans were more rational; he was wildly *exuberant* when he danced in the rain and *remorseful* when chastised for so doing, and he was deeply *depressed, plaintive*, and *frightened* when he had a cold and thought he would die. Yes, Kongor was clearly emotional, but he was also extremely rational. His failure to consciously realize his emotionality was probably largely a function of the Koron culture — a culture that not only deifies reason, but also unceremoniously eliminates all members who violate the Great Law that describes Koron behavior as rational.

In his quest to understand and report on the dominant Earth species, man, Kongor was considerably hampered by a third basic error. Although he was forever pointing out similarities between Blips and humans, he never stopped to consider that we might be two species of the same evolutionary ancestry — a possibility that strikes me as highly probable, not only because of the behavioral similarities between us, but also because of the remarkable physical resemblance. But Blips are a subservient race on Koros; humans are dominant on Earth. This simple fact probably blinded Kongor.

Poor Kongor. Rational and reasonable, yes, but not cold and unemotional. As time passed, he became more and more lovable. He laughed and played with the children (activities which he actively shunned when he first arrived); he rejoiced with the changing seasons; he danced in the snow and the rain; he wept at sad movies; he became excited as Christmas approached and was ecstatic as he opened his presents.

He probably knew that he had broken one of the Eleven Great Laws that day when I took him, for the last time, across the fields and into the small wood where he had hidden his landing craft. He rode on the back of my motorcycle, but he didn't laugh when we sailed over little hills or turned a particularly exhilarating corner.

He was sad and worried.

When we arrived at the spacecraft, he took out a spare sonarduct receiver which he left with me and which I now guard with my very life. Kongor then demonstrated how a sonarduct transmitter works; he contacted Koros in order to inform his superiors that he was proceeding to Mars according to instructions.

Then the blow fell!

His orders were changed! He was ordered to return directly to the Androneas system and to report to Koros for reevaluation. His superiors had read this report and suspected that he had broken one of the Eleven Great Laws.

He has returned to Koros. He was crying when he left, but his last words were, "I will convince them of my innocence. I will sonarduct the Eleven Great Laws back to you, and I WILL RETURN!"

We hope so.

Kongor

References

Allport, F. H. *Theories of perception and the concept of structure.* New York: John Wiley, 1955.

Anastasi, A. Heredity, environment and the question "how?" *Psychological Review,* 1958, **65**, 197–208.

Anderson, A. R. *Minds and machines.* Englewood Cliffs, New Jersey: Prentice-Hall, 1964.

Ashby, W. R. *An introduction to cybernetics.* London: Chapman & Hall, 1961.

Asimov, I. *The human brain.* New York: Signet, 1963.

Athey, I. J. & Rubadeau, D. O. (Eds.) *Educational implications of Piaget's theory.* Waltham, Mass.: Ginn-Blaisdell, 1970.

Ausubel, D. P. *The psychology of meaningful verbal learning.* New York: Grune & Stratton, 1963.

Ausubel, D. P. *Educational psychology: A cognitive view.* New York: Holt, Rinehart and Winston, 1968.

Ausubel, D. P. & Anderson, L. C. *Readings in the psychology of cognition.* New York: Holt, Rinehart and Winston, 1965.

Ausubel, D. P. & Robinson, F. G. *School learning: An introduction to educational psychology.* New York: Holt, Rinehart and Winston, 1969.

Ayllon, T. & Michael, J. The psychiatric nurse as a behavioral engineer. *Journal of the Experimental Analysis of Behavior,* 1959, **2,** 323–334.

Babich, F. R., Jacobson, A. L., Bubash, S., & Jacobson, A. Transfer of learning to naive rats by injection of ribonucleic acid extracted from trained rats. *Science,* 1965, **149**, 656–657.

Baer, D. M., Peterson, R. S., & Sherman, J. A. The development of imitation by reinforcing behavioral similarity to a model. *Journal of the Experimental Analysis of Behavior,* 1967, **10**, 405–416.

Baldwin, A. L. *Theories of child development.* New York: John Wiley, 1967.

Bandura, A. Behavioral modifications through modelling procedures. In Krasner, L. & Ullmann, L. P. (Eds.), *Research in behavior modification.* New York: Holt, Rinehart and Winston, 1967.

Bandura, A. *Principles of behavior modification.* New York: Holt, Rinehart and Winston, 1969.

Bandura, A., Grusec, J. E., & Menlove, S. L. The vicarious extinction of avoidance behavior. *Journal of Personality and Social Psychology,* 1967, **5**, 16–23.

Bandura, A., Ross, D., & Ross, S. A. Imitation of film mediated aggressive models. *Journal of Abnormal and Social Psychology,* 1963, **66**, 3–11.

Bandura, A. & Walters, R. *Social learning and personality development.* New York: Holt, Rinehart and Winston, 1963.

Barnard, C. W., Wolfe, H. D., & Graveline, D. E. Sensory deprivation under null gravity conditions. *American Journal of Psychiatry,* 1962, **118**, 921–925.

Bartlett, S. C. *Remembering.* Cambridge: Cambridge University Press, 1932.

Bennett, E. L. & Calvin, N. Failure to train planarians reliably. *Neuro-sciences Research Program Bulletin,* 1964, **2**, July–August issue.

Berlyne, D. E. *Conflict arousal and curiosity.* New York: McGraw-Hill, 1960.

Berlyne, D. E. *Structure and direction in thinking.* New York: John Wiley, 1965.

Berlyne, D. E. Curiosity and exploration. *Science,* 1966, **153**, 25–33.

Bernard, L. L. *Instinct: A study in social psychology.* New York: Holt, Rinehart and Winston, 1924.

Bexton, W. H., Heron, W., & Scott, T. H. Effects of decreased variation in the sensory environment. *Canadian Journal of Psychology,* 1954, **8**, 70–76.

Bijou, S. W. & Baer, D. M. *Child development I: A systematic and empirical theory.* New York: Appleton-Century-Crofts, 1961. (a)

Bijou, S. W. & Baer, D. M. *Child development II: Universal stage of infancy.* New York: Appleton-Century-Crofts, 1961. (b)

Bijou, S. W. & Sturges, P. S. Positive reinforcers for experimental studies with children — consumables and manipulatables. *Child Development,* 1959, **30**, 151–170.

Birnbrauer, J. S. & Lawler, J. Token reinforcement for learning. *Mental Retardation,* 1964, **2**, 275–279.

Birnbrauer, J. S., Wolf, M. N., Kidder, J. D., & Tague, C. E. Classroom behavior of retarded pupils with token reinforcement. *Journal of Experimental Child Psychology,* 1965, **2**, 219–235.

Bitterman, M. E. Toward a comparative psychology of learning. *American Psychologist,* 1960, **15**, 704–712.

Bitterman, M. E. Learning in animals. In H. Helson & W. Bevan (Eds.), *Contemporary approaches to psychology.* Princeton: Van Nostrand, 1967.

Bitterman, M. E. Thorndike and the problem of animal intelligence. *American Psychologist,* 1969, **24**, 444–453.

Bowlby, J. *Maternal care and mental health.* Geneva: World Health Organization Monograph Series, 1951.

Brehm, J. W. & Cohen, A. R. *Explorations in cognitive dissonance.* New York: John Wiley, 1962.

Brim, O. G., Jr., & Wheeler, S. *Socialization after childhood: Two essays.* New York: John Wiley, 1966.

Broadbent, D. E. Speaking and listening simultaneously. *Journal of Experimental Psychology,* 1952, **43**, 267–273.

Broadbent, D. E. *Perception and communication.* London: Pergamon Press, 1958.

Brown, J. S. Generalization and discrimination. In D. I. Mostossky (Ed.), *Stimulus generalization.* Stanford: Stanford University Press, 1965. Pp. 7–23.

Bruner, J. S. *Contemporary approaches to cognition.* Cambridge: Harvard University Press, 1957. Pp. 41–69. (a)

Bruner, J. S. On perceptual readiness. *Psychological Review,* 1957, **64**, 123–152. (b)

Bruner, J. S. *The process of education.* Cambridge: Harvard University Press, 1961.

Bruner, J. S. *On knowing: Essays for the left hand.* Cambridge: Harvard University Press, 1963.

Bruner, J. S. *Toward a theory of instruction.* Cambridge: Harvard University Press, 1966.

Bruner, J. S. *Processes of cognitive growth: Infancy.* Clark University Press, 1968.

Bruner, J. S., Goodnow, J. J., & Austin, G. A. *A study of thinking.* New York: John Wiley, 1956.

Bruner, J. S., Olver, R. R., & Greenfield, P. M. *Studies in cognitive growth.* New York: John Wiley, 1966.

Butler, R. A. & Harlow, H. S. Discrimination learning and learning sets to visual exploration incentives. *Journal of Genetic Psychology,* 1957, **57**, 257–264.

Campbell, D. T. & Stanley, J. C. *Experimental and quasi-experimental designs for research.* Chicago: Rand McNally, 1963.

Cannon, W. B. *Bodily changes in pain, hunger, fear and rage.* (2nd ed.) New York: Appleton-Century-Crofts, 1929.

Cannon, W. B. *The wisdom of the body.* New York: W. W. Norton, 1939.

Chaplin, J. P. & Krawiec, T. S. *Systems and theories of psychology.* New York: Holt, Rinehart and Winston, 1960.

Cherry, E. C. Some experiments on the recognition of speech, with one and with two ears. *Journal of the Acoustical Society of America,* 1953, **25**, 975–979.

Cherry, E. C. & Taylor, W. K. Some further experiments on the recognition of speech with one and two ears. *Journal of the Acoustical Society of America,* 1954, **26**, 554–559.

Commons, W. D. & Fagin, B. *Principles of educational psychology.* New York: Ronald Press, 1954.

Conrad, R. & Hille, B. A. The decay theory of immediate memory and pace recall. *Canadian Journal of Psychology,* 1958, **12**, 1–6.

Côté, A. D. J. Flexibility and conservation acceleration. Unpublished doctoral dissertation, University of Alberta, Edmonton, Alberta, 1968.

Craig, R. C. Directed versus independent discovery of established relations. *Journal of Educational Psychology,* 1956, **47,** 223–234.

Crespi, L. Quantitative variation of incentive and performance in the white rat. *American Journal of Psychology*, 1942, **55**, 467–517.

DeCecco, J. P. *The psychology of learning and instruction: Educational psychology.* New Jersey: Prentice-Hall, 1968.

Deese, J. & Hulse, S. H. *The psychology of learning.* (3rd ed.) New York: McGraw-Hill, 1967.

Delgado, J. M. R. *Physical control of the mind.* New York: Harper & Row, 1969.

Deutsch, J. A. & Deutsch, D. Attention: Some theoretical considerations. *Psychological Review*, 1963, **70**, 80–90.

Ebbinghaus, H. *Memory.* (1885) Translated by H. A. Ruger & C. E. Busenius. New York: Teacher's College, 1913. Reissued as paperback, New York: Dover, 1964.

Eriksen, C. W. & Johnson, H. J. Storage and decay characteristics of non-attended auditory stimuli. *Journal of Experimental Psychology*, 1964, **68**, 28–36.

Ferguson, L. W. The use of nonveridical heartrate feedback as an adjunct to modeling technique in the extinction of avoidance response. Unpublished doctoral dissertation, University of Alberta, Edmonton, Alberta, 1968.

Ferster, C. B. Positive reinforcement and behavioral deficits in autistic children. *Child Development*, 1961, **32**, 437–456.

Ferster, C. B. & deMyer, M. K. Method for the experimental analysis of the behavior of autistic children. *American Journal of Orthopsychiatry*, 1962, **32**, 89–98.

Festinger, L. *A theory of cognitive dissonance.* Stanford: Stanford University Press, 1957.

Festinger, L. Cognitive dissonance. *Scientific American*, October 1962.

Flavell, J. H. *The developmental psychology of Jean Piaget.* Princeton, New Jersey: Van Nostrand, 1963.

Fowler, H. *Curiosity and exploratory behavior.* New York: Macmillan, 1965.

French, J. D. The reticular formation. *Scientific American*, May 1957.

Freund, K. Some problems in the treatment of homosexuality. In H. J. Eysenck (Ed.), *Behavior therapy and the neuroses.* New York: Pergamon, 1960.

Furth, H. G. *Piaget and knowledge.* Englewood Cliffs, New Jersey: Prentice-Hall, 1969.

Furth, H. G. *Piaget for teachers.* Englewood Cliffs, New Jersey: Prentice-Hall, 1970.

Gagné, R. M. *The conditions of learning.* (1st ed.) New York: Holt, Rinehart and Winston, 1965.

Gagné, R. M. *The conditions of learning.* (2nd ed.) New York: Holt, Rinehart and Winston, 1970.

Galton, F. *Hereditary genesis: An inquiry into its laws and consequences.* New York: D. Appleton & Co., 1870.

Ginsberg, H. & Opper, S. *Piaget's theory of intellectual development.* Englewood Cliffs, New Jersey: Prentice-Hall, 1969.

Goldschmid, M. L. & Bentler, P. M. *Conservation concept diagnostic kit: Manual and keys.* San Diego, Calif.: Educational and Industrial Testing Service, 1968.

Greenspoon, J. The reinforcing effect of two spoken sounds on the frequency of two responses. *American Journal of Psychology*, 1955, **68**, 409–416.

Gunderson, K. The imitation game. In A. R. Anderson (Ed.), *Mind and machines.* Englewood Cliffs, New Jersey: Prentice-Hall, 1964.

Guthrie, E. R. *The psychology of learning.* New York: Harper & Row, 1935.

Guthrie, E. R. *The psychology of learning.* (Rev. ed.) New York: Harper & Row, 1952.

Guthrie, J. T. Expository instruction versus a discovery method. *Journal of Educational Psychology,* 1967, **58**, 45–49.

Harlow, H. F. Learning set and error factor theory. In S. Koch (Ed.), *Psychology: A study of a science.* Vol. 2. New York: McGraw-Hill, 1959.

Haslerud, G. N. & Meyers, S. The transfer value of given and individually derived principles. *Journal of Educational Psychology,* 1958, **49,** 293–298.

Hebb, D. O. *The organization of behavior.* New York: John Wiley, 1949.

Hebb, D. O. *A textbook of psychology.* (1st ed.) Philadelphia: W. B. Saunders, 1958.

Hebb, D. O. The American Revolution. *American Psychologist,* 1960, **15**, 735–745.

Hebb, D. O. *A textbook of psychology.* (2nd ed.) Philadelphia: W. B. Saunders, 1966.

Hebron, M. E. *Motivated learning.* London: Methuen, 1966.

Hellyer, S. Supplementary report: Frequency of stimulus presentation and short-term decrement in recall. *Journal of Experimental Psychology,* 1962, **64**, 650.

Heron, W. The pathology of boredom. *Scientific American,* January 1957.

Heron, W., Doane, B. K., & Scott, T. H. Visual disturbances after prolonged perceptual isolation. *Canadian Journal of Psychology,* 1956, **10**, 13–18.

Hess, E. H. Imprinting in animals. *Scientific American,* 1958, **198,** 81–90.

Hewett, F. *The emotionally disturbed child in the classroom.* Boston: Allyn and Bacon, 1968.

Hilgard, E. R. & Bower, G. H. *Theories of learning.* (3rd ed.) New York: Appleton-Century-Crofts, 1966.

Hill, W. S. *Learning: A survey of psychological interpretations.* San Francisco: Chandler Publishing Co., 1963.

Holland, J. G. & Skinner, B. F. *The analysis of behavior: A program for self-instruction.* New York: McGraw-Hill, 1961.

Hovland, C. I. Computing simulation of thinking. *American Psychologist,* 1960, **15**, 687–693.

Hovland, C. I. & Hunt, E. B. Computer simulation of concept attainment. *Behavioral Science,* 1960, **5**, 265–267.

Hull, C. L. *Principles of behavior.* New York: Appleton-Century-Crofts, 1943.

Hull, C. L. *Essentials of behavior.* New Haven: Yale University Press, 1951.

Hull, C. L. *A behavior system.* New Haven: Yale University Press, 1952.

Hulse, S. H., Jr. Amount and percentage of reinforcement and duration of goal confinement in conditioning and extinction. *Journal of Experimental Psychology,* 1958, **56**, 48–57.

Hunt, J. McV. *Intelligence and experience.* New York: Ronald Press, 1961.

Hurlock, E. B. *Child development.* New York: McGraw-Hill, 1964.

Irwin, O. C. & Weiss, L. A. The effect of clothing on the general and vocal activity of the new born infant. *University of Iowa Studies in Child Welfare;* 1934, **9**, 149–162.

Isaacs, N. *The growth of understanding in the young child.* London: The Education Supply, 1961.

Jacobson, A. L., Babich, F. R., Bubash, S., & Jacobson, A. Differential approach tendencies produced by injection of ribonucleic acid from trained rats. *Science,* 1965, **150,** 636–637.

James, W. *The principles of psychology.* New York: Holt, Rinehart and Winston, 1890.

Jensen, A. R. Social class, race and genetics: Implications for education. *American Educational Research Journal,* 1968, **5,** 1–42.

Keller, F. S. *Learning: Reinforcement theory.* (2nd ed.) New York: Random House, 1969.

Kendler, H. H. A concept of the concept. In A. W. Melton (Ed.), *Categories of human learning.* New York: Academic Press, 1964. Pp. 212–233.

Kessen, W. *The child.* New York: John Wiley, 1965.

Kintsch, W. *Learning, memory and conceptual processes.* New York: John Wiley, 1970.

Koffka, K. Perception: An introduction to gestalt theory. *Psychological Bulletin,* 1922, **19,** 531–585.

Koffka, K. *The growth of the mind.* New York: Harcourt, Brace & World, 1925.

Koffka, K. *Principles of gestalt psychology.* New York: Harcourt, Brace & World, 1935.

Kohler, W. *The mentality of the apes.* New York: Harcourt, Brace & World, 1927.

Kohler, W. *Gestalt psychology.* New York: Liveright Publishing, 1929.

Kohler, W. Gestalt psychology today. *American Psychologist,* 1959, **14,** 727–734.

Konorski, J. M. D. *Integrative activity of the brain.* Chicago: The University of Chicago Press, 1967.

Krech, D. Rosenzweig, M., & Bennett, E. L. Effects of environmental complexity and training on brain chemistry. *Journal of Comparative and Physiological Psychology,* 1960, **53,** 509–519.

Krech, D., Rosenzweig, M., & Bennett, E. L. Relations between brain chemistry and problem-solving among rats raised in enriched and impoverished environments. *Journal of Comparative and Physiological Psychology,* 1962, **55,** 801–807.

Krech, D., Rosenzweig, M., & Bennett, E. L. Environmental impoverishment, social isolation, and changes in brain chemistry and anatomy. *Physiology and Behavior,* 1966, **1,** 99–104.

Laurendeau, M. & Pinard, A. *Causal thinking in the child: A genetic and experimental approach.* New York: International Universities Press, 1962.

Lefrancois, G. R. The acquisition of concepts of conservation. Unpublished doctoral dissertation, University of Alberta, Edmonton, Alberta, 1966.

Lefrancois, G. R. Jean Piaget's developmental model: Equilibration-through-adaptation. *Alberta Journal of Educational Research,* 1967, **13,** 161–171.

Lefrancois, G. R. A treatment hierarchy for the acceleration of conservation of substance. *Canadian Journal of Psychology,* 1968, **22,** 277–284.

Lefrancois, G. R. *Psychology for teaching: A bear always faces the front.* Belmont, Calif.: Wadsworth Publishing Co., 1972.

Lewin, K. *A dynamic theory of personality.* Translated by B. K. Adams & K. E. Zener. New York: McGraw-Hill, 1935.

Lewin, K. *Principles of topological psychology.* Translated by F. Heider & G. N. Heider. New York: McGraw-Hill, 1936.

Lewin, K. Frontiers in group dynamics. *Human Relations,* 1947, **1**, 5–41.

Lewin, K. *Field theory in social science.* New York: Harper & Row, 1951.

Lindsley, O. R. Characteristics of the behavior of chronic psychotics as revealed by free operant conditioning methods. *Diseases of the Nervous System,* 1960, **21**(Monogr. Suppl.).

Lindsley, O. R. Free operant conditioning and psychotherapy. *Current Psychiatric Therapies.* Vol. 3. New York: Grune & Stratton, 1963, 47–56.

Loess, H. Pro-active inhibition in short-term memory. *Journal of Verbal Learning and Verbal Behavior,* 1964, **3**, 362–368.

Lorenz, K. *King Solomon's ring.* London: Methuen, 1952.

Lovaas, O. I. A program for the establishment of speech in psychotic children. In J. K. Wing (Ed.), *Early childhood autism.* Oxford: Pergamon, 1966.

Lovaas, O. I., Berberich, J. P., Perloff, B. S., & Schaeffer, B. Acquisition of imitative speech by schizophrenic children. *Science,* 1966, **151**, 705–707.

Luria, A. R. *The mind of a mnemonist.* New York: Avon Books, 1968.

Maier, H. W. *Three theories of child development.* New York: Harper & Row, 1965.

Marx, M. H. & Hillix, W. A. *Systems and theories in psychology.* New York: McGraw-Hill, 1963.

Maslow, A. H. *Motivation and personality.* New York: Harper & Row, 1954.

McConnell, J. D. Memory transfer through cannibalism in planarians. *Journal of Neuro-Psychiatry,* 1962, **3**(Monogr. Suppl. 1).

McDougall, W. *An introduction to social psychology.* London: Methuen, 1908.

McNeil, A. B. *Human socialization.* Belmont, Calif.: Brooks/Cole, 1969.

Melton, A. W. Implications of short-term memory for a general theory of memory. *Journal of Verbal Learning and Verbal Behavior,* 1963, **2**, 1–21.

Melton, A. W. *Categories of human learning.* New York: Academic Press, 1964.

Miller, G. A., Galanter, E., & Pribram, K. H. *Plans and the structure of behavior.* New York: Henry Holt & Co., 1960.

Miller, N. E. Learnable drives and rewards. In S. S. Stevens (Ed.), *Handbook of experimental psychology.* New York: John Wiley, 1951.

Miller, N. E. & Dollard, J. C. *Social learning and imitation.* New Haven: Yale University Press, 1941.

Moray, N. Attention in dichotic listening: Affective cues and the influence of instruction. *Quarterly Journal of Experimental Psychology,* 1959, **11**, 56–60.

Moray, N. *Cybernetics.* New York: Hawthorne Books, 1963.

Mouly, G. J. *Psychology for effective teaching.* (2nd ed.) New York: Holt, Rinehart and Winston, 1968.

Murdock, B. B., Jr. The retention of individual items. *Journal of Experimental Psychology,* 1961, **62**, 618–625.

Murray, H. A. *Explorations in personality.* New York: Oxford University Press, 1938.

Neisser, V. *Cognitive psychology.* New York: Appleton-Century-Crofts, 1967.

Newell, A., Shaw, J. C., & Simon, H. A. Empirical explorations with a logic theory machine. *Proceedings of the Joint Western Computer Conference,* Institute of Radio Engineers, 1957, 218–230.

Newell, A., Shaw, J. C., & Simon, H. A. Elements of a theory of human problem-solving. *Psychological Review,* 1958, **65**, 151–166.

Newell, A. & Simon, H. A. The logic theory machine: A complex information processing system. *Transactions on Information Theory,* Institute of Radio Engineers, 1956, IT-2, 61–69.

Norman, D. A. *Memory and attention: An introduction into human information processing.* New York: John Wiley, 1969.

O'Leary, K. D. & Becker, W. C. Behavior modification of an adjustment class: A token reinforcement program. *Exceptional Children,* 1967, **33,** 637–642.

Olson, D. R. The role of verbal rules in the cognitive processes of children. Unpublished doctoral dissertation, University of Alberta, Edmonton, Alberta, 1963.

Osgood, C. E. A behavioristic analysis of perception and language as cognitive phenomena. In *Contemporary Approaches to Cognition,* Cambridge: Harvard University Press, 1957.

Osgood, C. E., Suci, G. P., & Tannenbaum, P. H. *The measurement of meaning.* Urbana: University of Illinois Press, 1957.

Peel, E. A. *The pupil's thinking.* London: Oldbourne, 1960.

Peterson, L. R. & Peterson, N. J. Short-term retention of individual verbal items. *Journal of Experimental Psychology,* 1959, **58,** 193–198.

Phillips, John L. *The origins of intellect.* San Francisco: W. H. Freeman, 1969.

Piaget, J. *The language and thought of the child.* New York: Harcourt, Brace & World, 1926.

Piaget, J. *The child's conception of the world.* New York: Harcourt, Brace & World, 1929.

Piaget, J. *The child's conception of physical causality.* London: Kegan Paul, 1930.

Piaget, J. *The moral judgement of the child.* London: Kegan Paul, 1932.

Piaget, J. *Le développement de la notion de temps chez l'enfant.* Paris: Presses Univer. France, 1946.

Piaget, J. *The psychology of intelligence.* New York: Harcourt, Brace & World, 1950.

Piaget, J. *Play, dreams and imitation in childhood.* New York: W. W. Norton, 1951.

Piaget, J. *Logic and psychology.* New York: Basic Books, 1957.

Piaget, J. Logique et équilibre dans les comportements du suject. In L. Apostel, B. Mandelbrot, & J. Piaget (Eds.), *Logique et équilibre, études d'épistémologie génétique.* 1957, **2,** 27–117.

Piaget, J. The stages of the intellectual development of the child. *Bulletin of the Menninger School of Psychiatry,* March 6, 1961.

Piaget, Jean. *Biologie et connaissance.* Paris: Gallinard, 1967.

Piaget, J. *On the development of memory and identity.* Worcester, Mass.: Clark University Press, 1968.

Piaget, J. & Inhelder, B. Le développement des quantités chez l'enfant. *Neuchatel: Délachauxet Niestlé,* 1941.

Piaget, J. & Inhelder, B. *The child's conception of space.* New York: W. W. Norton, 1956.

Pollack, I. Message uncertainty and message reception. *Journal of Acoustical Society of America,* 1959, **31,** 1500–1508.

Postman, L. Reward and punishments in human learning. In L. Postman (Ed.), *Psychology in the making.* New York: Knox, 1962.

Premack, D. Reinforcement theory. In D. Levine (Ed.), *Nebraska symposium on motivation,* University of Nebraska Press, 1965. Pp. 123–180.

Raths, L. E. & Burrell, A. P. *Understanding the problem child.* West Orange, New Jersey: The Economics Press, 1963.

Razran, G. The observable unconscious and the inferable conscious in current Soviet psycho-physiology: Introspective conditioning, semantic conditioning, and the orienting reflex. *Psychological Review*, 1961, **68**, 109–119.

Reese, E. P. *The analysis of human operant behavior*. Dubuque, Iowa: W. N. C. Brown, 1966.

Risley, T. & Wolf, M. Establishing functional speech in echolalic children. *Behavior Research and Therapy*, 1967, **5**, 73–88.

Rogers, C. R. *Client-centered therapy: Its current practice, implications and theory*. Boston: Houghton Mifflin, 1951.

Rogers, C. R. *Freedom to learn*. Columbus, Ohio: Charles E. Merrill, 1969.

Rogers, C. R. & Skinner, B. F. Some issues concerning the control of human behavior: A symposium. *Science*, 1956, **124**, 1057–1066.

Rosenthal, R. & Fode, K. L. The effect of experimenter bias on the performance of the albino rat. *Behavioral Science*, 1963, **8**, 183–189.

Rosenthal, R. & Lawson, R. A longitudinal study of the effects of experimenter bias on the operant learning of laboratory rats. *Journal of Psychiatric Research*, 1964, **2**, 61–72.

Schachter, S. & Singer, J. Cognitive, social and physiological determinants of emotional state. *Psychological Review*, 1962, **69**, 379–399.

Schultz, D. P. *Sensory restriction: Effects on behavior*. New York: Academic Press, 1965.

Sears, R. R., Maccoby, E. P., & Lewin, H. *Patterns of child rearing*. Evanston: Row, Peterson, 1957.

Shurley, J. T. Stress and adaptation as related to sensory/perceptual isolation research. *Military Medicine*, 1966, **131**, 254–258.

Skinner, B. F. *The behavior of organisms: An experimental analysis*. New York: Appleton-Century-Crofts, 1938.

Skinner, B. F. *Walden Two*. New York: Macmillan, 1948.

Skinner, B. F. How to teach animals. *Scientific American*, December 1951, **185**, 26–29.

Skinner, B. F. *Science and human behavior*. New York: Macmillan, 1953.

Skinner, B. F. *Verbal behavior*. New York: Appleton-Century-Crofts, 1957.

Skinner, B. F. *Cumulative record*. (Rev. ed.) New York: Appleton-Century-Crofts, 1961.

Smedslund, J. The acquisition of conservation of substance and weight in children. I. Introduction. *Scandinavian Journal of Psychology*, 1961, **2**, 11–20. (a)

Smedslund, J. The acquisition of conservation of substance and weight in children. II. External reinforcement of conservation of weight and of operations of addition and subtraction. *Scandinavian Journal of Psychology*, 1961, **2**, 71–84. (b)

Smedslund, J. The acquisition of conservation of substance and weight in children. III. Extension of conservation of weight acquired normally and by means of empirical controls on a balance scale. *Scandinavian Journal of Psychology*, 1961, **2**, 85–87. (c)

Smedslund, J. The acquisition of conservation of substance and weight in children. IV. An attempt at extension of visual components of the weight concept. *Scandinavian Journal of Psychology*, 1961, **2**, 153–155. (d)

Smedslund, J. The acquisition of conservation of substance and weight in children. V. Practice in conflict situations without external reinforcement. *Scandinavian Journal of Psychology*, 1961, **2**, 156–160. (e)

Spence, K. W. *Behavior theory and conditioning.* New Haven: Yale University Press, 1956.

Spence, K. W. *Behavior theory and learning: Selected papers.* Englewood Cliffs, New Jersey: Prentice-Hall, 1960.

Sperry, R. W. The great cerebral commissure. *Scientific American,* January 1964.

Spitz, R. A. & Wolf, K. M. Anaclitic depression: An inquiry into the genesis of psychiatric conditions in early childhood. *P. A. Study of the Child II.* New York: International University Press, 1946.

Staats, A. W. *Human learning.* New York: Holt, Rinehart and Winston, 1964.

Staats, A. W. & Staats, C. K. Verbal habit families, concepts, and the operant conditioning of word classes. *Psychological Review,* 1961, **68**, 190–204.

Taylor, J. H. Innate emotional responses in infants. *Ohio University Studies,* 1934, **12**, 69–81.

Thorndike, E. L. *The psychology of learning.* New York: Teacher's College, 1913.

Thorndike, E. L. *The psychology of arithmetic.* New York: Macmillan, 1922.

Thorndike, E. L. The influence of first year Latin upon the ability to read English. *School and Society,* 1923, **17**, 165–168.

Thorndike, E. L. Reward and punishment in animal learning. *Comparative Psychology Monographs,* 1932, **8**, No. 39.

Thorndike, E. L. *The psychology of wants, interests, and attitudes.* New York: Appleton-Century-Crofts, 1935.

Thorpe, W. H. *Learning and instinct in animals.* (2nd ed.) London: Methuen, 1963.

Tinbergen, N. *A study of instinct.* Oxford: Clarendon Press, 1951.

Titchener, E. B. Postulates of a structural psychology. *Philosophical Review,* 1898, **7**, 449–465.

Toch, H. H. & Schulte, R. Readiness to perceive violence as a result of police training. *British Journal of Psychology,* 1961, **52**, 389–394.

Tolman, E. C. *Collected papers in psychology.* Berkeley: University of California Press, 1951.

Tolman, E. C. & Honzik, C. H. Insight in rats. *University of California Publications in Psychology,* 1930, **4**, 215–232.

Towler, J. O. Training effects and concept development: A study of the conservation of continuous quantity in children. Unpublished doctoral dissertation, University of Alberta, Edmonton, Alberta, 1967.

Travis, L. D. Conservation acceleration through successive approximations. Unpublished master's thesis, University of Alberta, Edmonton, Alberta, 1969.

Treisman, A. M. Verbal cues, language and meaning in selective attention. *American Journal of Psychology,* 1964, **77**, 206–219.

Turing, A. M. Computing machinery and intelligence. *Mind,* 1950, **59**, #236.

Underwood, B. J. & Schultz, R. W. *Meaningfulness and verbal learning.* Philadelphia: Lippincott, 1960.

Voeks, V. W. Postremity, recency, and frequency as bases for prediction in the maze situation. *Journal of Experimental Psychology,* 1948, **38**, 495–510.

Voeks, V. W. Formalization and clarification of a theory of learning. *Journal of Psychology,* 1950, **30**, 341–363.

Voeks, V. W. Acquisition of S-R connections: A test of Hull's and Guthrie's theories. *Journal of Experimental Psychology,* 1954, **47**, 137–147.

Wallace, J. G. *Concept growth and the education of the child.* New York: New York University Press, 1965.

Walters, R. H. & Llewellyn, T. E. Enhancement of punitiveness by visual and audio-visual displays. *Canadian Journal of Psychology,* 1963, **17,** 244–255.

Walters, R. H., Llewellyn, T. E., & Acker, W. Enhancement of punitive behavior by audio-visual displays. *Science,* 1962, **136,** 872–873.

Watson, J. B. Psychology as the behaviorist views it. *Psychological Review,* 1913, **20,** 157–158.

Watson, J. B. *Behaviorism.* (2nd ed.) Chicago: University of Chicago Press, 1930.

Wertheimer, M. *Productive thinking.* (1st ed.) New York: Harper & Row, 1945.

Wertheimer, M. *Productive thinking.* (Enlarged ed.) New York: Harper & Row, 1959.

Whitehead, A. N. & Russell, B. *Principia mathematica.* (2nd ed.). Vol. 1. Cambridge: Cambridge University Press, 1925.

Wiener, N. *Cybernetics.* (1st ed.) New York: John Wiley, 1948.

Wittrock, M. C. Verbal stimuli in concept formation: Learning by discovery. *Journal of Educational Psychology,* 1963, **54,** 183–190.

Wolpe, J. *Psychotherapy by reciprocal inhibition.* Stanford: Stanford University Press, 1958.

Wulf, S. Tendencies and figural variations (1922). In W. D. Ellis (Ed.), *A source book of Gestalt psychology.* New York: Harcourt, Brace & World, 1938.

Zeaman, D. & House, B. J. The role of attention in retardate discrimination learning. In N. R. Ellis (Ed.), *Handbook of mental deficiency.* New York: McGraw-Hill, 1963. Pp. 159–223.

Zelman, A., Kabot, L., Jacobson, R., & McConnell, J. V. Transfer of training through injection of "conditioned" RNA into untrained worms. *Worm Runners' Digest,* 1963, **5,** 14–21.

Zubek, J. P. *Sensory deprivation: Fifteen years of research.* New York: Appleton-Century-Crofts, 1969.

Zubek, J. P., & Wilgosh, L. Prolonged immobilization of the body: Changes in performance in the electroencephalogram. *Science,* 1963, **140,** 306–308.

Author Index

Acker, W., 300
Allport, F. H., 9
Anastasi, A., 29
Anderson, A. R., 266
Anderson, L. C., 222
Ashby, W. R., 266
Asimov, I., vii
Athey, I. J., 240, 260
Ausubel, D. P., 11, 19, 37, 152, 188, 206,
    222–228, 316, 317, 324–328, 329
Ayllon, T., 304

Babich, F. R., 43
Baer, D. M., 120
Baldwin, A. L., 29, 240
Bandura, A., 120, 287, 288, 290, 292, 293, 294,
    295, 298, 299, 300, 303, 305, 306, 307,
    326, 329
Barnard, C. W., 150
Bartlett, S. C., 38
Becker, W. C., 119
Bennett, E. L., 43
Bentler, P. M., 260
Berlyne, D. E., 151, 217
Bijou, S. W., 119, 120
Binet, A., 230
Birnbrauer, J. S., 119
Bitterman, M. E., 88, 89
Bower, G. H., 123, 126, 190
Broadbent, D. E., 44, 45, 47
Bruner, J. S., 11, 19, 151, 152, 188, 206–222,
    241, 274, 315, 316, 317, 327, 328, 329

Calvin, N., 43
Chaplin, J. P., 138, 231
Cherry, E. C., 43
Commons, W. D., 187
Conrad, R., 37
Côté, A. D. J., 257
Craig, R. C., 227
Crespi, L., 89

Darwin, C., 82
DeCecco, J. P., 120
Deese, J., 35
deMyer, M. K., 303
Deutsch, D., 45, 47
Deutsch, J. A., 45, 47
Dollard, J. C., 290, 291, 307

Ebbinghaus, H., 33–34, 35, 43, 46
Eriksen, C. W., 45

Fagin, B., 187
Ferguson, L. W., 305
Ferster, C. B., 303
Flavell, J. H., 240, 241
Fode, K. L., 187
Freund, K., 303, 305
Furth, H. G., 240, 260

Gagné, R. M., 326, 328–329
Galanter, E., 266, 271, 274, 278, 280, 281, 318
Galton, F., 82
Ginsberg, H., 240, 260
Goldschmid, M. L., 260
Greenspoon, J., 111
Grusec, J. E., 305
Gunderson, K., 267, 268, 269
Guthrie, E. R., 10, 17, 35, 76, 82–87, 92, 93,
    96, 130, 132, 206, 304, 311, 323, 327, 329
Guthrie, J. T., 227

Haslerud, G. N., 227
Hebb, D. O., 6, 10, 18, 32, 38, 77, 123,
    136–165, 180, 181, 206, 217, 222, 314,
    317, 327, 328
Hellyer, S., 37
Heron, W., 150, 151
Hewett, F., 120
Hilgard, E. R., 90, 123, 126, 190
Hill, W. S., 9, 123, 192, 311, 322, 329
Hille, B. A., 37
Hillix, W. A., 123
Holland, J. G., 120
Honzik, C. H., 204
House, B. J., 45, 47
Hovland, C. I., 271
Hull, C. L., 6, 10, 18, 89, 122–135, 206, 313,
    324, 327, 329
Hulse, S. H., 35, 89
Hunt, J. McV., 41, 260
Hurlock, E. B., 29

Inhelder, B., 38, 231, 253
Irwin, O. C., 81

Jacobson, A., 43
Jacobson, A. L., 43
James, W., 13, 43, 77
Jensen, A. R., 29, 82
Johnson, H. J., 45

Keller, R. S., 81
Koffka, K., 186, 189, 190, 192, 193, 203, 316

347

Subject Index